Mysteries of the Lib

A record of three years of exploration in the heart of that vast & waterless region

W. J. Harding King

Alpha Editions

This edition published in 2024

ISBN : 9789361474668

Design and Setting By
Alpha Editions
www.alphaedis.com
Email - info@alphaedis.com

As per information held with us this book is in Public Domain.
This book is a reproduction of an important historical work. Alpha Editions uses the best technology to reproduce historical work in the same manner it was first published to preserve its original nature. Any marks or number seen are left intentionally to preserve its true form.

Contents

PREFACE .... - 2 -
CHAPTER I .... - 5 -
CHAPTER II .... - 13 -
CHAPTER III .... - 20 -
CHAPTER IV .... - 29 -
CHAPTER V .... - 43 -
CHAPTER VI .... - 57 -
CHAPTER VII .... - 62 -
CHAPTER VIII .... - 70 -
CHAPTER IX .... - 79 -
CHAPTER X .... - 86 -
CHAPTER XI .... - 97 -
CHAPTER XII .... - 103 -
CHAPTER XIII .... - 109 -
CHAPTER XIV .... - 114 -
CHAPTER XV .... - 117 -
CHAPTER XVI .... - 122 -
CHAPTER XVII .... - 127 -
CHAPTER XVIII .... - 133 -
CHAPTER XIX .... - 144 -
CHAPTER XX .... - 153 -
CHAPTER XXI .... - 157 -
CHAPTER XXII .... - 166 -
CHAPTER XXIII .... - 176 -
CHAPTER XXIV .... - 186 -
CHAPTER XXV .... - 194 -

CHAPTER XXVI	- 199 -
CHAPTER XXVII	- 229 -
APPENDIX I	- 239 -
APPENDIX II	- 269 -
APPENDIX III	- 274 -
FOOTNOTES:	- 285 -

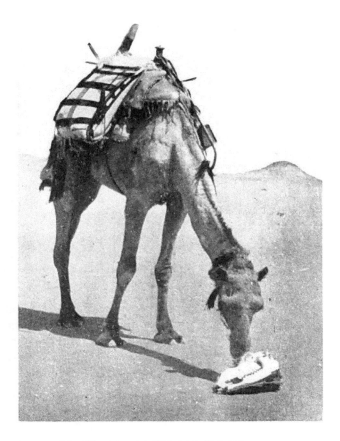

My Hagin, or Riding Camel.

The saddle bags, or *hurj*, are gaily coloured and the rider rests his legs on the leather pad over the withers, the camel being controlled by a single rein.

PREFACE

IT is not easy to condense into a reasonable compass an account of three years' work in an entirely unknown part of the world like the centre of the Libyan Desert.

Most of the scientific results I obtained during that time, however, have already appeared in the journals of the Royal Geographical Society, or other scientific bodies, so it has not been necessary to reproduce them. Many of the journeys, too, that were made into the desert had of necessity to retraverse routes that I had already covered, or were of too uninteresting a character to be worth describing, so no account of these was necessary. On the other hand, various incidents have been introduced into the narrative part of the book which, though they may appear comparatively unimportant in themselves, illustrate the character of the natives, and so supply data of an ethnographical character in one of its most practical forms.

The photographs which form the illustrations were all taken by myself. Unfortunately many others that I took were so seriously damaged by the sand, or heat, as to be unfit for reproduction. These have had to be replaced by sketches that I made from them—for these I can only offer my apologies.

The names by which the new places that we found in the central part of the desert are called will not be seen on any map. They are only those given to them by my men. But it has been necessary to use them in order to avoid repetition of such cumbersome phrases as "the-hill-that-appeared-to-alternately-recede-and-advance-as-we-approached-it," etc.

I received so much kindness and assistance in so many quarters in carrying out my work that it is a little difficult to decide where to begin in acknowledging it. To the War Office I am indebted for the gift of the graticules upon which my map was constructed; the Sudan Office in Cairo lent me tanks and gave me much useful intelligence. Major Jennings-Bramley, Capt. James Hay and the late Capt. (afterwards Colonel) O. A. G. Fitzgerald all gave me information and advice of great value.

Dr. Rendle and his staff of the Botanical Section of the Natural History Museum in South Kensington kindly identified for me a collection of plants that I brought back, and in addition allowed me the use of their library while working out the geographical distribution of the collection.

For the identification of part of my other collections I am also indebted to the staff of the Natural History Museum in South Kensington. A collection of insects made on my last journey sent to the Tring Museum were most kindly identified for me by Lord Rothschild.

I am under a deep debt of gratitude to the Royal Geographical Society for a most generous loan of instruments; and last, but by no means least, I have to express most cordial thanks to the Survey Department in Egypt for the loan of tanks and instruments and for much valuable advice and assistance. More especially I am under obligations to the following members of this department: To the late Mr. (afterwards Lt.-Col.) B. F. E. Keeling and Mr. Bennett, for calculating some of my astronomical observations; to Mr. J. Craig for his kindness in working out my boiling point and aneroid altitudes; to Dr. John Ball and Mr. H. E. Hurst, who gave me much assistance and so far enlightened my ignorance on the subject as to enable me to take some electrical observations on the sand blown off a sand dune; the former, too, most kindly lent me his electrometer for the purpose of the observations. Mr. Alfred Lucas of this department also kindly analysed some samples of crusted sand that I collected in order to discover the cementing material.

The Libyan Desert, that in the past has to a great extent defied the efforts of all its explorers, is bound before long to give up its secrets. Suitably designed cars, accompanied perhaps by a scouting plane, our enemies against which even the most avid desert is almost defenceless, though one cannot but regret the necessity for such prosaic mechanical aids, they unquestionably afford an ideal method of conducting long pioneer explorations in a waterless desert. But these things have only recently been invented, and there are still many problems that remain unsolved as to "what lies hid behind the ridges" in the vast area that we know as the Libyan Desert, and speculation is so full of fascination, that it seems almost a pity that those problems should ever be solved.

MAP FOR "MYSTERIES OF THE LIBYAN DESERT."

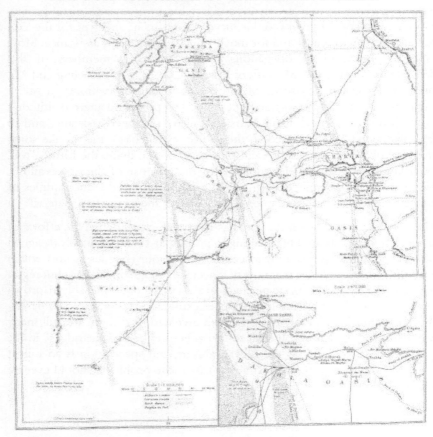

Seeley Service & Co. L^td.

CHAPTER I

OF the making of books on Egypt there is no end. The first on the subject was Genesis, and there has been a steady output ever since. But the literature of the Libyan Desert, that joins up to Egypt on the west, is curiously scanty, when the enormous area of this district is considered.

The Libyan desert may be said to extend from the southern edge of the narrow cultivated belt that exists almost everywhere along the North African coast, to the Tibesti highlands, and the northern limit of the vegetation of the Sudan. On the east the boundary of the desert is well defined by the Valley of the Nile; but on its western side it is extremely vague.

A broad belt of desert stretches all across North Africa from east to west. The western portion of this is known to us as "the Sahara." But "Sahara" is not really a name, but an Arabic word meaning a desert—*any* desert. By the natives this term is applied to the whole of this desert belt, and is used just as much to describe the Libyan Desert, as the more westerly part of it. The boundary line between what we know as the Sahara and the Libyan Desert has never been drawn, but it may be said to run roughly from the northern end of Tibesti to the base of the Gulf of Sidra. With such vague boundaries it is impossible to give an accurate estimate of its extent, but it may be taken that the Libyan Desert covers nearly a million square miles. It is probably the least-known area of its size in the world. There are still hundreds of thousands of square miles in its southern and central parts quite unknown to Europeans, the map of which appears as so much blank paper, or is shown as being covered with impassable sand dunes.

I had had some experience of desert travelling in the Western Sahara, so when, in 1908, I wrote to the Secretary of the Royal Geographical Society, suggesting a journey into the Western Sahara, and received a letter in reply proposing that I should tackle the Libyan Desert instead, as offering the largest available area of unknown ground, and should take up the study of sand dunes, for which it afforded an unrivalled opportunity, I jumped at the suggestion, which had not before occurred to me.

But after a jump of that kind one usually comes to earth again with something of a bang, and when, after making a more thorough enquiry than I had previously done into the nature of the job I had undertaken, I began to realise its real character and felt that in saying I would tackle this part of the world, I had done something quite remarkably foolish.

Many expeditions had set out from Egypt to explore this part of the world, but none up to that time had ever crossed the Senussi frontier, with the exception of Rohlfs', who, in 1874, before the Senussia was firmly established in the desert, attempted to reach Kufara Oasis. Even he, hampered perhaps by his enormous caravan, only managed to proceed for three days westward from Dakhla and was then compelled, by the insurmountable character of the dunes, to abandon the attempt and to turn up towards the north and make for the Egyptian oasis of Siwa. This difficulty of crossing the sand hills, the obstructing influence of the Senussi, who had reduced passive resistance to a fine art, and, perhaps, in some cases, want of experience in desert travelling, had rendered the other attempts abortive. Still, this seemed to be the most promising side from which to enter the desert.

I first took a preliminary canter by going again to the Algerian Sahara. This was, of course, some years before the war, in the course of which the Senussi—or the Senussia as they should be more strictly called—were very thoroughly thrashed. Just before the war, however, they were at about the height of their power and were a very real proposition indeed.

They had the very undesirable peculiarity—from a traveller's point of view—of regarding the part of the Libyan Desert, into which I was proposing to go, as their private property and of resenting most strongly—to put it mildly—all attempts to penetrate into their strongholds. There can be little doubt that at this period they had been contemplating for a long time an invasion of Egypt, and were only waiting for a suitable opportunity to occur of putting it into execution. In the circumstances, they naturally did not want Europeans to enter their country for fear that they should get to know too much. Moreover their fanaticism against Europeans had been considerably augmented by the advance of the French into their country from the south.

Even now most people seem hardly to realise the real character of the Senussia; for one constantly hears them alluded to as a "tribe" or merely as a set of unusually devout Moslems, who have chosen to take up their abode in the most inaccessible parts of Africa, in order to devote themselves to their religious life, without fear of interruption from outsiders. The fact is, that they are in reality dervishes, whose character, at that time at any rate, was of a most uncompromising nature towards all non-Mohammedans and was especially hostile towards Europeans, particularly those occupying any Moslem territories. Moreover they were not confined only to the Libyan Desert, but formed one of the most powerful of the dervish orders, with followers spread throughout practically the whole Moslem world from Sumatra to Morocco.

As I expected to come a good deal in contact with them in the Libyan Desert, after leaving the Algerian Sahara, I spent a considerable time in the public libraries of Algeria and Tunis, in collecting such information as was available on the Senussia and other dervishes of North Africa.

For the benefit of those unacquainted with the subject it may be as well to explain the nature of these dervish orders. They resemble in some ways the monastic communities of Christianity, and are usually organised on much the same lines. Their *zawias*, or monasteries, vary in size from unpretentious buildings, little better than mud huts, to huge establishments, which in size and architecture favourably compare with the finest institutions of their kind in Europe.

Each dervish order has its own peculiar ritual. Many of them are entirely non-political and of a purely religious character; but there are others, such for instance as the notorious Rahmania and Senussia, who are of a strongly political character, usually hostile to Europeans. Frequently, however, their influence is not apparent, as they keep discreetly in the background; but it has been repeatedly shown that it has been intriguing sects such as these, who have been at the bottom of the numerous risings and difficulties that Europeans have had to contend with in dealing with their Moslem subjects.

Other political orders—such as the Tijania—are actually favourable towards Europeans; while others again lend their support to some particular branch of the community, acting for instance, as in the case of the Ziania, as protectors to travellers or, as the Kerzazia do, supporting the dwellers in the oases against the attacks of the *bedawin* who surround them, and so forth.

As these dervish orders are largely dependant upon the *refar*, or tribute, that they exact from their followers, for their support, with few exceptions, each sect does its utmost to increase the number of its adherents and to prevent them from joining any other order. This naturally leads to a considerable rivalry between them, and when two of them pursue an exactly opposite policy—as for instance in the case of the Tijania and the Senussia—this rivalry develops into a deadly feud. It is the impossibility of inducing rival dervishes to combine, more perhaps than anything else, that makes that wild dream of Pan-islam, by which all Mohammedans are to unite to get rid of their European rulers, such a hopelessly impossible scheme.

A very large proportion of the Moslem natives of North Africa belong to one, or more, of these orders. But it is seldom that a native can be found to discuss at all freely the particular one to which he belongs. A knowledge, however, of them and of the peculiarities by which the followers of each sect can be identified, is most useful. The information that I picked up on this subject before going to Libya I found of the greatest possible value, as it often enabled me to gauge the probable attitude towards me of the men with whom I came in contact, and even to put a spoke in their wheel, before they even realised that I had any ground for suspicion.

On leaving Tunis, I went on to Egypt, where, before actually setting out for the desert, I spent some time in Cairo, putting the finishing touches to my equipment and picking up what information I could about the part into which I was going. It is extraordinary how many of my informants regarded the desert as "a land of romance." No doubt in many cases distance lends enchantment to the view, and covers it with a certain amount of glamour; but a very slight experience of these arid wastes is calculated completely to shatter the spell. Romance is merely the degenerate offspring of imagination and ignorance. There can be few parts of the world where one is so much up against hard cold facts as one is in the desert.

On the whole, the information that I was able to collect was of a very unsatisfactory character. I could learn practically nothing at all definite about the desert—at least nothing that seemed to be reliable, except that the dunes of the interior of the desert were quite impassable.

But I soon found out that though I was learning nothing, other people *were*. The truth of the local saying that "you can't keep anything quiet in Egypt" was several times forced upon me in rather startling ways. Most of the news that natives learn probably leaks out through the reckless way in which some Europeans talk in the presence of their English-speaking servants. But even allowing for careless conversation of this kind, it is astonishing how quickly news sometimes travels. This rapid transmission of secret news is a well-known thing in North Africa, and one that has always to be reckoned with. In Algeria they call it the "arab telegraph," and many extraordinary cases of it are recorded.

As a result of my enquiries I was able to draw up a sort of programme for my work in the desert, the main objects in which were as follows:—

(1) To cross that field of impassable dunes.

(2) If I succeeded in doing so, to cross the desert from north-east to south-west.

(3) Failing the latter scheme, to survey as much as possible of other unknown parts of the desert.

(4) To collect as much information as possible from the natives about the unknown portions of the desert that I was unable to visit myself.

Before leaving Cairo, I engaged two servants. My knowledge of Arabic at that time was scanty, and what there was of it was of the Algerian variety—a vile patois that is almost a different language to that spoken in the desert—an interpreter was consequently almost a necessity. I took one—Khalil Salah Gaber by name—from a man who was just leaving the country. He was loud in his praises of Khalil, stating that he was an extremely good interpreter and "very tactful."

Since then I have always been distinctly suspicious of people who are noted for their tact—there are so many degrees of it. Tactful, diplomatic, tricky, dishonest, criminal, all express different shades of the same quality, and Khalil's tact turned out to be of the most superlative character!

I also engaged a man called Dahab Suleyman Gindi as cook. Dahab—unlike Khalil, who was a *fellah* or one of the Egyptian peasants—was a Berberine, the race from which the best native servants are drawn. He was a small, elderly, rather feeble-looking man with an honest straightforward appearance, who not only turned out to be a very fair cook, but who also made himself useful at times as an interpreter, as he knew a certain amount of English.

After my preparations were completed, I stayed on for a while to see something of the sights of Cairo. Its cosmopolitan all-nation crowd made it an interesting enough place for a short stay. But after one had spent a little time there, and done all the usual sights, dirty, noisy Cairo and the other tourist resorts began to pall upon one. After all, they are only a sort of popular edition of the country, published by Thomas Cook and Son. Beyond lay the real Egypt and desert, a land where *afrits*, *ghuls*, *genii* and all the other creatures of the native superstitions are matters of everyday occurrence; where lost oases and enchanted cities lie in the desert sands, where the natives are still unspoiled by contact with Europeans, and where most of the men are pleasing, and, though the prospect is vile, that could not destroy the attraction that lay in the fact that about a million square miles of it were quite unknown, and waiting to be explored.

Before I had been very long in Cairo, I had had enough of it—it was so much like an Earl's Court exhibition—and at the end of my stay, I cleared out for the desert with a feeling of relief.

The train for Kharga Oasis left Cairo at 8 p.m. After a long dusty journey I found myself deposited at the terminus in the Nile Valley of the little narrow gauge railway that runs across the desert for some hundred miles to Kharga Oasis.

There is a proper station at this junction now, but at that time, in 1909, the line had only been recently opened, and the junction consisted merely of a siding, a ramshackle little wooden hut for the station-master, and a truly appalling stink of dead dog, the last being due to the fact that owing to an attack of rabies in the district, the authorities had been laying down poisoned meat to destroy the pariah dogs of the neighbourhood, who all seemed to have chosen the vicinity of the station as the spot on which to spend their last moments.

Having shot out my baggage at the side of the permanent way, the train disappeared into the distance and left me with about half a ton of kit to get up to Qara, the base of the oasis railway, where I had been told I could get put up. After a delay of nearly an hour, during which time, as it was bitterly cold, I began to feel the truth of the native saying that "all travel is a foretaste of hell," some trollies put in an appearance. Moslems, it may be mentioned, believe that there are seven hells, each worse than the last—and they say they are all feminine!

As soon as the trollies had been loaded up, a start was made for Qara, some five miles away, where I spent the next few days, while collecting the camels for my caravan.

To assist me in buying the beasts, I engaged a local Arab, known as Sheykh Suleyman Awad, a grim, grizzled old scoundrel of whom I saw a good deal later on. In his youth he had had a great reputation as a *gada*—a term corresponding pretty closely to our "sportsman," and much coveted by the younger *bedawin*.

He had gained this reputation in a manner rather characteristic of these Arabs. Once, when a young man, he was having an altercation with a couple of *fellahin*, who after showering other terms of abuse upon him, finally wound up by calling him a "woman." An insult such as this from a couple of mere *fellahin*, a race much despised by the Arabs, was too much altogether for Suleyman, who promptly shot them both. It was a neat little repartee, but Suleyman had to do time for it.

The *bedawin* in that part of Egypt are semi-sedentary, living encamped in the Nile Valley on the edge of the cultivation. Most of them live in tents woven of thick camel and goat hair, others in huts of *busa*—dried stalks of maize, etc.—a few of the more wealthy Arabs have houses, built of the usual mud bricks, and own small areas of land which they cultivate. At certain seasons of the year, they migrate into the oases, returning again to their camping places in the Nile Valley in the spring, to avoid the camel fly that puts in its appearance in the oases at that season, and is capable of causing nearly as much mortality among the camels as the tsetse fly does among horses in other parts of Africa.

After spending a day or two trying to buy camels round Qara, I at length secured five first-rate beasts in the market at Berdis.

Each Arab tribe has its own camel brand or *wasm*, the origins of which are lost in the mists of antiquity. Some of these marks, however, are identical in shape with the letters of the old Libyan alphabet of North Africa, and with its near relation the Tifinagh, or alphabet of the modern Tawareks, and it is possible that there may be some connection between them.

The camels I bought at Berdis came from the Sudan. They were large fawn-coloured beasts with a fairly smooth coat, and all showed the same brand—a vertical line on the near side of the head by the nostril, and a similar line in the bend of the neck. They belonged, I believe, to the Ababda tribe.

Sheykh Suleyman eventually produced a decent-looking camel from somewhere, which I bought, and that, with the five I had procured from Berdis, constituted my whole caravan—and an excellent lot of beasts they were.

I engaged a couple of drivers to look after them—Musa, a young fellow of about eighteen years of age, and a little jet-black Sudani, called Abd er Rahman Musa Said, who turned out to be a first-rate man, and stayed with me the whole time I spent in the desert. Both of these men belonged to Sheykh Suleyman's tribe.

The choice of a guide is a serious question, as the success or otherwise of an expedition depends very largely upon him, and I found considerable difficulty in finding a suitable man. I nearly engaged one who applied, as he seemed to be the only one of the candidates who knew anything at all about the desert beyond the Egyptian frontier. But Nimr—Sheykh Suleyman's brother—sent me word by Abd er Rahman, that he was not to be relied on as he "followed the Sheykh"—the usual way among natives of describing a man who was a member of the Senussia, and as he refused a cigarette I offered him, I declined to employ him. Smoking, it may be noticed is forbidden to the followers of Sheykh Senussi, and the offer of a cigarette is consequently a useful—though not always infallible—test of membership of this fanatical fraternity.

My suspicions were confirmed on the following morning, when this man came in to hear my answer to his application. The camel he rode was branded on the neck with the *wasm* of the Senussia—a kind of conventionalised form of the Arabic word "Allah" (**IWI**)—a damning piece of evidence showing not only that he belonged to the sect, but that his mount was supplied by the Senussia itself. He was probably one of their agents.

I was beginning to despair of finding a guide, when I received a telegram from the *mudir* (native governor) of Assiut, to whom I had applied for a reliable man, saying that he had got one for me, and asking whether I wished to see him.

The man arrived the next day. I took a fancy to him at once, which even his many peccadilloes never quite destroyed. His appearance was distinctly in his favour. He was a big man, nearly six feet high, which is very tall indeed for an Arab. He looked about sixty years old, and carried himself with that "grand air" which so many of the *bedawin* show, and which goes so well with the flowing robes of the East. Unlike most *bedawin* he was spotlessly clean.

His name he said was Qway Hassan Qway. It is quite impossible to convey an accurate idea of the pronunciation of Arabic names by mere European systems of writing, but his first name as he pronounced it, sounded like "choir" with a sort of gulping "g" instituted for the "ch." He added the gratuitous piece of information that his grandfather had been a *bey*—a sort of military title corresponding roughly to a knighthood. He was clearly not in the habit of hiding his light under a bushel. But as he was very highly recommended by the *mudir*, and I liked the look of him, I engaged him.

"Guide" is perhaps hardly the correct term to describe the capacity in which he was expected to act, for he did not even profess to have any knowledge of the desert beyond the Egyptian frontier. But as it seemed hopeless to attempt to find anyone who did, I employed him as a man of great experience in desert travelling, who would act as head of the caravan and help me with his advice in any difficulty that arose.

I took him round and introduced him to my other men. At my suggestion he arranged with Sheykh Suleyman to hire a riding camel from him, as he said that he had not one of his own that was strong enough for a hard desert journey.

In spite of his engaging manners, for some reason that was not apparent, both Sheykh Suleyman and Abd er Rahman obviously took a strong dislike to him. I was rather pleased at this, as a little friction in one's caravan makes the men easier to manage. At the time, I put it down to his belonging to a different tribe; but, judging from what afterwards occurred, I fancy it was really due to their knowing something against him, which, native-like, they did not see fit to tell me.

Qway being thus provided for, I dispatched my caravan by road to Kharga Oasis, and followed them myself a day or two afterwards by the bi-weekly train.

CHAPTER II

FOR the first few miles the line ran over the floor of the Nile Valley. Some twenty-eight miles from Qara, we emerged from the wady through which the railway ran on to the plateau above. *Jebel*, the word generally used in Egypt to signify desert, means literally mountain; the desert near the Nile Valley consisting of the plateau through which the Nile has cut its course.

The view on the plateau was impressive in its utter barrenness—no single plant, not even dried grass, was to be seen. Though the actual surface of the desert was very uneven, the general level was extremely uniform. The whole plateau consisted of limestone, in the slight hollows and inequalities of which patches of sand and gravel had collected. Here and there very low limestone hills, or rather mounds, were to be seen, none of them probably exceeding twenty feet in height. Everywhere on the plateau the effect of the sand erosion was most marked. The various types of surface produced being known to the natives as *rusuf, kharafish, kharashef* and *battikh*, or "water melon" desert, the nature of which will best be seen from the photographs.

The descent from the plateau into the depression in which Kharga Oasis lies, lay, like the ascent from the Nile Valley on to the plateau, through a wady. Kharga Oasis was at that time very little known to Europeans. Until the advent in the district of the company who had constructed the railway, the oasis had only been visited, I believe, by a few scientists and Government officials.

The desert beyond it had been so little explored that, within about a day's journey from the oasis, I found a perfect labyrinth—several hundred square miles in extent—of little depressions, two or three hundred feet in depth, opening out of each other, that completely honeycombed what had previously been considered to be a part of the solid limestone plateau. Unfortunately, I was never able entirely to explore this curious district. It almost certainly contains at least two wells, or perhaps small oases—'Ain Hamur and 'Ain Embarres.

It is difficult to convey to anyone who has not seen them a clear idea of these oases in the Libyan Desert. Kharga is an oblong tract of country measuring roughly a hundred and forty miles from north to south by twenty from east to west. It is bounded on the east, north and west by huge cliffs or hills. Only about a hundred and fiftieth of its area, in the neighbourhood of the various villages, hamlets and farms scattered over its surface, is under cultivation. These cultivated areas are irrigated by artesian wells, many of which date back to a very remote period. But Kharga Oasis and its antiquities have already been described by two or three writers, so no lengthy account of them is necessary. It contains a number of temples and other ruins, the most important of which is the Temple of Hibis.

The temple has an excellent mummy story connected with it. Those engaged in excavating the temples and tombs of Egypt—an occupation locally known as "body snatching"—are well aware that in their work they always have "the dead agin them," and there are few places where this has been so well exemplified as in the Temple of Hibis.

At the time of my arrival in Kharga it was being restored by an American archæologist, named W———. Before it was taken in hand, sand had drifted by the wind up against the walls, until it reached very nearly to their summit. In order to find out the extent of the buildings, W——— caused a trench to be dug parallel to one of the main walls.

Before this was completed, his men told him that they did not wish to continue working in that part, giving as their reason that a sheykh, i.e. a holy man, had been buried there, and since he was of exceptional holiness, lights had been seen hovering over his grave at night, and a man who had dug there before had fallen ill.

After some difficulty W——— succeeded in inducing the men to continue their work. But a sacred mummy is an uncanny thing to tackle. Sure enough, after his men had been digging a little longer, some earth slipped down into the trench, and with it came half the mummy, the other half remaining in the ground by the side of the trench. The men "downed tools" at once, and stood aghast at this calamity. The mummy's feelings must have been seriously outraged for he lost no time in getting to work—the native who had actually dug him up was subject to fits, and had one and died *that night.*

The next morning the mummy had disappeared and all the men were back at work again, just as though nothing had happened. After some little time W——— began to make cautious enquiries as to what had happened to the mummy; but he elicited no information whatever. His enquiries were met with a blank stare of surprise—"mummy? What mummy? There had been no mummy there." When a native knows nothing like that, it is quite hopeless to try and get anything out of him.

W———'s men went on with their work as though nothing had happened. One of them had atoned for the little accident to the mummy, so they knew that the rest of them were safe . . . but they seemed solicitous about W——— 's health, and W——— soon found that he had not done with that mummy. Before the end of the season, he and the European working with him, who had had most to do with the mummy, went down with very bad Kharga fever—a virulent form of malaria—from which W——— himself nearly died.

Some time afterwards he discovered that his men had gone down before him, on the night the mummy had been dug up, and had collected his remains and given him a decent Mohammedan burial. He found out where he was buried and built a really magnificent tomb-top over his grave. It must be nearly ten feet long, six feet wide and two feet high. It was built of the very best mud bricks the oasis could produce—and he even whitewashed it. Since then the mummy has been pacified and has left W——— in peace.

When I found out where the mummy was buried, I *bakhshished* him, by shoving a five-piastre piece into the ground by the side of his grave—a proceeding that met with Dahab's highest approval—and I had a more successful trip that year than any other. But it doesn't say much for the intelligence of the mummy, for that five-piastre piece was a bad one.

For the benefit of the sceptical, I wish to add that this story is true—*absolutely true*—any native in Kharga will tell you that—besides there is the whited sepulchre to prove it; so for a mummy story it is very true indeed.

After a stay of some days in Kharga to allow the caravan to come through from the Nile Valley, we started off for our journey to Dakhla Oasis. Our road at first ran roughly from east to west. Shortly after our start it passed through a patch some two miles wide of curious clay ridges. These, which seemed all to be under twenty feet high, were evidently formed by the erosion of the earth by the wind-driven sand, for they all ran from north to south, in the direction of the prevailing wind. Just before reaching the western side of the oasis, our road passed through a gap in a belt of sand dunes, which, like the clay ridges, also ran in the same north to south direction of the prevailing wind.

These sand belts consist of long narrow areas covered with dunes, running across the desert in almost straight lines, roughly from north to south. This Abu Moharik belt, through which our road ran, has a length which cannot be much less than four hundred miles; but, though it varies somewhat in width at different points along its course, its average breadth is probably not much more than five miles, that is to say, about an eightieth of its total length. These belts consist almost entirely of more or less crescent-shaped dunes. In places the sand hills of which they are composed are scattered and stand isolated from each other, with areas of sand-free desert between them. In other parts the dunes are more closely packed; many of the crescents join together to form large clusters, and the spaces between the dunes are also sometimes covered with sand.

Beyond the dune belt, we turned sharply towards the south and soon came on to the northern end of the cultivated area surrounding Kharga village. From Kharga we journeyed southward to the village of Bulaq, passing on our way the sandstone temples of Qasr el Guehda—or Wehda, as it is often locally pronounced—and Qasr Zaiyan. Both were surrounded by a mudbrick enclosure filled with the remains of a labyrinth of small ruined brick buildings and contained some hieroglyphics and some fine capitals to the pillars.

Shortly after leaving Qasr Zaiyan, we entered a sandy patch covered with vegetation consisting of graceful branched Dom palms, acacias, palm scrub and grasses, in which some of the cattle of the breed, for which the oasis was noted, were grazing. Half an hour's journey through this scrub-covered area brought us to the palm groves and village of Bulaq, on the south side of which I pitched my camp. Bulaq, though one of the largest villages of the oasis, with a population of about one thousand, is quite uninteresting. Its palm groves and cultivated land lie on its eastern side; on the north, south and west it is bounded by open sandy desert. It is chiefly noted as being the main centre in the oasis for the manufacture of mats and baskets, made chiefly from the leaves of the numerous Dom palms growing in the neighbourhood.

After breakfast the next day we struck camp and set off due west across the dune belt. It took us only an hour and a quarter to negotiate. Between the dunes were many interspaces entirely free from sand, so by keeping as much as possible to these and winding about, so as to cross the sand hills at their lowest points, we managed to get through the belt and emerged on to a gravelly sand-free desert beyond.

This, my first experience of the dunes of the Libyan Desert, was distinctly encouraging. Not only were the sand hills much smaller than I had been led to suppose, but their surface was crusted hard, and we crossed them with little difficulty; on emerging on the farther side, I set out for Dakhla Oasis, feeling far more hopeful of being able to cross the heavy sand to the west of that oasis than I had ever been before.

After crossing the dune belt, we altered our course and turned up nearly due north so as to make for the well of 'Ain Amur. The desert over which we were travelling was of pebbly sand, with an occasional rocky hill or ridge of black sandstone, and presented few points of interest. We camped at five, and I had a good opportunity of studying the peculiarities of my men, and of the kit they had brought with them for the journey.

Qway's equipment was about as near perfection for the desert as it was possible to get it. His camel saddle was a *rabiat*, over this was a red leather cushion on which he sat. On this he placed his *hurj*, or pair of saddle-bags, of strong carpet-like stuff, one of which hung down on either side; above this lay a folded red blanket, and over this again he spread his *furwa*, or black sheepskin—an indispensable part of a camel rider's equipment, which he not only places over his saddle, where it forms a soft and comfortable seat, but on which he sits when dismounted, lies on or covers himself with at night and throws over his shoulders on a cold day. Over the camel's withers in front of the saddle was a second small pad, also of red leather, on which to rest his legs as he crossed them in front of him as he rode, hanging from his *rabiat* on either side was a sack of grain for his camel, the pockets of his *hurj* resting on the top of the sacks.

Slung on to his saddle was a most miscellaneous collection of articles. A Martini-Henry rifle I had lent him, with a text from the Koran engraved on it in gold lettering, lay along his camel's back under his *hurj* on one side, and was balanced by a red parasol on the other. A goat-skin for carrying water, a small crock full of cheese, his camel's nose-bag, or *mukhlia*, in which, when leaving an oasis he generally carried a few eggs packed in straw that he had managed to cadge from some village as we passed, his *'agal,* or camel hobble, and a skin of flour, were all tied on to some part or other of his saddle.

In his *hurj* Qway carried a most extraordinary collection of things: a small circular mirror and a pair of folding nail scissors, with which at the end of a day's march he frequently spent some time in trimming his beard and moustache—he was always spotlessly clean and neat—a clothes-brush, with which he always brushed his best clothes; his best shoes; an awl with the point stuck into a cork for operating on the camels; a packing needle and one or two sewing needles, with their points similarly protected, a little bag containing thread and buttons; a lump of soap; part of a cone of sugar; tea, salt, red pepper, pills and one or two other mysterious Arab medicines, all carefully tied up separately in different pieces of rag, some cartridges I had given him for his rifle, any onions he had been able to cadge in the last oasis, and a quantity of dried dates, constituted only a few of the miscellaneous assortment of things that his camel bags contained.

The kit of the camel drivers, who were of course on foot, was much more simple. Between them they brought a skin of flour, an enamelled iron basin to make their dough in; a slightly dished iron plate (*saj*) to bake their bread on, and two or three small tin canisters, in which they carried sugar, salt and tea, when they had any, and which were thrown into the ordinary sack in which they carried the small amount of surplus clothing they possessed.

Dahab carried his belongings in a bag rolled up in a rug on which he slept, his kit being of a very workmanlike nature. Khalil's outfit, however, was largely of an ornamental character, including such trifles as a pink satiny pillow thickly studded with gold stars and covered with a pillow-case trimmed with lace!

In the rough usage inseparable from a desert journey everyone's clothing becomes more or less damaged. The other men during our halts got their clothes patched and mended, but Khalil never repaired the numerous rents that soon began to appear in his garments. He ultimately became such a scarecrow that when, on one extremely hot day, he seated himself on a rock during our noontide halt, he sprang up again a great deal quicker than he sat down, the reason being that the rock was greatly heated, and, to put it poetically, he had not been "divided from the desert by the sewn."

While in the Valley, Khalil had been quite a success, for he made a very fair interpreter. But no sooner did he get into the desert, than he appeared at once in his true character, of a dragoman of the deepest die. He was a sore trial, until I got rid of him.

The first few days in the desert with a new caravan are always trying. The men have not got into their work, and the camels, being strangers to each other, spend most of their time in fighting. A savage camel is a dangerous beast and it is of no use playing with him. The right place to hit him is his neck. Hit him hard with something heavy, and go on doing it and he becomes partially stunned and is then amenable to reason. Still, as the gifted author of "Eothen" put it, "you soon learn to love a camel for the sake of her gentle womanish ways."

The Arabs have different names that they apply to camels according to their age—a one-year-old beast is called *ibn esh Sha'ar*, or sometimes *ibn es Sena*; a two-year-old, *ibn Lebun*; a three-year-old, *Heg*; a four-year-old, *Thenni*; a five-year-old, *Jedda*; a six-year-old, *Raba'a*; a seven-year-old, *Sedis*; and an eight-year-old, *Fahal*. The names apply to both male and female beasts. After eight years a male is called *jemel* (camel) simply, and the female *naga*.

On some very bad roads, where there is much rock surface to be crossed, many of the caravan guides carry an awl, string and pieces of leather, for the purpose of resoling a camel's foot should the whole skin of it peel off, as it sometimes will. Qway resoled a foot of one of my camels once that went dead lame from this cause.

The operation was a simple one and seemed to be quite painless. He bored holes diagonally upwards through the thick skin on the edge of the sole of the foot, cut out a piece of leather slightly larger than the camel's footprint, and then passed pieces of string through the holes he had bored, and through corresponding holes in the piece of leather and tied the ends of the string together. One or two of the strings got cut through by the rock and had to be replaced. The camel, however, without much difficulty was able to hobble back into the oasis, and after some weeks' rest to allow the skin on the sole of his foot to grow again, completely recovered.

Camels vary considerably in colour. Among those I bought in my first season in Egypt were a beast of a rather unusual chestnut colour and two other fawn-coloured brutes, one of which had a shade of grey in its complexion, and the other was inclined towards a roan tint. These were called by my men the red, blue and green camels respectively.

The "green" beast was the one I used to ride. He was not a bad mount, but as he had not been ridden before I bought him, and guiding a camel by means of a single rein is always rather like trying to steer a boa-constrictor with a string, my stick at first had to be used pretty often.

In the afternoon of our third day, after leaving Kharga, we passed a mass of eroded chalk jutting up above the sandy ground, which, being a recognised landmark was known to natives from its shape as *Abu el Hul*—"the Sphinx." From there we proceeded to the well of 'Ain Amur, close to which I found a few patches of light blue sand.

A journey of a day and a half westwards over the tableland, on the north cliff of which 'Ain Amur is placed, brought us to the top of the slope from the level of the plateau to Dakhla Oasis.

This *negeb*, or descent, proved to be rather difficult to negotiate. The sand had drifted up against the cliff we had to climb down, and once on the bank of sand the camels, by walking diagonally down the slope, were able to reach the bottom without difficulty. But at the top of the sand bank, the rocks of which the cliff was composed, overhung to form a sort of cornice, and the path on to the sand slope below it lay through a cleft in the cornice, so narrow that the baggage had to be lifted temporarily up from the camels' backs to enable them to pass through the passage.

It took us half an hour to negotiate this place; but having at length managed it without any catastrophe, we camped in a bay in the cliff soon after reaching the bottom.

Soon after sunset a wild goose flew over the camp on to the plateau, coming from the south-west. Many were the speculations as to where it had come from, as no water was known to exist in the desert from which it came anywhere nearer than the Sudan.

CHAPTER III

ABOUT two in the afternoon of the following day we reached "Ain El Jemala," the first well of Dakhla Oasis, situated near the edge of a large area of scrub, which was said to be a favourite haunt of gazelle. We halted here to water the camels. We then pushed on past the village of Tenida, to Belat.

The *'omda* (village head-man) came round during the afternoon, bringing some of the leading men of the village with him to welcome me to the oasis, and to invite me to dine with him, greeting me with the picturesque formula invariably used in the desert to anyone returning from a journey—"praise be to Allah for your safety."

After dinner a man was brought in who had come from Mut, the capital town of the oasis, bringing me a note from the *mamur*, or native magistrate, welcoming me to his district, and saying that, though he had heard I had come, no one had been able to pronounce my name. He asked me to get someone to write it down in Arabic. Dakhla Oasis, though it lies just within the Egyptian frontier, had been visited by very few Europeans up to that time, and my arrival in this out-of-the-way spot consequently created somewhat of a stir in its little community.

I entrusted Khalil with the answer to the letter. The "ing" sound in my name is one which no Arab-speaking native has ever been able to master. At length, after much discussion, Khalil got the letter written; the result being that I ever afterwards went in the oasis under the name of "Harden Keen."

From Belat we pushed on to Smint el Kharab, or ruined Smint, where are some mud-built ruins, some of which have paintings on their interior walls, apparently of Coptic origin. From Smint el Kharab we pushed on to the village of Smint itself. Here we were of course invited to lunch by the *'omda*— an invitation of which I was for once glad to avail myself, as we had made an early start, and the caravan, which had been told to wait for me outside the village, had by some misunderstanding, gone on to Mut.

My first impressions of the inhabitants of these oases, with their cordial welcome, was certainly a most favourable one. Their hospitality, however, I found at times somewhat overwhelming.

'OMDA'S HOUSE, TENIDA.

As to the nature of this hospitality there appears to be some misunderstanding. In many cases one's host is a private individual, or, if he be an *'omda*, entertains one in his private capacity. But usually when invited to partake of a meal or to stay with an *'omda*, one is in reality the guest of the entire village, though the fact may not be apparent. The *'omdas* of Dakhla Oasis have the right to take a small proportion of the flow of any new well sunk in their district, to pay for the hospitality they show to the strangers that come to their village. In cases where there are no new wells, they collect from the heads of the different families the expenses that they have incurred in this way; so that in reality the cost of one's entertainment falls on the whole village.

The majority of the natives of these oases are miserably poor, and it goes much against the grain for a European to have to live upon them in this way. But to refuse their hospitality would be considered as a slight, if not as an actual insult, and so would any attempt to offer them any payment in return.

The meals, as a rule, were quite well cooked, and usually better than I got in camp. It was the tea and cigarettes that were such a trial. The one luxury the inhabitants of the oasis allow themselves is tea; even the poorest of them consume enormous quantities. The quality of the tea in the better class houses is irreproachable. The best of it is said to come from Persia, and I was told that as much as £1 a *rotl* (the Egyptian pound) is paid for it. In addition to red tea, a green tea, and also a brown and a black are used. The last I only tasted once; it seemed to be of an inferior quality. The richer natives will often offer two or even three different kinds in succession.

After drinking, it is quite the correct thing to sit silent for some time licking and smacking one's lips, "tasting the tea" as it is called, as a compliment to the quality supplied by one's host. The natives have another way of showing their appreciation of the fare set before them, which, however, it would be better not to describe.

The greatest ordeal I had to face was not the tea but the cigarettes. My host would extract from somewhere in the voluminous folds of his clothing a large shiny papier mâché tobacco-box, inlaid with mother-of-pearl, from which he would produce some tobacco and cigarette papers and proceed to roll me a cigarette, which he then *licked down*.

Eventually I found a means to avoid them. If the cigarette was offered me before the tea, I placed it above my ear—the correct position to carry it in the oases—and explained that I would smoke it later, so as to avoid spoiling the tea. If it was handed to me after the tea drinking, I was able to postpone lighting it for a time by saying that I would not smoke it just then, as I was still "tasting" the tea; then, while still licking and smacking my lips, with the cigarette still unsmoked above my ear, I found that it was time to take my departure. Once safely outside my host's house in the desert, the cigarette would fall down from my ear and be promptly scrambled for by my men.

In Smint, however, no cigarettes were forthcoming. The reason was not far to seek. Close to the village the Senussi had built a *zawia*, and a large number of the inhabitants of the village had already been converted to the tenets of the sect, or, as the natives put it, they "followed the sheykh." The members of this sect are forbidden to smoke.

SENUSSI ZAWIA AT SMINT.

In company with the *'omda* we went to call on the sheykh of the *zawia*. After speaking to us for a minute or two, he rather sulkily invited us to enter and treated us to the usual tea.

The *zawia* was an entirely unpretentious looking mud-built building, and might have been only the house of a well-to-do villager. The head of it—Sheykh Senussi by name—was quite a young man in the early twenties, and had probably been given the position owing to the fact that he had married a daughter of Sheykh Mohammed el Mawhub, the chief Senussi sheykh in Dakhla, who himself had a *zawia* at Qasr Dakhl, the largest town in the oasis, situated in its north-western corner.

He was said to be an Arab from Tripoli way, a statement that was borne out by his clothing, which consisted of the ordinary white *hram* of a Tripolitan Arab of the poorer class. He was very silent during the whole of our visit, and when he did condescend to speak it was generally to sneer or laugh at some remark that we made. The interview was consequently cut as short as possible.

Re-soling a Camel's Foot.

The sharp rocks of the desert sometimes flay the entire skin from the sole of a camel's foot, the Arabs replace this with a piece of leather sewn on to the camel's foot. (p. 35).

After Qway had succeeded in extracting some barley for his camel off the *'omda* we started again, for Mut, which lay about six miles away to the west.

In many parts the scenery of these oases is extremely pretty. Our road to Mut lay through cultivated fields, alternating with areas of salt-encrusted land, and sprinkled with palm plantations and low earthy hills. Away to the north at the foot of the cliff that bounds the oasis lay the palm groves of the village of Hindau. The fields, with their ripening grain and green crops of *bersim* (clover), the yellow ochreous hills, the clumps of graceful date palms with their dark green foliage, set against a background of cream-coloured sand dunes and purple cliffs, made a lovely picture in the light of the setting sun.

As we neared Mut, however, the country became less productive. Large areas of land thickly encrusted with salt and barren stretches of desert replaced the fertile fields and palm groves in the neighbourhood of Masara and Smint. Owing probably to the sinking of new wells at a lower level in the village of Rashida, the water supply of Mut has for many years been falling off, and now, although the place is the capital town, the district in which it lies is one of the poorest in the whole oasis.

We reached Mut in the dusk soon after sunset. Built on a low hill, and seen in the failing light, the place gave rather the impression of an old medieval fortified town. We skirted round its southern side, past a number of walled enclosures used to pen the cattle in at night, and, passing through a gap in the south-western corner of the wall that surrounds the town, arrived at a large rambling mud-built building, mainly used as a store, in which I had received leave to stay. It was a gloomy-looking place, and had evidently been built with a view to defence. Entering through a gate in the wall, secured by a bar, and turning to the right past some low outbuildings, we found ourselves in a narrow court, surrounded on three sides by high two-storied buildings—the upper part having apparently been used at some time as a harem by one of its former inmates.

Doors opened from either end of a gallery that joined the two wings. One led into the centre of three rooms on the western side that looked over the desert, and the other into some small chambers which, as one had a fire-place in it for cooking, I allotted to Dahab and Khalil, retaining the three western rooms for my own use.

OLD HOUSES IN MUT.

These proved to be high, spacious and airy, and commanded a fine view over the desert. The windows were large and fitted with a sort of trellis. This not only made the rooms more private, but considerably reduced the glare of the desert. So beyond the fact that the floors in many places seemed unsafe, and that the place was said to swarm with scorpions, I had little fault to find with my lodgings.

I walked out in the dusk as soon as we had settled into our quarters in the old store, to see what I could of the town. Many of the streets were roofed over, as in Kharga Oasis, but the tunnels were not nearly so long and very considerably higher, so that, except for the unevenness of the roadway, we had no difficulty in getting about. We were, however, compelled to carry a lantern in order to find our way.

There was not much to be seen; but the monotonous thudding of the women pounding rice, the continuous rumbling sound of the small stone hand mills by which they were grinding grain, the smell of wood smoke, the soft singing of the women and an occasional bar of ruddy light, crossing the roadway from some partly open doorway, showed that most of the inhabitants were in their houses preparing their evening meal.

Rice enters largely into the bill of fare of the natives of the oases, and is pounded by the women with a large stone held in both hands, which is brought down with all their strength into a small basin-shaped hollow scooped out of the rocky sandstone floor upon which the town is built.

The following morning I received a state visit from the *mamur* (magistrate), Ibrahim Zaky by name, the doctor, Gorgi Michael, a Copt from Syria, and the *zabit*, or police officer. The *mamur* and doctor spoke English fairly well.

Like most of the native officials who are to be found in the oases, the *mamur* was rather under a cloud, and had been sent to Dakhla as a punishment for some misdeeds of his in his last appointment. These oases posts are cordially disliked by the natives, as in these remote districts they are entirely cut off from the gay life of the towns of the Nile Valley. The appointments, however, have certain advantages. Being so far removed from the towns of the Nile Valley may be dull, but it frees them from the constant supervision of the English inspectors, a state of things of which an Egyptian is usually not slow to take advantage, by extorting *bakhshish* from the wretched *fellahin* of their district—often to a most outrageous extent.

One of the English inspectors had very kindly written to the *mamur* to inform him that I was coming into his district, and to tell him to help me in any way he could. The *mamur's* term of office in Dakhla being nearly at an end, he was extremely anxious to get my good word with the inspector in order that he might be appointed to a better district. He was accordingly most oppressive and unremitting in his attentions—until the government removed him to another and still worse district.

He was by no means enthusiastic about his life in the oasis, and, from his account of the natives, he evidently looked upon them as being little removed from beasts. He explained that he had left his wife behind in Egypt, but as he found that he did not get on well without one, he had married a young girl from Mut. He complained bitterly of the expense she had put him to, for as he expressed it in his rather defective English, it had "cost him £25 to make her clean!"

After the Egyptian officials had departed, a succession of *'omdas* from all over the oasis dropped in to pay their respects and to ask me to come round to their villages.

After the *'omdas* came various minor fry. First the camel postman, a burly, black-bearded Arab, called 'Ali Kashuta, looked in, drank a gallon or two of tea, took a handful of cigarettes out of the box that was handed to him, told me several times that he was my servant, and obviously didn't mean it; and then asking if I had any letters for post, departed, leaving a breezy independent atmosphere behind him, which was a pleasant contrast to the fawning attitude of the other natives.

Then came the clerk to the Qadi, Sheykh Senussi, who was also a member of the Senussi sect. He was a very learned person and a poet in his leisure moments. He drank tea, but didn't smoke, and was all smiles and compliments.

Next came the postmaster. He had been to school in the Nile Valley and spoke English quite well. He explained—what I was beginning to realise—that I was causing much mystification to the good people of the oasis; they could not make me out at all. The postmaster, however, who had been educated in Egypt, knew all about it. He had read about a man called "Keristoffer Kolombos," who had found America, and he thought that I must be in the same line of business. I told him that he was quite right. He beamed all over, and immediately departed to break the good news to an expectant oasis that the great problem had been solved. Before going he wished that Allah would preserve me on my journey, and hoped that I should find another America in the Libyan Desert.

In the afternoon I went round to tea with the *mamur* in the *merkaz*, or official residence.

One of his guests was a tall intelligent looking man, who was introduced to me as the *'omda* of Rashida, the *mamur* adding in English that he was one of the most hospitable men in the oasis; but very fond of whisky.

The latter statement unfortunately proved to be true. According to the *mamur*, he was a most depraved and habitual drunkard. This, however, was an exaggeration.

Between him and this *'omda* there was very little love lost. Shortly before my arrival they had quarrelled furiously. I never heard the cause of the dispute—it was probably a case of *cherchez la femme*, for Dakhla is one of those unfortunate places where, as Byron so nearly expressed it, "man's love is of his wife a thing apart, 'tis woman's whole persistence." These small-minded natives will squabble over the most trivial matters and keep the quarrel going for years. Often a tiff of the most puerile kind will become a family matter and end in a regular hereditary feud. In the Nile Valley this often leads to bloodshed. In the oases, however, the quarrel usually takes the form of the two sides to abusing and telling lies about each other behind their backs, wrangling whenever they chance to meet, and endeavouring at every possible opportunity to subject their opponent to an *ayb* (insult, slight, snub) often of a most elaborate description.

Shortly before my arrival the *'omda*, getting sick of the squabble, or finding that the *mamur* was making things too unpleasant for him, had held out the olive branch by sending him a basket of early mulberries—a fruit much appreciated in the oasis. The *mamur* had made this an opportunity to humiliate his opponent. He had thrown the fruit out of his window into the square in front of the mosque, where all the inhabitants had seen it. It was generally considered that he had scored heavily by doing so, and that this was one of the best *aybs* that had been seen for years. The whole oasis had been talking about it.

The partisans of the *'omda* were consequently much discomforted; but endeavoured to cover up their defeat by explaining that it hadn't really been a good *ayb*—the *mamur* had not thrown the whole of the mulberries away, as he had stated, but had taken out all the best ones and had only thrown away the rotten ones out of his window; so as an *ayb* it didn't count at all.

The ill-feeling between these two at length rose to such a pitch that some of the leading men in the oasis decided to try and effect a reconciliation between them, and a ceremony known as "making the peace" took place.

The two opponents were invited to meet together in the presence of some of their friends, who had argued with them, and at length the quarrel had been patched up. They had then fallen on each other's necks and embraced and had agreed to feed together. They had partaken of a huge feast in which whisky apparently played a prominent part, and had both got drunk and started quarrelling furiously again, in their cups. The next morning, when they were both probably feeling rather cheap, the peace-makers had got to work again and explained to them that they had not played the game, and again a reconciliation had been effected; but there was still a good deal of latent ill-feeling between them which vented itself mostly in backbiting, under a show of friendship.

CHAPTER IV

BY Qway's advice I started feeding my camels on *bersim*, preparatory to our journey into the dunes. There are two kinds of *bersim* grown in the oasis: *bersim beladi*[1] and *bersim hajazi*.[2] *Bersim hajazi*, however, should not be fed to camels in its green state, as it very frequently causes them to get hoven.

The *bersim* was bought off the natives by the *kantar*, of a hundred Egyptian pounds. At first there was some difficulty in getting it weighed. Abd er Rahman, however, proved equal to the emergency. He discovered a rock, which was supposed to weigh a *kantar*, and which was the standard weight for the whole oasis. He then rigged up a pair of scales, consisting of two baskets fixed to either end of a beam, suspended from a second beam.

In the evening of the first day I spent in Mut I climbed to the top of a low hill close to the town to look at the dune field that I hoped to cross. A more depressing sight it would be impossible to imagine. Not only were the sand hills in the neighbourhood of the town much higher than those we had encountered on leaving Kharga Oasis, but they extended as far as it was possible to see to the horizon, and obviously became considerably larger in the far distance, where they were evidently of great height.

I returned to my rooms with the gloomiest forebodings, wishing I had never been such a fool as to tackle the *belad esh Shaytan*, or "Satan's country," as the natives call this part of the desert, and wondering whether, when I attempted to cross those dunes, I should not end, after a few hours' journey, in having to return completely beaten with my tail tightly tucked between my legs, to the Nile Valley. I lay awake for most of the night in consequence.

But daylight as usual made things look more cheerful. Anyway I could have a shot at it, and as my camels did not seem to be in very good order I decided to give them a rest and to feed them up into the best possible condition, before subjecting them to what appeared to be an almost impossible task. In the meantime I thought I might as well see something of the oasis, and at the same time collect what information I could about the desert.

So a few days after my arrival at Mut I set off with the *mamur*, the policeman and the doctor to stay for a night with the *'omda* of Rashida, leaving the caravan behind me.

For the first two hours after leaving Mut, till we reached the village of Qalamun, our road lay over a barren country largely covered with loose sand, which proved to be rather heavy going.

Qalamun is rather a picturesque village, and seems to have been built with an eye to defence. A great deal of land in the neighbourhood is covered with drift sand, which in places seems to be encroaching on to the cultivation, though not to be doing any serious damage. An unusually large proportion of land in the neighbourhood is planted with date palms, and, as the water supply seems to be fairly abundant, the place has a prosperous well-to-do air. In some cases the wells appear to be failing, as a few *shadufs* for raising the water were to be seen. These and a few Dom palms gave the neighbourhood a rather distinctive appearance. Of course we visited the *'omda*. The sheykhs of this village—the Shurbujis by name—claim to have governed the oasis ever since the time of the Sultan Selim, "The Grim."

On leaving Qalaman we made straight for Rashida, most of our road lying through cultivated fields, planted mainly with cereals. Before reaching the village, we passed a large dead tree—a *sunt*, or acacia, apparently—which is known as the "tree of Sheykh Adam," and is supposed to possess a soul. The wood is reported to be uninflammable.

Shortly before reaching Rashida, we were met by the *'omda* and some of his family, who had ridden out to meet us, all splendidly mounted on Syrian horses, gorgeously caparisoned with richly embroidered saddles and saddle cloths. These joined on to our party and rode back with us to Rashida.

Kharashef.

Sand Grooved Ridge.

The wind driven sand grooves away the rock, sometimes leaving large ridges standing above its surface. (p. 308).

In Old Mut.

This shows the fortified character of the houses formerly built in the oases of the Libyan desert as a defence against raids. (p. 41).

The village is one of the prettiest and most fertile in the oasis. It is built on a low ridge lying at the south-east corner of a very extensive grove of palms, in whose shade were planted great numbers of fruit trees: figs, mulberries, apricots, oranges, tangerines—known in Egypt under the curious name of *Yussef effendi*, i.e. Mr. Joseph—bananas, almonds, pomegranates, limes, lemons, olives and sweet lemons, the last bearing a large, tasteless, but very juicy fruit, something like a citron in appearance.

THE TREE WITH A SOUL, RASHIDA.

The village lies close to the cliff. The interior of the village was of the normal type, and, beyond presenting an unusually prosperous appearance and having the walls of some of its houses painted on the outside in geometrical patterns, usually in red and white, did not differ from the other villages in the oasis.

The *'omda's* house was delightfully situated, with palm trees growing almost up to the walls. He took us up into his guest chamber, a long narrow room neatly whitewashed and furnished almost entirely in the European manner, with deck-chairs, sofas round the walls, a large gilt hanging lamp, bent wood chairs and three-legged tables. The windows were draped with European curtains and the floor covered with Eastern rugs and carpets. A large mirror in a gilt frame and an oleograph portrait of the Khedive completed the list of furniture.

On entering the room one's eye was at once caught by the words "*Ahlan wa Sahlen*"—welcome—painted on the opposite wall. And welcome that hospitable *'omda* certainly made us. The windows had been kept closely shuttered all the morning to keep out the heat and the flies; but these were opened on our arrival. Then the *'omda* entered and proceeded to spray the room and its inmates with scent. Shortly afterwards the inevitable tea and cigarettes made their appearance.

After compliments, enquiries as to the health of all parties present and the usual polite preliminaries had been got through—a process that took some minutes—the conversation turned upon horses. Only a few of the richer natives of the oases are able to afford them, and the remainder, when they do not walk, ride on donkeys. Powerful quarters, round cannon bones and a small head, with an especially small muzzle and widely distended nostrils, seemed to be the points they valued most.

After luncheon, when the heat of the day was past, we were taken by the *'omda* to see some of the sights of the village. First we were led to a big mud ruin known as the 'Der abu Madi. He told us he had dug up a number of mummies about a mile to the north of the village, which he said had been buried in earthenware coffins. Fragments of one of these coffins that he produced showed that they must have been about three inches thick and had evidently been baked in a kiln. Many of the mummies had been wrapped round with a cloth of some sort, with their arms lying straight along their sides, and had then been wound tightly round with a rope. The remains of one of them was shown us. It was, however, entirely knocked to pieces, as the *'omda* and his family had stuck it upright on the ground and then amused themselves by turning it into an "Aunt Sally." One or two coins and the skull of a gazelle had been dug up from one of the graves. The coins unfortunately were so worn and decayed that they could not be recognised. There seems to be plenty of work for an archæologist in Dakhla—and still more for an inspector of antiquities.

We were next taken off to see the great sight of Rashida—the Bir Magnun, or "foolish well." When this well was being sunk about forty years ago the labourers stopped working for the day, not knowing that they had almost reached the water-bearing stratum, with the result that the water forced its way through the small distance from the bottom of the bore hole to the top of the water reservoir, and gushed up with such violence that it forced the tubing, above the bore hole, partly out of the ground and flooded the whole country round.

On first arriving in the oases, I made enquiries on all sides from the natives for information as to what wells, roads or oases were to be found in the unknown parts of the desert, beyond the Senussi frontier. For a long time I could extract no information from any of them, and it was not till I got to Rashida, and happened to ask the *'omda* whether he knew anything about the oasis of Zerzura, that I got any information at all. There is no stopping a native of Dakhla when he gets on that subject, and one begins dimly to realise how very little the East has changed since the days when the "Arabian Nights" were written.

Many of the wealthier natives of the oases, and also, I believe, of the Nile Valley, spend an appreciable portion of their time in hunting for buried treasure. The pursuit is an absorbing one, to which even Europeans at times fall victims. Curious as it may seem at first sight, the native efforts are not infrequently attended with some success.

The reason is not far to seek. In former days, when the country was ruled by a lot of corrupt Turkish officials, a native, who was known to be possessed of any wealth, at once became the object of their extortionate attentions. He consequently took every precaution to hide his riches from these rapacious officials. The plan which he very often adopted was to bury his valuables in the ground. Not infrequently he must have died without imparting to his relations the whereabouts of his cache. The treasure buried in this way in Egypt would probably amount to an enormous sum in the aggregate, if it could only be located.

Then, too, the sites of old Roman settlements are to be found all over Egypt. The careless way in which the Romans seem to have scattered their petty cash about the streets of their towns is simply amazing. You can hardly dig for an hour in any old Roman site without coming across an old copper coin or two.

Let a native find a few coins in this way, and he will spend weeks, when no one is looking, in prowling around the neighbourhood in the hopes of finding more. Should he be lucky enough to find an earthenware pot containing a handful or two of old coins hidden in the past from a Turkish pasha, it is pretty certain that he will become a confirmed fortune-hunter for the remainder of his life. There is no doubt that quite considerable sums— several pounds' worth at a time—are occasionally found in this way. The natives are extraordinarily secretive about this kind of thing, and have been so long under a corrupt Government that they can hold their own counsel far better than any white man—for even now in out-of-the-way districts such as the oases, where the English inspectors cannot properly supervise the native officials, the extortionate ruler is at times most unpleasantly *en evidence*.

In their hunts for buried riches the natives are frequently guided by old "books of treasure." Every self-respecting native, who is wealthy enough to procure one, possesses at least one copy.

Before leaving Kharga I was fortunate in meeting E. A. Johnson Pasha, so well known as the translator of the whole of Omar Khayyám's "Rubaiyat" into English verse—Fitzgerald, of course, only translated a portion of it. He was the proud possessor of the only complete copy known to exist of a book of this description, dating from the fifteenth century.

One of the problems of the Libyan Desert, beyond the western frontier of Egypt, is that of the oasis known as Zerzura, or "The oasis of the Blacks." It was, I believe, first heard of by Rohlfs, who, in his attempt to go westward from Dakhla Oasis to Kufara, found the sand dunes impassable for his big caravan, and so had to turn up to the north and make for the oasis of Siwa instead. During this journey he encountered three blacks, who said that they were escaped slaves from the oasis of Zerzura, a place that they described as being some distance to the west of his route.

On mentioning this place to Johnson Pasha, he told me of this old book, and said that it contained a description of the road to this oasis, and of what might be found there by anyone who was fortunate enough to reach it. His book also described the road to the mines of King Cambyses.

He very kindly gave me a translation of the portions of this queer old volume that related to these two places. There were two descriptions of the road to Zerzura in a section of the book headed "In the Oases" They ran as follows:—

"Go to the Der el Banat (the girls' convent), near it you will find a hollow place, three *mastabas* (platforms), a round hill and three red stones. Burn incense here." Then follow two lines of cipher writing and cabalistic signs, which presumably give instructions for following the road, and the description ends.

The second reference was much more to the point. It was as follows: "Account of a city and the road to it, which lies east of the Qala'a es Suri, where you will find palms and vines and flowing wells. Follow the valley till you meet another valley opening to the west between two hills. In it you will find a road. Follow it. It will lead you to the City of Zerzura. You will find its gate closed. It is a white city, like a dove. By the gate you will find a bird sculptured. Stretch up your hand to its beak and take from it a key. Open the gate with it and enter the city. You will find much wealth and the king and queen in their palace sleeping the sleep of enchantment. Do not go near them. Take the treasure and that is all."

The book also contained two separate directions for finding the mines of King Cambyses. One of them instructed the reader thus: "Go to the Der el 'Ain, west of Esna, where there is a medical spring, and go north from the Der and the well five farasangs, which make a barid and a quarter, to where there is a red hill with a beacon mark on the top of it. You are to go up and look towards the east. You will see a pillar divided into two halves. Dig there." Then the aggravating book—just when it comes to giving the final definite directions for finding the mines, breaks off into line upon line of cabalistic signs, as it did in the case of Zerzura.

The second instruction for finding the mines, however, is much more explicit, and goes into minute details of the road to be followed, so much so that it would appear to be impossible for anyone to miss it.

It runs as follows: "By the town of Esna, north of Edfu. If you go there seek the mines of King Kambisoos (Cambyses). Ask for the Holy Der, which is called '———' but to give away directions for finding such wealth of treasure would be foolish. King Cambyses was a son of Cyrus the Great—the Conqueror of Babylon—and ruled over the Medes and Persians when the

Persian Empire was at about its height. He was a real big King, and the much-vaunted mines of King Solomon—a mere petty Sultan by comparison—probably bear about the same relation to those of King Cambyses as a threepenny-bit bears to the present National Debt. The mere description of them in Johnson Pasha's book of treasure makes one's mouth water."

First the directions lead you—in the clearest possible way—to a valley called the Wady el Muluk (the valley of the kings). Here you find the crucibles and all the apparatus and tools necessary for smelting, merely waiting to be used. You go a little farther on and you come to the "high class mine"—and very high class it is. You have only to dig half a cubit deep into it and you come at once on to a mineral "like yellow earth in stony ground." First you find it in lumps the size of beans, which "is sent by Allah," and you are directed to take "His good fortune." Then if you dig deeper, you will find it in lumps the size of melons. This you are explicitly told "is gold of Egypt. There is none better"—a statement it would be rash to contradict.

Having dealt with these particular mines, the old Arab astrologer directs his son, to whom the book is addressed, to go on to where two great rocks stand up, with a hollow before them, stating that in the hollow will be found "a black earth with green veins like silver rust," and directs him to take it. It is "sent by Allah." Unfortunately he omits to mention the nature of this mysterious mineral.

He then directs his son to "go with the blessing of Allah" to another place, where he states "You will find, oh! my son, before you a high hill in which they used to get the peridots." Next he tells him how to go on to the "Emerald pits which are three in number," and after that, directs him to the "Copper mine which is in a cave closed by a door," adding that the copper ore is "green earth very like green ginger and having veins in it like blood."

With the dazzling prospect of acquiring such untold wealth as that to be obtained in the very "high class mines," described in books of treasure such as this, is it to be wondered that the natives of Egypt spend so much time in looking for them?

Treasure hunting must be a most fascinating pursuit. But it is seldom a remunerative one. Still it is a curious fact that peridots used formerly to be known in the trade as "Esna peridots," which rather points to the fact that they were brought in to be marketed in that town, perhaps by the road alluded to in this book.

When I broached the subject of Zerzura to the *'omda* of Rashida, he said he did not know of any place called the Der el Banat (convent of the girls), but the old name of the Der Abu Madi was, he said, the "der el Seba'a banat" (convent of the seven girls), and that there was supposed to be a book and a mirror buried somewhere near there. By following the directions contained in the book, and then looking in the mirror the way to Zerzura would, he said, appear.

He told me—I don't guarantee his veracity—that three years before, while he was staying in an hotel in Egypt, a waiter had come up to him and asked him if he were not the *'omda* of Rashida. On hearing that he was, he told him that he wanted to go to the "Der el Seba'a Banat," as he had read in a book of treasure that seven hundred cubits to the north of the Der, there were three *mastabas* round a round hill, and that under each of them was buried a pan of large gold coins called *gurban*. He then showed him a specimen which the *'omda* said was very old, larger than a five-piastre piece and very thick and heavy. The waiter told him he had found the coin in the Nile Valley by following the directions given in his book of treasure, and offered, if he would go into partnership with him, to give him half of anything they found.

The *'omda* had apparently refused this offer, and started digging on his own account; but having failed to find the treasure, he was very anxious for me to go into partnership with him, and said that by combining our instructions we ought to be able to find something. I was not, however, sufficiently sanguine as to the result to feel justified in entertaining his offer—still three pans full of *gurban*. . . !

After a night spent at Rashida we started for Qasr Dakhl, stopping on our way to visit Budkhulu, a poor little place with but a scanty water supply. Like Rashida it lies close to the cliff that bounds the oasis; but being situated at a considerably higher level than either Qasr Dakhl or Rashida, the number of modern wells sunk in these two districts are said by the inhabitants to have greatly diminished their water supply. Its *'omda* was only noted for his drunken habits.

On leaving Budkhulu we rode past the little hamlet of Uftaima, and soon afterwards entered a stretch of soft sandy ground, a mile or two in width, beyond which we could see Qasr Dakhl with its palms and fields. This is the biggest town in the oasis, and is said by its inhabitants to produce the richest dates in Egypt.

Approached from the south-east, Qasr Dakhl looked a singularly picturesque and fertile place. The view of it from this side, across a reed-grown pool, reflecting the palm plantation with the village and blue scarp in the background, was one of the prettiest to be seen in the oasis.

The Gate of Qalamun.

The houses all join up to form a continuous wall as a defence against raids, having palm leaf hedges round some of the roof tops. (p. 48).

The 'Omda of Rashida and his Family.

The natives spend a great deal of their time on the flat house tops. Note the painted decoration of the wall in the background and the open work crest of the walls. (p. 50).

Just before entering the town, we passed the Bir el Hamia, one of the chief wells of the district, and the one from which most of the drinking water of Qasr Dakhl is drawn. The water from the well, effervescing strongly, rushed from beneath a stone platform that had been built over its mouth into a large clear pool, in which a number of the inhabitants were bathing as we passed, the water from this well being hot, is considered to have medicinal properties. It is said to have formerly been much hotter than at present; it is even stated that eggs could be boiled in it.

The *'omda* invited the whole party to lunch with him, and an excellent lunch it proved to be. The sheykhs of this village claim to be descended from the Qoreish tribe of Arabia, to which the prophet, Mohammed, belonged, and state that they settled in the oasis about A.D. 1500. They give themselves no small airs in consequence.

After lunch, from which for a wonder Qway excused himself on the plea that he wished to go and call on a friend, the inevitable tea was brought in, and with it arrived several of the leading men in the place, who all sat down on the floor in a line along one of the walls of the guest chamber.

Hoping to elicit some information, I asked if anyone had ever heard of the oasis Zerzura. Hadn't they! Half a dozen of them began to tell me all about it at once. Cows, I was told, had several times come into the oasis from the desert. They were very wild, but otherwise exactly like the cows of the oasis. They came from Zerzura. *Kimri sifi* (palm doves) and crows came into the oasis in the spring. They also came from Zerzura. Both the *kimri* and the cows came from the south-west; but the whole desert there was covered with sand and no one could go there. The last cows had come in only seventeen years before.

Another man told me that a woman leading a boy had once staggered into the oasis from the south, nearly dead from thirst, and that the descendants of the boy were still living in Mut. The woman and boy came from Zerzura too. In Mut, however, I was told practically the same story; but was there most positively informed that the boy's descendants were not living in Mut, but in Qasr Dakhl, so I found it a little difficult to know what to believe.

Having exhausted the subject of Zerzura we got on to that of Rohlfs, who had visited the oasis in 1874. An aged individual said he saw Rohlfs—or "Ro-hol-fus" as he called him—and remembered him quite well. He knew all about him. He had got a "book of treasure," and had come out to Dakhla to dig for buried riches in the Der el Hagar—a stone temple near Qasr Dakhl—and had employed a great many men in the excavation. But the treasure was guarded by an *afrit* (spirit), and for a long time he was unable to find it, and he got very angry and disappointed. At last, one day he sent everyone out of the temple, except a black man whom he kept with him. The rest of the men went and sat on the ground a little way off waiting developments, as they were sure that he was going to write a talisman or do something to propitiate the *afrit*.

DER EL HAGAR, DAKHLA OASIS.

For a long time nothing happened. Then loud cries for help, followed by the most piercing and blood-curdling shrieks were heard coming from the temple, and they knew that the talisman must be working, and guessed that the *afrit* was getting the worst of it.

Nothing more happened for some time. Then they heard a crackling sound, followed by dense clouds of black smoke arising from the temple. The crackling sound and the smoke continued for some time, and then Rohlfs emerged from the temple, looking very pleased and smiling, announced that he had found the treasure at last, and invited them all to come and see it.

They all trooped in and found that he had discovered the opening to the treasure chamber, which was a trap-door covering a flight of steps that led down into a vault that was filled with gold and silver and diamonds and treasure of all kinds, and Rohlfs was very pleased.

Then they looked for the black man, but could not see him. At last, in another part of the temple, one of them discovered the glowing embers of an enormous fire, and in it were the charred skull and some bones—the black man had been sacrificed by Rohlfs to propitiate the *afrit*!

Several of the men present concurred in this story. None of them, though they were living in Qasr Dakhl, had been present on the occasion; but they had heard of it, and everybody in the oasis knew about it.

They did not quite know what had happened to the treasure, but Rohlfs had a very large caravan with him, and all the camels were loaded when he left, so they supposed he took it all away with him.

All this was told with the utmost gravity, and with considerable detail, and they all unquestionably believed the story themselves. Yet it was all supposed to have happened close to their own village, and many of them were not only living at the time, but must have been young men and not children. They, none of them, thought any the worse of Rohlfs for this sacrifice—in fact they seemed to think all the better of him for having overcome the *afrit*.

CHAPTER V

AFTER lunch—and the tea that followed—we started off to pay a visit to Sheykh Mohammed el Mawhub, the representative of the Senussi in the oasis, at his *zawia* (monastery) close to the town.

His history is interesting, as throwing some light on the methods of the Senussi sect. He was born somewhere between 1840 and 1850, at Jalo, in Tripoli, and early in life became a member of the Senussia. While still quite a young man, probably under thirty, he was sent by the head Senussi sheykh to try to convert the inhabitants of Dakhla Oasis.

He arrived with practically no possessions beyond the clothes he stood up in, and began to expound the doctrines of his order to the inhabitants. He soon succeeded in collecting a following, upon whom, after the manner of his kind, he lived.

His next step was to apply to the authorities in the oasis for a permit to sink a well, and, having obtained it, asked his followers to help him in the work. The first well he sank—Bir Sheykh Mohammed—lies some four miles to the west of the village of Qasr Dakhl, and, when sunk, turned out to be an extremely good one. Soon afterwards, he sank a second well—Bir el Jebel—rather nearer to the village, which proved to be an even better one than Bir Sheykh Mohammed. This well was also sunk mainly by voluntary labour. The two wells together irrigated a considerable area. Close to them *ezbas* (farms) were built, which were inhabited by Sheykh Mohammed's sons. These farms being on the road from Dakhla to Kufara, the headquarters of the Senussi, and well removed from the village, without any of the ordinary *fellahin* of the oasis near them, enabled the Mawhubs to come and go to Kufara, a journey always conducted by them with a considerable amount of mystery, without fear of being observed by the other natives of the oasis.

While the property round these wells was being developed, the building of his *zawia* was also being proceeded with. This also was largely carried on by voluntary workers, not only from the members of his sect, but also from other villages, who, without actually belonging to the community, were sympathetic towards it and considered it a pious act to assist in the building of a religious edifice to be devoted to the service of Allah. Later on other wells were sunk.

The *zawia* consisted of a courtyard surrounded by a very high wall of mud bricks that was not even plastered. The whole building had no pretensions to any architectural beauty. I glanced into the court through the door as we passed it. A man, sitting on the floor of a small room opening out of it close to the entrance, and three small boys he was teaching, were the only inhabitants to be seen.

Sheykh Mawhub's house was of the same simple character as the rest of his *zawia*. We were led up into a guest chamber of the usual type, with settees round the walls, and were left for some time to our own devices. After about ten minutes' waiting a Sheykh Ibrahim—whom I recognised as the schoolmaster I had seen in the courtyard of the *zawia*—came in and announced that tea was coming shortly, and that Sheykh Mawhub himself would follow it—he evidently considered this a mark of considerable condescension on the part of the sheykh.

Tea in due course appeared, and Sheykh Ibrahim, having seen that we had all been duly served, departed and another interminable delay occurred.

At length we heard sounds of slow shuffling footsteps, punctuated by halts and questions and answers in a low voice in the distance, and the *mamur* whispered to me that he thought it must be Sheykh Mawhub who was coming. He seemed to stand rather in awe of him.

The sheykh himself at last appeared in the doorway, respectfully—it would hardly be too much to say reverently—supported by Sheykh Ibrahim. He seemed to be in the last stage of nervousness. He just touched hands with us in an almost lifeless manner, and then, still supported by Sheykh Ibrahim, sat down huddled up on a settee in the far corner of the room, being tenderly tucked into his place by the attendant sheykh. Hardly had he settled himself into his corner than, rather to my surprise, Qway came in, just spoke to him casually and then went and sat down as near as possible to the tea. It was evident that Sheykh Mawhub was the friend that Qway had asked leave to visit, and that he had already seen him, as the usual greetings were omitted on his entry.

A very resplendent young man followed close on Qway's heels, went up and kissed Sheykh Mawhub's hand, and then immediately went out again and stationed himself just opposite the door with his back to the wall of the passage, where he remained watching the assembled guests. This proved to be Sheykh Ahmed, the eldest son of Sheykh Mawhub.

It was noticeable that the native Government officials, who, while at Rashida and during the journey through the oasis, had behaved in the usual boisterous manner of their kind, laughing and chaffing each other and perpetually bawling out orders, apparently for no other object than to hear their own voices and assert their authority, were all most subdued and almost timid in the presence of Sheykh Mawhub.

His stage management was excellent, and he was certainly rather an impressive looking individual. Since his access of prosperity, and the advent of his sons to manhood, he had led an extremely retired life and become practically a recluse, seldom emerging from his *zawia* or seeing anyone except his followers, leaving the management of his property largely to his sons and the men, such as Sheykh Ibrahim, who were attached to his *zawia*. It was popularly supposed that he devoted his whole life to study, the affairs of the sect to which he belonged and to his religious observances. It was probably this method of life, combined with the influx of so many strangers, that accounted for his obvious nervousness.

The old sheykh, from the time of his entry, entirely dominated the meeting. His manner was so quiet and subdued as to be almost an affectation. He spoke at first in such a low voice as to be scarcely audible, and replied to the remarks of the officials as briefly as possible.

The *mamur* took it upon himself to explain to the sheykh that I was going off to map the desert, and had been making enquiries about Zerzura; so, as he had introduced the subject, I asked Sheykh Mawhub if he had ever heard of the place. He thought for a moment, and then said he had. It was an enchanted oasis, and all the inhabitants and cattle had been turned into stone, and would only come to life when someone had been sacrificed there.

He then for a few moments gazed out of the window at the sky with the rapt expression of a stained-glass saint, and added in a tone of dreamy reminiscence that a Greek had once tried to look for Zerzura, but that he had not been able to find it, and had died of poison on his way back to Europe. He then came down to earth again and glanced at me in an absent-minded way; but I thought that I detected something like a twinkle in his bleary eyes.

Afterwards we got on the subject of natural history. The sheykh woke up and became interesting. I had a long conversation with him on a variety of subjects. Towards the end he rather overcame his reserve and seemed to be trying to please, for on my expressing regret that my knowledge of his language was insufficient to enable me to converse with him, except through an interpreter, he volunteered to teach me Arabic, if I would come to his *zawia*.

I own I was tempted. The chance of completing my education in a Senussi monastery was unique; but it would have been an "eye-washy" sort of job, and I had other work to do—besides I doubted his motives, so I declined. He seemed genuinely disappointed. He had hoped, I suppose, to keep me learning Arabic in his *zawia*, instead of going off to explore the Libyan Desert that the Senussi looked upon as their private property.

After some further conversation, the sheykh invited us all to be his guests for the night at the *ezba* belonging to his son, Sheykh Ahmed.

Sheykh Ahmed's *ezba* lay some five miles to the west of the *zawia*. The first part of the way was mainly over uncultivated land. As soon as he was removed from the restraining influence of his father's presence, Sheykh Ahmed shook off his odour of sanctity and appeared in his true character of a very cheery and slim young scamp. He and his two brothers, Sheykhs Mohammed and 'Abd el Wahad—both of whom joined us before reaching the *ezba*—had by no means the reputation in the oasis for sanctity that their father possessed. Sheykh Ahmed was reported to be an extremely slim fellow to deal with, and, even among the natives, had the character of being "the biggest liar in the oasis." 'Abd el Wahad, the youngest brother, was still in his 'teens, and had not then attracted the gossip of the oasis. But Sheykh Mohammed was considered to be even more tricky than his elder brother.

It was the old, old story; too much pious teaching in the youth is apt to lead to a reaction later on. One meets clergymen's sons, for instance, who are famous for many things, but excessive piety is seldom one of them. History being based on human nature is proverbially apt to repeat itself, and those *in loco parentis* would, I fancy, always do well to remember that Robert the Devil was the son of Richard the Good—he frequently is!

Old Sheykh Mawhub's religion was obviously a very real and genuine thing, but that of his sons was, from all I heard and saw, largely a matter of conforming to the outward formalities of their order. But the prestige of the sect they belonged to was so great that, with the simple inhabitants of the oasis, their backslidings were overlooked, and almost regarded as one of the privileges of their holy character. In North Africa it is only necessary to label yourself as a holy man, to say enough prayers and fast occasionally, and you can do pretty much what you like in the meantime.

A ride of something over an hour brought us, just as the sun was setting, to Sheykh Ahmed's *ezba*. His guest house, like that of the *'omda* of Rashida, was built on to his private dwelling, where his wives and family lived. The house, and its guest house, were surrounded by a series of open yards forming the farm buildings, and used as places in which to house the stock at night, as threshing-floors and so on.

A Tea Party in Dakhla Oasis.

Enormous quantities of very strong tea are drunk by the natives, the making of which is a regular ceremony. Note the large copper urn on the left. (p. 39).

The guest chamber was a long narrow room about twenty-five feet from east to west by twelve from north to south. Two windows and the door opened on to a kind of terrace, while on the opposite side three windows looked out, to the north, on to a garden, in which was the well that watered the *ezba*, and where a number of palms and other fruit trees were planted, over the tops of which could be seen the cliff bounding the oasis in the blue distance.

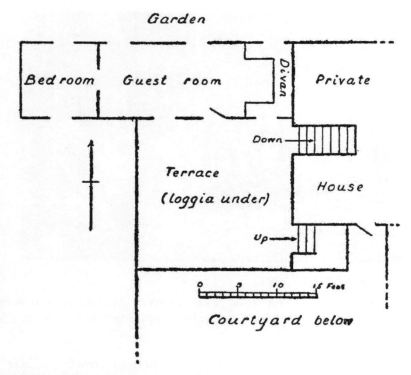

SHEYKH AHMED'S GUEST HOUSE.

The windows were draped with red curtains, and a doorway, leading into a small bedroom on the western end of the room was covered by a pair of heavy and rather dusty velveteen curtains of the same colour. The floor was carpeted, a few mats being placed here and there over the carpet. The roof, which seemed to be built in the usual way with palm trunk rafters supporting *jerids* (palm leaf stems), was covered with a thin coating of plaster, whitewashed like the walls and painted with broad red stripes—a form of decoration which, though roughly executed, was both effective and tasteful, and, taken with the subdued hues of the rugs on the floor, formed a colour scheme of which a European artist need not have been ashamed.

Knowing the reputation that the Senussi bear for leading the simple life, and their supposed aversion to adopting any European innovations, the contents of the room filled me with complete surprise.

On a plate by an open window, so as to be in the draught, stood the inevitable *gula*—a porous terra-cotta bottle for cooling water, to be found in every native's house in Egypt. Nailed to the wall were circular paper fans of Japanese make and two or three of a curious hatchet shape, ornamented with bits of red cotton stuff, such as are made in the oasis. A gaudy red and black print of Mecca was nailed to the wall opposite to the door, and a second long print in silver on silk, which stretched nearly across the eastern wall, showed another view of the same subject in villainous perspective, together with some other scenes of Eastern towns that I was unable to identify, the spaces between the views being filled up with texts and Arabesque ornamentations.

The remainder of the furniture was pure European—a shelf, with a mirror beneath it fixed to the wall, might have been bought in Tottenham Court Road; a hammock chair and some of bent wood with cane seats of the usual type, a couple of deal tables, on one of which stood a nickel-plated paraffin lamp and a sparklet bottle, and on the other a few books, an ordinary black japanned tray, with a glass water bottle and tumblers, and a gramophone. On one side of the gaudy print of the sacred Ka'aba at Mecca, was a coloured oleograph of the Khedive, and on the other was one of King Edward VII!

Having seen us all settled comfortably in our places, Sheykh Ahmed excused himself from attending on us any further, explaining that it was time for the *maghrib* prayer, and departed downstairs, where shortly afterwards we heard him fervently leading the prayers in the room beneath us.

Soon after he returned with a servant bringing the inevitable tea. Having seen that we were all served, Sheykh Ahmed departed again to change his clothes, and returned in a more gorgeous raiment than before.

While waiting for dinner to appear, Sheykh Ahmed's two brothers—Sheykh Mohammed and Sheykh 'Abd el Wahad—came in, went up and kissed his hand and then remained standing till he waved them permission to sit down.

The Senussi—or the better class among them at any rate—keep up the ceremonious manners of the old patriarchal system of the Arabs. Sheykh Ahmed, for instance, would not even stay in the room with his father in the *zawia*, much less sit down in it without his permission. His younger brothers, in his own home, kissed his hand when they came into the room and waited his permission to sit down. They stood up whenever he did, and remained standing till he went out of the room, or till he signed them to be seated. When Sheykh Mohammed, the second brother, came in, the youngest, Sheykh 'Abd el Wahad, at once stood up.

When dinner arrived the two younger brothers left, to go, I understood, to Sheykh Mohammed's *ezba*, which was not far from that of Sheykh Ahmed. Sheykh Ahmed himself helped to lay the cloth. A folding iron table was brought up to near where we were sitting, and an enormous round tray in red enamel, having views of Switzerland in panels all round it, was laid on the table. A cloth was spread over it, and on this the dinner was laid. At nearly all the '*omdas*' houses we stayed at we ate with our fingers in the native way;

but at Sheykh Ahmed's *ezba* we had nickel-plated spoons and forks, plates, tumblers and knives with plated handles.

Sheykh Ahmed himself, in accordance with the strict Arab etiquette, with his sleeves carefully rolled up to prevent them from being soiled by coming in contact with the dishes, waited on his guests at first—he was a good "bun hander"—and it was not till I invited him to join us, that he took his seat at the table and joined in the conversation. I was unfortunately unable to follow a good deal that he said, as my Arabic at that time was not of the best, but from the laughter that greeted many of his remarks, he was clearly an amusing and witty talker. He joined freely in the chaff of the Egyptian officials, and had evidently a gift of quick repartee.

The Mawhub family prided themselves upon keeping the best table in the oasis, and the dinner that he provided for us was, without any exception, the best meal I ever had the good fortune to take part in, and I took a large part in it.

The *mamur* was one that the Senussi hoped to convert to their sect—if they had not already done so. Much of their influence in Egypt was gained by this form of "pacific penetration." Sheykh Ahmed was no fool, and probably realised that the easiest road to an Egyptian's heart is through his tummy. He had accordingly borrowed his father's cook from the *zawia* at Qasr Dakhl to do honour to the occasion. This man was said in the oasis—probably correctly—to have been at one time a chef to the Sultan of Turkey, and Turkish cooking is probably the best in the world.

I do not know whether we in Europe borrowed our monastic system from the Arabs, whether they got it from us, or whether we both got it from some common source; but certainly there are a great many points of resemblance between ours and theirs. The reputation for "good living," enjoyed by the monasteries of the Middle Ages in Europe, when

"No baron or squire or knight of the shire

  Lived half so well as a holy friar."

has its exact counterpart in most of the Moslem monasteries at the present day. That cook from *zawia* of the Senussi sect—so famed for their abstemious simple life!—in Qasr Dakhl, was a past-master in his art, and that dinner must have been one of his finest efforts.

First arrived a large basin full of broth with two or three young chickens that had been boiled in it. The broth was strongly flavoured with lemon, which is an acquired taste.

Then came the *pièce de résistance*—a turkey. The police officer who was sitting next to me, who was himself an excellent cook, and quite knew what he was talking about, said it had been boiled in milk and then buttered, covered over with some sort of paste and put into the oven for a few minutes. It was stuffed with almonds, rice, raisons and *ferikh*, a sort of pop-corn, made, I believe, of green corn fried in butter. The stuffing had also some sort of spice in it that I was not able to identify.

The meat seemed to have lost all its fibre and almost melted in one's mouth; the skin was crisp and tasted like pastry; the stuffing—but to give an idea of what that stuffing was like is beyond me—no one but a poet could describe it.

After the turkey came chickens, roasted and also stuffed. Rissoles, flavoured with some delicious herbs, followed.

By the time the rissoles had been finished, I already felt that I had done more than justice to Sheykh Ahmed's hospitality, and that to attempt to pay him any further compliments in this direction might be attended by serious consequences. I hoped that the end of the meal might be in sight. But not a bit of it.

"The hardships of the lonely white man in Africa" have often been described, but they have never been really done justice to—they're frightful! After the rissoles came an endless succession of sweets, made as only a Turkish cook can make them. A spongy kind of blancmange eaten with jam. Jam-tarts—the jam being apparently made from dates. Crisp, thin flakes of pastry, covered with whipped cream, coloured pink and eaten with honey. A kind of very sweet nougat, also eaten with cream, followed by unmistakable Turkish Delight, thickly covered with powdered white sugar, which was infinitely superior to the best "Rahat lakum" that could be bought even in Cairo—rahat lakum, by the way, was a name that no one seemed to have even heard.

After dinner of course came tea, and following that *kerkadi*, or Sudan tea—a drink made from the dried flowers of a plant that grows somewhere in the Sudan.

The latter I had heard of in Egypt, but had never seen, so hearing that Sheykh Ahmed had some, I asked for it. It is not only considered by Moslems to be quite correct to ask your host to produce any little thing in this way, but it is even considered as a compliment.

The *kerkadi* was first made cold. A few flowers were dropped into a tumbler and stirred round for a few minutes till a pale pink decoction was produced, and then sugar was added to sweeten it.

When made in this way it produced a drink with a curious slightly acid flavour, that would have been very pleasant and refreshing on a hot day. It can also be drunk hot, in which case it is made exactly in the same manner as ordinary tea. But it is not nearly so good when made in this way, and when it has been left standing for some time it takes a strong acrid flavour, that would not be likely to appeal to European tastes. But as a cold drink it is surprising that it is so little known.

The policeman told me in a whisper that the tea which preceded the *kerkadi* was of extremely fine quality, adding native-like that Sheykh Ahmed must have paid a guinea a pound for it. He was very likely correct, for this is by no means an unusual price for one of the richer natives of the oasis to give for his favourite Persian tea.

When dinner and tea were over, and our cigarettes had been lighted, the Coptic doctor took possession of the gramophone, and we were regaled by Arab songs and tunes. Songs, band pieces and an occasional recitation followed each other for about half an hour. At length a very dreary tune was put on, and, as everybody voted it a bore, Sheykh Ahmed went over to the pile of records and began sorting them over, saying that he would find something better.

The record that he put on the machine proved to be a dialogue between a man and his wife, who after a few sentences started to quarrel violently, abusing each other and calling each other all the filthy and disgusting names that even the Arabic language could produce. This record evidently appealed to the audience, for they fairly roared with laughter at some of the remarks. As soon as it was finished and had been repeated, Sheykh Ahmed put on a song, which I was quite unable to follow, but which, from the remarks of the audience, must have been of an exceedingly racy character.

That gramophone was a great institution, but one that in my second year in the desert nearly led to unpleasant complications. On my return to Cairo, after my first season in the desert, I ordered half a dozen records to be sent to Sheykh Ahmed as *bakhshish*—leaving the choice of them to the shop assistant, as being more likely to know what would appeal to native tastes.

I visited Sheykh Ahmed again during my second season, and the gramophone was once more brought out and my records produced. Sheykh Ahmed had kept them in a separate place from the others in his collection, and I suspect had never put them on his gramophone before. But he placed them, one by one, on his machine and sat over it, beating time to the music, politely pretending to be thoroughly enjoying them. From this I gathered that he was entirely unaware of the nature of the music that his gramophone was producing—for they were certainly not records that I should have selected to send to a Senussi sheykh.

Some years later, owing to a slight difference of opinion with the Government authorities, Sheykh Ahmed found it convenient to clear out suddenly with his family and belongings to Kufara.

If some future visitor to that oasis should hear proceeding from a native house a fine baritone voice, announcing that he will "sing him songs of Araby and tales of fair Kashmir," or a choir of voices, accompanied by a brass band, exhorting him to further efforts by the inspiring strains of "Onward, Christian soldiers! marching as to war," he will be able to locate Sheykh Ahmed's house, and will know where those records came from.

I called at the shop, when next I was in Cairo, to ask why records so entirely inappropriate for a present to a Senussi sheykh had been sent to him. During the course of a rather heart-to-heart talk on the subject, the shop assistant explained that, as he had not expected me to go out again to the oasis, he had chosen those records as "a joke." It certainly had a humorous side; the sight of that unsuspecting Senussi sheykh politely beating time to "Onward, Christian soldiers!" was quite worth seeing!

But to return to my first visit to Sheykh Ahmed's *ezba*. When that gramophone's repertoire came to an end, a lengthy and serious discussion took place as to whether our digestion of the dinner was sufficiently far advanced to allow us to go to bed. Although it was then past two o'clock in the morning, the conclusion that was unanimously arrived at was that we should give our digestions some further time to continue their work before we retired. The company had evidently determined to make a night of it.

It was decided at first that we should have a little more music. The policeman during the morning had manufactured a sort of penny whistle out of a piece of cane. The *mamur* got hold of an iron tray, which he proceeded to use as a *tamtam*. The Coptic doctor, having had the advantage of an education under European teachers at the Qasr el 'Aini hospital in Cairo, was more civilised in his choice of an instrument—he managed to get hold of a comb from somewhere, and, with a piece of paper added, proved to be a first-rate performer. Having thus improvised a jazz band, they proceeded to make the night hideous by singing over again some of the songs they had heard on the gramophone.

At length, tiring of that amusement, they proceeded to play a childish game, in which one of them thought of something and the others, by questioning him in turn, tried to find out what it was. This caused considerable amusement, and the fun waxed fast and furious. The game was evidently a popular one. But the things that that sanctimonious Senussi sheykh thought of—well! they *were* Eastern! so much so that I eventually went to bed, and left them still playing—so austere were the Senussi!

Making Wooden Pipes.

These oases are irrigated by artesian wells of unknown antiquity, they are all lined with wooden pipes. Similar wells are being sunk to this day. (p. 312).

A Street in Rashida.

Sometimes the upper stories of the houses are built over the streets to keep the roadways cool in hot weather. (p. 49).

After a somewhat disturbed night's rest, I was aroused by a renewal of the concert by the jazz band. Coming out of my room I found the whole party in various stages of undress, sitting on the mattresses on which they had spent the night, smoking cigarettes, singing, banging trays and waiting the arrival of the barber to shave them. Sheykh Ahmed, himself, was not to the fore, he had retired to his private house for the night, and had not then put in an appearance.

The arrival of the barber and two servants with washing appliances put an end to the pandemonium. The barber went the round of each of the native guests in turn, shaving them and trimming their hair, while the remainder washed their hands as the attendants poured water over them. These preliminaries having been got through they proceeded to dress.

Sheykh Ahmed, gorgeously arrayed as usual, soon came in from his house, and proceeded with the help of the servants to lay the table for breakfast.

The meal having been concluded, tea made its appearance, and this having been consumed, we were taken by our host to see his well and garden. In one of the small-walled enclosures built round his house, he showed us his oven, round which were lying a number of rough earthen plates, pots and basins. The oven itself was a small beehive-shaped erection, slightly ornamented on the dome with raised patterns, among which a device like an inverted Y was conspicuous. This may possibly have been his *wasm*—tribal cattle brand.

The Senussi sect itself has a *wasm* of its own, consisting of the word "Allah," to show that the beasts and slaves branded with it are consecrated to His Service. I have never seen any slaves marked with this brand, but have often seen their camels, which had been marked in this way. In each case, however, the word took the form **IWI**. This may have been due only to bad writing on the part of the man who branded the beast, but it may also be a kind of conventionalised form of the correctly written word.

Sheykh Ahmed's two brothers arrived just before his house party broke up. So when we had gone back to the guest chamber to pack our belongings, I took the opportunity of photographing them together. I afterwards tried to induce Sheykh Ahmed to be photographed in his white praying clothes; but I made rather a *faux pas* there. He looked very angry for a moment, then stiffly replied that that was impossible as it was *haram*—forbidden by his religion. But he soon recovered his temper and was all smiles by the time we left.

CHAPTER VI

THE *mamur*, who was personally conducting our party, had arranged that we should look in at Gedida. On the way there we passed the village of Mushia, lying in an area of blown sand, which in some places seemed to be encroaching on the cultivation. Most of the land was planted with palms, of which there were said to be about twenty-six thousand. The village itself proved to be uninteresting, its most noticeable peculiarity being the painting of geometrical patterns which decorated the outer walls of some of the houses. The inhabitants showed more signs of progress here than in most of the villages of the oasis, as a number of *sagias*—waterwheels—had been erected to irrigate the cultivated land, where the partial failure of the wells had rendered this necessary.

At Gedida, however, they seemed more conservative. The water supply was failing, owing, according to the inhabitants, to the large amount of water yielded by the big modern wells at Rashida, and many of their palms were dying for want of irrigation. A few *shadufs* had been introduced to raise the water; but the inhabitants complained bitterly of the hard labour required to work them. When asked why they did not use *sagias*, they apathetically replied that no one knew how to make them, and seemed to think it would be too much trouble to import them from the Nile Valley.

At Gedida I heard another story of Zerzura. It appears that many years ago—the exact number was not stated—when the forebears of the present inhabitants all lived scattered about the district in little hamlets and *ezbas* some very tall black men, with long hair and long nails, came up out of the desert and stole their bread at night. In the morning the natives followed their tracks out into the desert, found the wells they had drunk from when coming into the oasis, and filled them up with salt to prevent them from being used again. They then returned to Dakhla Oasis, and, banding together, built the village of Gedida (the "new town") for mutual protection.

We reached Mut just at sunset, passing a number of the natives driving in their cattle to be housed in the little walled enclosures that surround the town.

I found Abd er Rahman waiting to report on the state of the camels. Everything he said had gone well, except that the green camel had bitten the blue one, and that the red one had been attacked by mange. Abd er Rahman, however, said that he had buttered him well—which, he added, had made him very angry, and he hoped now that he was cured.

The *'omda* of Rashida dropped in during the afternoon. On leaving, he expressed a fervent wish that I might find Zerzura, and that I should find a lot of treasure there. I soon found that it was quite useless to attempt to persuade any native into the belief that I was only intending to make maps and collect scientific information. Even the more intelligent of them—such as the native officials, the Mawhub family and the *'omda* of Rashida—were quite unable to realise that anyone could be so foolish to do work of that kind unless he were paid to do so, and they were such confirmed treasure seekers themselves, and so secretive in their methods of conducting their hunt for buried riches, that they all considered that the reason I gave for my journey was only a cloak to disguise the fact that I was really looking for treasure.

In making my plans to set out into the unknown part of the Libyan Desert beyond Dakhla, I found myself at once confronted by a serious difficulty of a distinctly unusual nature. Generally, when a traveller starts on a journey, he has some definite object in view—he is going to climb a particular mountain, to follow a certain river to its source, to complete the survey of some lake that has been found, or to look for some place that has been reported to exist on native information—but in this part there was no such object available.

With the exception of the Kufara group of oases, on its extreme western side, practically the whole Libyan Desert to the south and west of Dakhla was quite unknown, so the south-west quarter was the one that appealed to me most, as any journey made in this direction would lead right into the heart of the largest area of unknown ground in Africa, or for the matter of that outside it, and it was in this quarter, too, that the maps showed the great dune-field, the crossing of which was one of the main objects of my journey, so this was the part I decided first to tackle.

It was then that I found myself faced with the problem. What was to be my objective? Between west and south there are a great many bearings upon which one can march. In which direction should I go?

The prospect of being able to find a well, perhaps only a two-foot shaft in the ground—very probably silted up with sand—by wandering out haphazard into several hundred thousand square miles of desert is remote.

The maps gave little assistance in solving the problem. Many of them left this space entirely blank. Those that placed anything there at all, described it as being entirely covered with large dunes, or as some of them put it, "impassable dunes."

The nearest point to Dakhla in this south-western quadrant, that was marked in the maps, was an oasis which native information placed eighteen days' journey to the south-west. Eighteen days, that is over ordinary desert, which might mean thirty at least if large dunes had to be crossed, and from what I had seen of those dunes it was doubtful if they were negotiable at all. It was said to be inhabited; but even its name was unknown. It was also said to have an old road leading from it towards Egypt. This looked somewhat promising, but the place was too far off to be of any use as a first objective, as until its position was accurately known, so that I could be certain of finding it at my first attempt, it would be necessary for me to arrange to get back again in the event of my not being able to reach it—and this would have necessitated a thirty-six days' journey away from water, over easy desert, or two or three months over large dunes.

When it is considered that a camel, laden only with grain, will consume its own load in about a month, and that the amount of water that would have to be taken in addition on a journey of this description would be far heavier than the grain required, it will be easily realised that such a journey as this would be quite impossible without adopting some system of depots or relays, which, owing to the risk of their being tampered with, I felt disinclined to do until I knew more about the district. Before I could hope to reach this place, it was necessary for me to find some nearer oasis, or well, from which I could start afresh; so it was clear that this intermediate oasis, or well, must be my first objective. But where was this place to be found?

In the absence of more reliable information, it occurred to me that possibly some indication of its whereabouts might be gathered from the legends of Zerzura. The story of Rohlfs' excavations in the Der el Hagar, told me by men who had actually been living in the neighbourhood at the time when they were said to have taken place, showed the extent to which even comparatively recent events are contorted by the natives.

But the name Zerzura itself was suggestive. Zerzur means literally a starling, but is a term often loosely applied to any small bird. Assuming the name to be derived from this source, it would have some such meaning as "the place of little birds," a name that seemed of such a fanciful nature that it appeared to me unlikely to be applied to any definite place, and, taken in conjunction with the somewhat mystical character of the stories with which the oasis was associated, I concluded that either no place of that name ever existed, or, which seemed more likely, that Zerzura was a generic name applied to any unknown or lost oasis, and that the various legends I had heard of it were, in some cases at all events, garbled versions of events that had really occurred in the past; and judging from the speed with which the story of Rohlfs' excavations had been distorted, a past that was not necessarily very remote.

Zerzura was said to lie to the south-west of Dakhla, and the other indications, small as they were, all pointed to this being the most promising direction in which to go. Not only was the unknown oasis, with the road running back towards Egypt, marked on the map as lying approximately in this direction, but what was probably the best indication of all, a large migration of birds came up annually from this part of the desert. Certainly there was not much to go upon in deciding to adopt this route, but in the absence of more reliable information, I was compelled to follow such indications as there were. Later on—in my last season in the desert—I was able to collect from various natives a large amount of data as to the unknown parts, from which I was able to construct a more or less complete map. But the information came too late for me to make use of it. It may perhaps be of service in affording an objective for future travellers. If I had had this intelligence to go upon when I first went out into the desert I should have tackled the job in an entirely different manner.

The red camel having recovered from his buttering, and being declared by Qway to be cured of the mange, I decided to start at once.

Much curiosity existed in the oasis as to the direction in which I intended to go. The majority of the natives, influenced perhaps by my enquiries about Zerzura, were firmly convinced that I was bent upon a hunt for the hidden treasure to be found there, and any statement that I made to the contrary only had the effect of strengthening them more strongly in their opinion. No native, when he is starting treasure seeking, ever lets out where he is going, he tries to mislead his neighbours as to his real intentions, and any statements I made as to the object of my journey were invariably regarded from this standpoint.

The *mamur* came to see me off, and, just before starting, asked me in what direction I intended to go. I told him the south-west. The *mamur* was too polite to contradict me, but his expression showed his incredulity quite plainly—incredulity and some admiration. His thoughts put into words were: "Liar, what a liar. I wish I could lie like that."

On my return he was one of the first to come round to "praise Allah for my safety." Having got through the usual polite formalities, he asked me where I had *really* been. When I said I had gone to the south-west as I had told him I should, he looked extremely surprised and glanced across to Qway, drinking tea on a mat near the door, for confirmation. Qway laughed. "Yes, he did go to the south-west," he said.

"But—but—but—," stammered the *mamur*, "that's where you said you were going."

Even then I don't think he quite believed it. When asked questions of this kind, I invariably told the exact truth and never made any secret of my plans. I knew quite well they would not believe me, and at first they never did. Afterwards, when they began to realise that my statements were correct, they looked on me, I believe, as rather a fool. They did not seem to understand anyone speaking the truth, when he merely had to lie in order to deceive.

This raises a somewhat intricate question in morality. When you know that if you speak the truth, you will not be believed, and so will deceive as to your real intentions, isn't it more strictly moral to lie?

I had made somewhat elaborate preparations for crossing the dunes. I had brought with me several empty sacks to spread on the sand for the camels to tread on, and for my own use I had a pair of Canadian snow-shoes, with which I had found it perfectly easy to cross even the softest sand.

I walked out to have a nearer look at the dunes. At close quarters they seemed to me even more formidable than when viewed from a distance. Not only were they of considerable size, but, what was infinitely worse, the sand of which they were composed was so loose and soft that the camels would have sunk in almost to their hocks. It was obvious that, if the whole dune-field was of this character, to get a caravan over many days' journey of this soft sand was an almost hopeless task.

However, I made up my mind to give it a trial. So the evening before starting out into the desert, I sent Qway off on his *hagin* to find the best place for us to enter the dune belt, with the result that, instead of setting out towards the south-west, he led the caravan towards the north-west, where he had found a low point in the sand hills, but it was with a good deal of trepidation that I set foot on the first dune we came to, and realised that I had embarked on the desperate attempt to solve the riddle of the sands of the "Devil's Country"—it was an awful prospect.

CHAPTER VII

THE first dune we had to negotiate was only about eight feet high and, as the sand at this point was crusted hard, in a minute or two, without the slightest difficulty, we were across the first sand hill of that field of "impassable dunes"—and the last!

We at once found ourselves on a sand-free patch lying between the dunes. By following a winding course across the belt we were able to reach its farther side in about an hour and a half, without having to negotiate any further sand. The sand hills were not nearly so closely packed together as they appeared to be from a distance.

We emerged into a long lane between the dunes quite free from drift sand, running parallel with the sand belt and stretching away to the south, till it ended in the distance in a hill on the skyline. On the far side of this lane was another belt of sand hills, which, being closely packed together and of considerable height, would have caused some difficulty to cross. So instead of keeping a south-westerly direction, which would have necessitated crossing these difficult dunes, I followed the sand-free lane to the south and coasted along them, hoping to find an easier place where the dunes had become lower or more scattered. An old disused road ran west from Mut into the dunes, presumably leading direct to Kufara. We found the continuation of this road where it crossed the lane and again ran under the dunes to the west of it. At that point it bore 265° mag.

We soon joined the tracks of five camels proceeding in the same direction as ourselves, and apparently only three or four days old. We followed these tracks, which ran along the lane between the dunes and presently, to everyone's profound astonishment, came upon the unmistakable track of a two-wheeled cart. They eventually led us to a very low gritstone hill.

As wheeled conveyances are entirely unknown in the oasis the presence of the tracks was a perfect mystery. It was not till my return to the oasis that I learnt their history. At least forty years before, the father of the *'omda* of Rashida had imported a cart into the oasis from the Nile Valley, in order to fetch from the gritstone hill two millstones we had seen in a mill in his village.

The permanence of tracks in certain kinds of desert is well known to anyone with any experience of desert life. The marks in this case ran over a level sandy surface thinly covered with darker pebbles. The cart must have crushed the pebbles deeply into the soft sand on which they lay, and the ruts thus formed rapidly filled up again with drift sand during the first sandstorm, showing as two conspicuous white lines, owing to the absence along the tracks of the darker pebbles, and forming marks that might easily last for a century, unless they happened to be situated in a part of the desert where the sand erosion was gradually wearing away the surface of the ground.

Close by the hill from which the millstones had been quarried the tracks of the five camels we had seen turned off towards the west. As the lane we had been following ran up north in the direction of Qasr Dakhl and the only camels in the oasis were those kept by the Senussi living there, there was little doubt that the tracks we had seen were those of a party of Senussi from the *zawia* on their way, probably with letters, to Kufara.

The Senussi invariably conducted their visits to and from their headquarters with the greatest secrecy, for fear that, when proceeding there, they might be followed and the road that they took might thus become known. The route followed by this party was eminently well suited to preserve their secret, as, while following the lane, they must have been entirely concealed from the inhabitants of the oasis by the intervening line of dunes that we crossed. So we had evidently stumbled upon one of their secret roads to Kufara.

About four o'clock we reached the hill we had seen on the skyline at the end of the lane between the dunes, and as it was the highest in the neighbourhood I climbed to its top with Qway and Abd er Rahman, sending the caravan round its base to wait for me on its southern side.

From the summit we could see over a wide range of country. In the far north lay Dakhla Oasis with the scarp behind it. The continuation of this cliff beyond Qasr Dakhl could be seen stretching far away to the west as a faint blue line that appeared to get lower towards the west.

The desert to the west of Dakhla was almost entirely covered by dunes, which seemed to be higher farther to the north and in the extreme west, where they were noticeably redder in colour than the cream-coloured sand hills in the neighbourhood of the oasis.

Everywhere to the south-west, in the direction in which we were going, the desert was very level, and to my great surprise entirely free from drift sand, with the exception of one or two isolated dunes that could be seen in the distance. Instead of the sand-covered desert to the south-west of Dakhla shown on the maps, the whole surface consisted of bare Nubian sandstone—there was no sign of the limestone that caps the plateau near the Nile Valley. The hill on which we stood was considerably higher than Dakhla, and from our elevated position we could see a great distance; but not a trace was there to be seen of the "great sea of impassable sand" that was shown on the maps of the south-west of the oasis. Never had an unsuspecting traveller been so hopelessly misled by an imaginative geographer. The great area covered with huge dunes that was supposed to exist here, extending to thousands upon thousands of square miles, simply did not exist at all. It was an absolute myth!

The sand belts of this desert creep forward towards the south under the influence of the prevailing north wind—not as I once saw stated in a novel at the rate of many miles in the course of a night—but with a steady advance of, say, twenty yards in a year. Long belts, like the Abu Moharik already referred to, are known to extend for hundreds of miles, and it had consequently been assumed that the dunes that Rohlfs had found ran for a similar distance.

From where we stood the reason that these belts were so curtailed was perfectly clear. The ground level rose fairly rapidly all the way from Dakhla, and the area lying to the south-west of our position constituted an elevated plateau, along the northern edge of which ran a chain of hills of considerable height. The sand belts found by Rohlfs had all banked up against these hills, except in one or two places where a line of isolated crescent dunes had crept through a gap in the range and emerged on to the plateau.

The contrast between this part of the desert, as shown on the map, entirely covered with these "impassable" dunes, to cross which was a problem that during the past few months I had been racking my brains in attempts to solve, and the desert as it existed in reality—with only one small ridge of sand about eight feet high and perhaps forty yards broad to be crossed, which had presented no difficulty at all, could hardly have been greater. I felt considerably annoyed with the compilers of those maps for causing me so much wasted scheming. The discovery, however, of the sand-free character of the desert, was of the greatest importance for the purpose of my journey, as it naturally made our road far easier to traverse.

As the "impassable sea of sand" had proved to be a myth, and the Senussi did not appear to be anything like as fanatical as I had been led to expect, I began to hope that the other unsurmountable difficulties foretold would also vanish in the same way, and that I should have no other impediments to surmount than the shortage of water and other problems that always have to be faced in every desert journey.

Abd er Rahman had been minutely examining the whole desert towards the south-west from the top of the hill. Suddenly he touched my arm and drew my attention to two *'alems* (landmarks) lying in the distance.

I looked through my glass in the direction that he indicated, but could see no *'alem* at all. However, as he persisted they were there, we went down to the bottom of the hill to look for them.

For a long way from the foot of the hill, the whole surface of the desert was covered with loose slabs of sandstone rock. Abd er Rahman led us across this up to a little pile of three stones about a foot high that, with the keen sightedness of the *bedawin*, he had spotted from a distance of some two hundred yards, although it lay on the ground so covered with loose slabs of stone that I had not been able to see it myself, even when pointed out by Abd er Rahman, until I got within a few yards of it.

These little heaps of stone, sometimes only a few inches high, are placed at intervals along the desert roads to act as landmarks to those who use them. Occasionally, instead of being placed on the road itself, they are erected on a hill, or rising ground, close by it. The *bedawin*, even if unacquainted with the district, will often travel great distances, relying for their guidance on the *'alems* erected along the roads by previous travellers.

Some hundred yards farther on we found the second *'alem* that Abd er Rahman had seen. It consisted of a similar pile of stones. I took a bearing along the line of the two and then we proceeded to march along it. But the road proved to be very bad going, the camels slipped and tripped over the loose stone slabs, till once or twice I thought one would be down. But after a time we got on to easier ground, and began to make better progress.

In making a compass traverse, it is, I believe, usual to estimate the speed at which the caravan is travelling for each section of the road. I personally found this method so unsatisfactory that, after many attempts, I at length was forced to abandon it and to keep my route book on a method of my own, which I found to give much better results.

I assumed a uniform speed of two and a half miles per hour, which is about the rate of a caravan of loaded camels over normal ground. Then, after having passed over an unusually difficult section of the road, where I knew we had not been marching up to our standard speed, I estimated the amount of time we had lost, and entered it in the route book as a "halt," to be deducted from the amount of time actually occupied in crossing it. I found that a compass traverse, booked in this way, not only fitted considerably closer to the astronomical positions I found, but the actual plotting of the traverse itself was very much simplified—and the risk of errors in consequence much reduced—by having a uniform speed to work upon.

Shortly before we camped for the night we crossed a very faint old road running almost due east and west. These old roads—of which we found a large number—remain visible for an extraordinarily long time, where they happen to run over certain kinds of desert.

We found the going over the plateau unusually bad. Not only had we to cross large areas of *kharafish* (sharp, sand-eroded rock), but we repeatedly came across a particularly obnoxious form of it known, I believe, as *sofut*—a type of erosion consisting of knife-edged blades of sandstone standing up two or three inches above the ground, which proved to be a severe trial to the soft-footed camels, who tripped and staggered along, uttering the most melancholy groans.

Another type of surface we had occasionally to cross was that known as *noser*. At first sight this appeared to be a perfectly level expanse of hard crusted sand. But appearances were deceptive. The sand was only a few inches thick and overlay a bed of stiff clay which, under the influence of the great summer heat, had cracked into fissures often a foot or more wide and extending for several feet down into the ground. The smooth sandy surfaces showed no trace of these chasms. But if the heavy camels, while walking over the ground, happened to place one of their feet over a fissure, they immediately broke through the weak crusted sand, and stumbled forward into the hole below, on more than one occasion coming right down and throwing their loads. Fortunately we had no worse casualties; but strained sinews, and even broken legs are by no means uncommon from this cause.

We continued marching along the bearing I had taken between the two *'alems*, so far as the unequalities of the desert would allow us, for though the general level of the plateau was maintained over a large area, it had many minor undulations. But by looking ahead in the direction of the bearing we were generally able to decide where the road ran.

Here and there we came across *'alems*, showing that we were still on the right track; but it was not until we had followed it for nearly two days that we again saw any part of the road itself.

Then, however, we found a stretch of it lying in a sheltered position, which we were able to follow for over two miles. In one place where, being sheltered, it was rather more plainly visible than usual, I counted no less than forty-three parallel paths. At one time it must clearly have been one of the main caravan roads of the desert. But we saw no more *'alems*, nor did we come across any more stretches of the road on that journey.

The farther out on the plateau we got the greater were the number of the hills we saw. They were all of the same Nubian sandstone of which the plateau itself consisted—I saw no trace anywhere in this part of the desert of the limestone that caps the plateau to the north and east of Dakhla and Kharga. The hills were of the usual desert type, either flat-topped, domed, or pyramidal. Here and there we came across some with a more jagged outline, but these were rare. In parts these hills were extraordinarily numerous, from one point I counted over two hundred and fifty of them, in spite of the fact that about 60° of the horizon were cut off by the proximity of a long ridge. The largest of them that I saw was not much more than three hundred feet in height. The general level of the plateau was approximately that of the tableland of the top of the cliff to the north of Dakhla.

On our fourth day out from Mut we got into a considerable area of very rough ground, largely consisting of sharp-edged *sofut*, with the result that by evening two of the camels were limping slightly, owing to the injuries to their feet from the sharp rock, and as I could see much lower ground to the south, I turned off on setting out on the fifth morning in that direction.

After two hours' march we reached the bottom of a small wady, which my aneroid showed to be 110 feet deep. As, shortly before reaching it, we had seen the track of a rat, my men christened it the *"wady el far"* or "Valley of the Rat." It was still quite early in the day, but as one of the camels was still limping, I decided to camp, and sent Qway off on his *hagin* towards the south-west to scout.

The Most "Impassable" Dune.

The whole of the central part of the Libyan desert was supposed to consist of an "impassable sea" of sand dunes, but on a journey to about the middle of the desert, the only dune that had to be actually crossed was the small one shown above. (p. 82).

On his return to the camp I asked Qway what he had seen during his ride. He said he had ridden for two hours towards the south-west, and then he had reached the edge of a plain on the far side of which was a high black mountain. Beyond that he said was a very deep valley, which he had been unable to see into, but which was overhung by a mist. As the mountain lay about four hours' ride away, and the valley about two hours beyond it, he had returned to the camp to report what he had seen.

This sounded most promising news, and I was anxious to go off at once and have a look at the *"wady esh shabur,"* or "Valley of the Mist," as Khalil poetically called it, so I took Qway off to look at our water-tanks.

But the inspection was not too encouraging. We were distinctly short of water. Qway thought we should have just enough to take us out to his "Valley of the Mist," and back again to Dakhla, if all went well, but he pointed out that we had one lame camel and another limping slightly, and that at that season it was quite possible that we might get some hot days with a *simum* blowing, and he consequently thought that it would be far better to be on the safe side and go straight back to Dakhla, rest the camels, and then come out and go on to the valley on the next journey.

As this was obviously sound advice, we struck camp, packed up and prepared to set off at once towards Dakhla, leaving several sacks of grain behind us, which greatly eased the burden of the camels and allowed us to leave the two limping beasts unloaded.

The wady in which the camp had been pitched evidently lay on the southern fringe of the plateau, and opened out on its eastern side down a sandy slope on to the lower ground beyond. The plateau, I knew, did not extend much farther to the east, so with two damaged camels in the caravan, I thought it best to avoid a return over the very rough road we had followed on our outward journey, and to strike instead in an easterly direction, round the south-east corner of the tableland, over the smooth sandy desert lying at the foot of the scarp of the plateau.

This road, though somewhat longer than the one we had followed on our outward journey, proved to be excellent going; it lay almost entirely over smooth hard sand. We continued to follow an easterly course till the middle of the next morning, when, on reaching the edge of the dune belt that runs along the western boundary of Dakhla, we turned up north towards Mut, and coasted along it.

The road was almost featureless. A few low rocky hills were seen on the lower ground for a while after leaving the "Valley of the Rat," but even these soon ceased. From this point onwards we saw nothing of interest, with the exception of some pieces of petrified wood, lying on a greenish clay, until we reached our destination at Mut, in Dakhla Oasis. In the desert round about Kharga and Dakhla we several times came across the petrified remains of trees, though they never occurred in large patches.

Qway proved to be right in his forebodings of hot weather, and we had two days of fairly warm *simum* wind. We, however, managed to get in without suffering unduly from thirst—but I felt rather glad that we had not tried to reach that valley.

The state of my caravan necessitated my giving them some days' rest, to enable them to recover their condition, and to allow their feet to get right again after the hard usage they had received on the sharp rocks of the plateau, before setting out again into the desert.

In the meantime I conducted an experiment to try and locate the position of the place from which the palm doves—the *kimri sifi*—were said to come. Their migration was just at its height, and several times, while on the plateau, we put them up from the rocks on which they had alighted to rest during their flight.

The *kimri sifi* always arrived in the oasis just before sunset, and as they generally made for a particular well to the south-west of Mut, I went there one evening with a compass and gun to wait for them. I took the bearing with my compass to the direction in which a number of them came. These bearings tallied very closely, the average of them being 217° mag.

I then shot a few of them just as they were alighting, and cut them open. They had all been feeding on seeds—grass seeds apparently—and olives. The seeds were in an almost perfect condition, but the olives were in such an advanced state of digestion as to be hardly recognisable.

I next bought some doves of the ordinary kind kept in the oasis from the villagers, and confined them in a cage. At sunrise the following morning I fed them on olives and then, towards midday, took them out one by one, at intervals of an hour, killed them, and cut them open to see the state of the olives. Those of the one killed at three o'clock seemed in the state most resembling those taken from the *kimri sifi* I had shot, showing that it required about nine hours' digestion to reduce them to that condition.

The *kimri sifi* is a weak-flighted bird, and, judging from the numbers we put up in the desert from places where they had settled down to rest, spends a considerable part of the day during the flight to Mut from the oasis where the olives grow, resting upon rocks in the desert. I consequently concluded that its average speed, including the rests, during its journey from the olive oasis, would be about twenty-five miles an hour.

Applying the principles of Sherlock Holmes to the case I deduced—I believe that to be the correct word—that the oasis the *kimri* came from lay in the direction of the mean of the bearings I had taken, viz. 217° mag., at a distance of nine times twenty-five, or two hundred and twenty-five miles, and that it contained olive trees. Some years later an Arab told me that there *was* an oasis off there that contained large quantities of olive trees. Boy scouts will, I trust, copy!

CHAPTER VIII

HAVING given my caravan sufficient time to recover from their previous journey, I set out again into the desert. On this occasion the camels were much more heavily loaded, as I had determined to cover as much ground as possible.

But we had not proceeded for more than four hours from Mut when one of the camels fell dead lame again. As it was obviously hopeless to think of taking him along with us, and we had proceeded such a short distance, I decided to turn back and make a fresh start.

On reaching Mut we fired the camel and then the poor brute was cast loose. He hobbled painfully about for a few minutes, and then with a grunt knelt down on the ground. Musa, with the idea perhaps of relieving his sufferings, squatted on his heels in front of him, and proceeded to warble to him on his flute.

This was an expedient to which he often resorted in order to soothe the beasts under his charge. Frequently, after an unusually heavy day in the desert, when the camels had been fed, he would squat down among them and discourse wild music from his reed flute to them, till far into the night. As this generally had the effect of keeping me awake, I rather objected to the proceeding.

On this occasion his musical efforts seemed curiously to take effect. The camel for some time remained shuffling uneasily on the ground, probably in considerable pain. But after a time he became quieter, and before long he stretched his long neck out upon the ground and apparently went to sleep.

The day after our operation on the camel we started off again for the "Valley of the Mist" and Qway's high black mountain.

The weather at the beginning of April is always variable. A strong northerly wind sprang up towards evening, on the third day out, and made things rather uncomfortable. The sky at dusk had a curious silvery appearance that I had noticed often preceded and followed a sand storm. It was presumably caused by fine sand particles in the upper reaches of the atmosphere. The wind dropped after dark, as it frequently does in the desert, but it sprang up again in the morning with increased strength. During the night it worked round from north towards the east, and by morning had got round still farther, and was blowing a gale from the south, right into our teeth.

Soon after our start, we found considerable difficulty in making any headway against it, and before long we were marching into a furious gale. One of the beasts, which was perhaps rather overloaded, was several times brought to a standstill by a violent gust. An unusually powerful one that struck him fairly brought him down on his knees. We got him on his feet again, but had gone but a short way when another camel followed his example. Then the first one came down again and this time threw his load.

It was obviously useless to attempt to proceed, so having reloaded the camel, we retraced our steps to a hill at the foot of which we had camped. It was, of course, quite out of the question to pitch the tent, so it was left tied up in a bale, together with the other baggage, while we climbed up on to a ledge that ran round the hill, about twenty feet above its base. Here we were above the thickest of the clouds of sand that swept over the surface of the ground so densely that it was hardly possible to see more than a few yards in any direction.

Towards the afternoon the wind increased if anything in force, and small stones could be heard rattling about among the rocks on the hill. It veered round once more till it was blowing again from the north. The gale had considerably fallen off by sunset. I accordingly, rather to my subsequent regret, decided to spend the night at the bottom of the hill.

When I got out my bedding, I picked up a woollen *burnus* and shook it to get rid of the sand. It blazed all over with sparks. I put the end of my finger near my blankets, and drew from them a spark of such strength that I could very faintly feel it. When I took off the hat I was wearing I found that my hair was standing on end—this I hasten to state was only due to electricity.

The wind died out towards morning. I had, however, to get up several times before midnight to shake off the sand that had accumulated on my blankets, to prevent being buried alive, for it drifted to an extraordinary extent round the flanks of the hill.

We had started off some time the following morning before it struck me that there was something wrong with the baggage, and I found that the tent had been left behind. We found it at the foot of the hill completely buried by the sand that must have banked up during that gale to the height of two or three feet against the hill.

The horrors of a sand storm have been greatly overrated. An ordinary sand storm is hardly even troublesome, if one covers up one's mouth and nose in the native fashion and keeps out of the sand. A certain amount of it gets into one's eyes, which is unpleasant, but otherwise there is not much to complain about. On the other hand, there is an extraordinarily invigorating feeling in the air while a sand storm is blowing—due perhaps to the electrified condition of the sand grains, which, from some experiments I once made on the sand blown off a dune, carry a fairly high charge of positive electricity.

The storm I have described was certainly unpleasant, but it had one compensation—Musa left his reed flute lying on the sand, and my *hagin* promptly ate it! That camel seemed to be omnivorous. Feathers, tent pegs and gun stocks all figured at various times in his bill of fare. But bones were his favourite delicacy; a camel's skeleton or skull by the roadside invariably drew him off the track to investigate, and he seldom returned to his place without taking a mouthful. In consequence, among the numerous names by which he was known in the caravan—they were all abusive, for his habits were vile—was that of the *ghul*, or cannibal.

We got off at five in the morning the day following the sand storm, and, after a six hours' march, reached the sacks of grain in the "Valley of the Rat." As the day was rather warm, we rested the camels here for four hours and then pushed on for Qway's "high black mountain" and the "Valley of the Mist."

I had hoped great things from Qway's description of them, but unfortunately I had not taken into account the want of proportion of the *bedawin* Arabs. The "high black mountain" was certainly black, but it was only seventy feet high!

From the top of this "mountain" we were able to look down into the "Valley of the Mist." Here, too, great disappointment met me. The wady was there all right—it was an enormous depression, about two hundred and fifty feet lower than the plateau. But the vegetation and the huge oasis, that I had been expecting from Qway's account of the "mist," were only conspicuous by their absence. The wady was as bare as the plateau; and considering the porous nature of the sand that covered its floor, and the height above sea-level as compared with the other oases, it could hardly have been otherwise. It was clearly, however, of enormous size, for it stretched as far as we could see south of an east and west line, as a vast expanse of smooth sand, studded towards the south and east by a few low rocky hills, but absolutely featureless to the south-west and west.

The "mist," upon which Qway laid such stress, I found was not due to moisture at all, but to refraction, or rather to the absence of it. The hot sun blazing down on to a flat stony desert, such as the plateau over which we had been travelling, causes a hazy appearance in the nature of a mirage on the distant horizon. But, when looking from the top of a tableland over a deep depression some distance away, this hazy appearance is absent, as the line of sight of the spectator lies the height of the cliff above the floor of the depression, instead of being only a few feet above it. Though the "Valley of the Mist" was invisible from the point where Qway had first seen his "high black mountain," his experienced eye had seen that a depression lay beyond it, owing to the absence of this haze, which, however, is only to be seen under certain conditions.

With some difficulty we managed to get the caravan down from the plateau on to the lower ground, and then coasted along towards the west, under the cliff, in order to survey it. This scarp ran practically due east and west, without a break or indentation until we came to a belt of dunes which poured over it, forming an easy ascent on to the plateau, up which we proceeded to climb.

At the top the sand belt passed between two black sandstone hills, from the summit of one of which a very extensive view over the depression was obtainable. It was at once clear that there was no prospect of finding water—still less an oasis—for at least two days' journey farther to the south, for there was nothing whatever to break the monotony of the sand-covered plain below us. As the water supply was insufficient to warrant any further advance from Mut, we had to return—always a depressing performance.

We found, however, one hopeful sign. The pass that led over the dune belt on to the plateau—the "Bab es Sabah," or "gate of the morning," as the poetical Khalil called it, because we first sighted it soon after dawn—had at its foot an *'alem*. When I plotted our route on the map, I found that this *'alem* lay almost exactly in line with the old road we had followed on our first journey out from Mut, showing that the pass had been the point for which it had been making. The place to which this road led would consequently be sure to lie near, or on the continuation of the bearing from the pass to the place where we had seen the two first *'alems*. This was a point of considerable importance, as there seemed to be little chance of finding any remains of the road itself on the sandy soil of the depression, unless we should happen to land on another *'alem*. The bearing we had been marching on before was such a short one that there was always the risk that, owing to the obstruction to the direct road of some natural feature, the short section of it, along which the bearing was taken, was not running directly towards its ultimate destination.

While hunting round about the camp, I found embedded in the sand two pieces of dried grass, much frayed and battered. So on leaving the camp next day, we followed the line of the sand belt to the north, as showing the direction of the prevailing wind, in hopes of finding the place from which the dried grass embedded in the dune had come.

View near Rashida.

Note the wooded height in the background and the scrub-lined stream in foreground from the well under the large tree on the right. (p. 49).

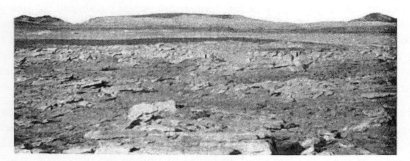

A Conspicuous Road—to an Arab.

Two small piles of stone, or *'alems* can, with difficulty, be seen. Arabs can march for hundreds of miles through a waterless desert, relying on landmarks such as these. (p. 86).

Battikh.

A type of sand erosion, known as *battikh* or "watermelon" desert. (p. 308).

We left the camp about half-past seven. Soon after four we entered what is known as a *redir*—that is to say, a place where water will collect after one of the rare desert rains. It was a very shallow saucer-like hollow, a few feet in depth, the floor of which consisted of clay. The farther side of this was covered with sand, and here we found the grass for which we had been searching.

It was very thinly scattered over an area a few hundred yards in diameter. It was quite shrivelled and to all appearances completely dead. But it was the first vegetation we had seen on the plateau to the south-west of Dakhla. This *redir* showed a noticeable number of tracks of the desert rats, and was probably one of their favourite feeding grounds.

Having solved the problem of the grass, as our water supply was getting low, we turned off in a north-easterly direction, making for Dakhla. The plateau surface changed for the worse, and a considerable amount of *sofut* had to be crossed; but fortunately the camels held out. We crossed two old roads running up north, apparently to Bu Mungar and Iddaila. Here and there along these old disused roads we saw circles, four or five feet in diameter, sparsely covered with stones about the size of a hen's egg, scattered on the sandy surface, that obviously had been placed there by human agency. Qway explained that these were the places where the old slave traders, who used these roads, had been in the habit of laying their water-skins. A *gurba*, raised slightly off the ground in this way, so that the air can circulate round it, keeps the water much cooler than when laid with a large part of its surface in contact with the ground.

Other evidence of the old users of these roads were to be seen in an occasional specimen of an oval, slightly dished stone about two feet long, known as a *markaka*, on which they used to grind, or rather crush, their grain with the help of a smaller hand stone, and also in the quantities of broken ostrich shells that were frequently seen. These shells can be found in many parts of the desert, and are said to be the remains of fresh eggs brought by old travellers from the Sudan to act as food on the journey. It has been argued, from their existence, that ostriches ran wild in these deserts. But it is difficult to see upon what food such a large bird could have subsisted.

On the second day after leaving the *redir*, we got on to another old road, and continued to follow it all day. This road eventually took us to a clump of four or five green *terfa* bushes, and a second one of about the same size was reached soon afterwards. These little clusters of bushes proved afterwards to be of the greatest assistance to us, as they not only afforded the camels a bite of green food, but were the source from which came most of the firewood that we used in the desert. Evidently others had found them useful too in the past, for no less than four old roads converged on to them—a striking instance of the value of green food and firewood in the desert. Some broken red pottery was found amongst these bushes.

Shortly after leaving them we found the track of a single camel going to the west—obviously to Kufara. But beyond this single track, and that of the five camels we had seen on our first journey from Mut, we never saw any modern traces of human beings on the plateau.

The weather, which had been very hot, fortunately grew suddenly cool, and once or twice a few drops of rain fell. This change in the temperature was most welcome, as the camels were becoming exhausted with their long journey away from water, and showing unmistakable signs of distress. The change to colder weather, however, revived them wonderfully.

The road, unluckily, became much worse, and we got on to a part of the plateau thickly covered by loose slabs of purplish-black sandstone, many of which tinkled like a bell when kicked.

On the day before we reached Dakhla there was a slight shower in the morning just after we started, and the weather remained cool, with a cold north wind and overcast sky all day. We were consequently able to make good progress, and by the evening had reached the north-east corner of the plateau and were within a day's journey of Mut.

Just before camping there was a sharp shower accompanied by thunder and lightning, enough rain falling during the few minutes it lasted to make my clothing feel thoroughly damp.

The tent was pitched on a sandy patch, and had hardly been erected before the rain, for about a quarter of an hour, came down in torrents, with repeated flashes of vivid lightning, which had a very grand effect over the darkened desert.

I was just going to turn in about an hour afterwards when my attention was attracted by a queer droning sound occurring at intervals. At first I thought little of it, attributing it to the wind blowing in the tent ropes, which the heavy rain had shrunk till they were as taut as harp strings. The sound died away, and for a few minutes I did not hear it.

Then again it swelled up much louder than before and with a different note. At first it sounded like the wind blowing in a telegraph wire; but this time it was a much deeper tone, rather resembling the after reverberation of a great bell.

I stepped out of the tent to try and discover the cause. It was at once clear that it could not be due to the wind in the tent ropes, for it was a perfectly calm night. The thunder still growled occasionally in the distance and the lightning flickered in the sky to the north. After the hot scorching weather we had experienced, the air felt damp and chilly enough to make one shiver.

The sound was not quite so distinctly audible outside the tent as inside it, presumably owing to the fact that the rain had so tightened the ropes and canvas that the tent acted as a sounding board. At times it died away altogether, then it would swell up again into a weird musical note.

Thinking that possibly it might be due to a singing in my ears, I called out to my men to ask if they could hear anything.

Abd er Rahman, whose hearing was not so keen as his eyesight, declared that he could hear nothing at all. But Khalil and Qway both said they could hear the sound, Qway adding that it was only the wind in the mountain. It then flashed across me that I must be listening to the "song of the sands," that, though I had often read of, I had never actually heard.

This "song of the sands" was singularly difficult to locate. It appeared to come from about half a mile away to the west, where the sand came over a cliff. It was a rather eerie experience altogether.

Musical sands are not very uncommon. The sound they emit is sometimes attributed, by the natives, to the beating of drums by a class of subterranean spirits that inhabit the dunes. In addition to those sands that give out a sound of their own accord, there is another kind that rings like a bell when struck. A patch of sand of this kind is said to exist on the plateau to the north of Dakhla Oasis. I never personally came across any sand of this description, but much of the Nubian sandstone we found on the plateau to the south-west of Dakhla Oasis gave out a distinctly musical sound when kicked, and in the gully that leads up to the plateau at the Dakhla end of the 'Ain Amur road, I passed a shoulder of rock that emitted a slight humming sound as a strong south wind blew round it.

The following day we reached Mut without any further incident. We, however, only just got in in time as our water-tanks were completely empty, after our journey of eleven days in the desert.

Knowing that many of the natives in Dakhla suspected me of being engaged on a treasure hunt, and of looking for the oasis of Zerzura, I had played up to the theory by continually asking for information on the subject. On our return from such a long journey into the desert several natives, assuming that we must have found something, came round to enquire whether I had actually found the oasis.

Khalil, who had heard the account in the "Book of Treasure," called my attention to the fact that the road we had followed on our return journey, until it lost itself in the sand dunes on the outskirts of Dakhla, at that time was leading straight for the Der el Seba'a Banat, and gave it as his opinion that, if we only followed the road far enough in the opposite direction, it would be bound to lead us to Zerzura. For the benefit of any treasure seekers who wish to look for that oasis, to embark on a treasure hunt, I will mention another and still more significant fact—that road exactly follows the line of the great bird immigration in the spring—showing that it leads to a fertile district, and moreover—most significant fact of all—many of those birds are wild geese!

CHAPTER IX

IN the journey from which we had just returned, we had been a rather long time away from water for that time of year, and the camels were in a very exhausted condition from the hard travelling in the heat on a short allowance of water. It was then May, and March is usually considered in Egypt as being the last month for field work, so I decided to give them a rest to recover their condition, and then go back to Kharga Oasis and the Nile Valley.

The men, with the exception of Khalil, had all settled down to the routine of desert travelling, and were working well. The mainstay of the caravan was Qway. He was a magnificent man in the desert, and was hardly ever at fault.

Finding that the caravan was rather overloaded at our start for our third journey, I left, on our second day out, a tank of water and two sacks of grain in the desert, to be picked up on our way back to Mut. From that point we had gone three days to the south. We had then gone two days south-west; then two days west; another day towards the north-west, and then three days north-east. All but the first four days of this journey had been over ground which was quite unknown to him; but when at the end of this roundabout route I asked him to point out to me where our tank and sacks had been laid, he was able to indicate its position without the slightest uncertainty.

At first sight the faculty that a good desert guide has of finding his way about a trackless desert seems little short of miraculous. But he has only developed to an unusual degree the powers that even the most civilised individual possesses in a rudimentary state.

Anyone, for instance, can go into a room that he knows in the dark, walk straight across from the door to a table, say, from there to the mantelpiece, and back again to the door without any difficulty at all, thus showing the same sense of angles and distances that enabled Qway, after a circuitous journey of a hundred and sixty miles, to find his way straight back to his starting-point. The Arabs, however, have so developed this faculty that they can use it on a much larger scale.

The *bedawin*, accustomed to travelling over the wide desert plains, from one landmark to another, keep their eyes largely fixed on the horizon. You can always tell a desert man when you see him in a town. He is looking towards the end of the street, and appears to be oblivious of his immediate surroundings. This gives him that "far-away" look that is so much admired by lady novelists.

It would be rash, however, to assume that a desert guide does not also notice what is going on around him, for there is very little indeed that he does not see. He may be looking to the horizon to find his next landmark during a great part of his time, but he also scans most closely the ground over which he is travelling, and will not pass the faintest sign or footprint, without noticing it and drawing his own conclusions as to who has passed that way and where they were going. He may say nothing about them at the time; but he does not forget them.

Nor will he forget his landmarks, or fail to identify them when he sees them a second time; a good guide will remember his landmarks sufficiently well to be able to follow without hesitation, a road that he has been over many years before, and has not seen in the interval.

Frequently, after passing a conspicuous hill, I have seen Qway glance over his shoulder for a second or two, to see what it would look like when he approached it again on the return journey, and to note any small peculiarities that it possessed.

In addition to this sense of angles and distances, these desert men have in many cases a wonderfully accurate knowledge of the cardinal points of the compass. This seems at first sight to amount almost to an instinct. It is, however, probably produced by a recollection of the changes of direction in a day's march which has, through long practice, become so habitual as to be almost subconscious.

A good guide can not only steer by the stars and sun, but is able to get on almost equally well without them. On the darkest and most overcast night, Qway never had the slightest doubt as to the direction in which our road lay—and this too in a part of the desert which he had previously never visited.

I often tested the sense of direction possessed by my men when we got into camp, by resting a rifle on the top of a sack of grain and telling them to aim it towards the north, afterwards testing their sighting by means of my compass.

Qway and Abd er Rahman were surprisingly consistent in their accuracy, and there was very little indeed to choose between them. There was considerable rivalry between them on this point in consequence. They were very seldom more than two degrees wrong on one side or the other of the true north.

Qway was an unusually intelligent specimen of the *bedawin* Arabs—a race who are by no means so stupid as they are sometimes represented. There was little that he did not know about the desert and its ways, and he was extraordinarily quick to pick up any little European dodges, such as mapmaking to scale, that I showed him; but on questions connected with irrigation, cultivation, building, or anything that had a bearing on the life of the *fellahin*, he was—or professed to be—entirely ignorant. He regarded them as an inferior race, and evidently considered it beneath his dignity to take any interest at all in them or their ways. He seldom alluded to them to me without adding some contemptuous remark. He never felt at home in the crowded life of the Nile Valley, declared that he got lost whenever he went into a town—this I believe to be the case with most *bedawin*—that the towns were filthy, the inhabitants all thieves, liars, "women" and worse, and that the drinking water was foul, and even the air was damp, impure, and not to be compared with that of his beloved desert.

The opinion of the Egyptians of the Nile Valley is equally unfavourable to the Arabs. They regard them as an overbearing, lawless, ignorant set of ruffians whom they pretend to despise—but they stand all the same very much in awe of them. After all, their views of each other are only natural; their characters have practically nothing in common, and criticism usually takes the form of "this man is different from me, so he must be wrong."

Qway, in the caravan, was invariably treated with great respect. He was usually addressed to as "*khal* (uncle) Qway," and he was not the man to allow any lapses from this attitude, which he considered his due as an Arab and as the head-man of the caravan. Any falling off in this respect was immediately followed by some caustic reference on his part to the inferiority of slaves, "black men," or *fellahin*, as the case required.

Abd er Rahman and the camel men all did their work well, and the difficulties due to the sand and the attitude of the natives that I had been warned that I should have to face, all appeared to be greatly exaggerated. With Qway as my guide, I hoped with the experience I had already gained, to make an attempt the next year, with a reasonable prospect of success, to cross the desert, or at any rate to penetrate much farther into it than I had already done, and reach some portion that was inhabited.

But just when I was preparing to return to Egypt, an event happened that put an entirely new complexion upon things, and upset the whole of my plans.

During our absence in the desert, a new *mamur* arrived in Dakhla Oasis and came round to call on me. He was rather a smart-looking fellow, dressed in a suit considerably too tight for him, of that peculiar shade of ginger so much affected by the Europeanised Egyptians. He had the noisy boisterous manner common to his class, but he spoke excellent English and was evidently prepared to make himself pleasant.

Before he left, he informed me that the postman had just come in, and that news had arrived by the mail of the revolution in Turkey. This revolution had long been simmering, with the usual result that the scum—in the form of Tala'at and the Germanised Enver—had come up to the top. The Sultan had been deposed, and it was considered likely that he would be replaced by some sort of republic. The whole Moslem community was in a very excited state in consequence.

A day or two later the Coptic doctor dropped in. He told me that he had just seen Sheykh Ahmed, from the *zawia* at Qasr Dakhl—whose guest I had been at his *ezba*—who had told him that if the revolution in Turkey succeeded and the Sultan really were deposed, the Senussi Mahdi would reappear and invade Egypt. The Mahdi, it may be mentioned, is the great Moslem prophet, who according to Mohammedan prophecies, is to arise shortly before the end of the world, to convert the whole of mankind to the faith of Islam.

This, if it were true, was important news. The position was one fraught with considerable possibilities. In order to understand the situation some explanation may perhaps be useful to those unacquainted with Mohammedan politics.

Egypt at that time was a part of the Turkish Empire—our position in the country being, at any rate in theory, merely that of an occupation, with the support of a small military force. The Sultan of Turkey was consequently, nominally, still the ruler of the country.

But in addition to being Sultan of Turkey, Abdul Hamid was also the Khalif of Islam—an office that made him a sort of Emperor-Pope of the whole of the Mohammedans. His claim to be the holder of this title was in reality of a somewhat flimsy character; but whatever his rights to it may have been according to the strict letter of the Moslem law, he was almost universally regarded by the members of the Sunni Mohammedans as their Khalif, that is to say, as the direct successor, as the head of Islam, of the Prophet Mohammed himself, in the same way that the Pope is regarded as the direct successor to St. Peter.

A revolution always loosens the hold that the central Government has over the outlying parts of a country, and in a widespread and uncivilised empire like that subject to the Sultan of Turkey, where centuries of misgovernment have produced a spirit—it might almost be said a habit—of revolt, serious trouble was bound to follow, if the Sultan should be deposed and his place be taken by a republic. Not only would Egypt and Tripoli be deprived of the ruler to whom they owed their allegiance, but the whole native population of North Africa, with the exception of an almost negligible minority, would be left without a spiritual head. This would have been clearly a situation that opened endless possibilities to such an enterprising sect as the Senussia, whose widespread influence through North Africa is shown by the numerous *zawias* they have planted in all the countries along the south of the Mediterranean and far into the interior of the continent.

Egypt, as the richest of these countries, was likely to offer the most promising prize. The *fellahin* of Egypt, when left to themselves, are far too much taken up in cultivating their land to trouble themselves about politics, and though of a religious turn of mind, are not fanatical. But, as recent events have shown, they are capable of being stirred up by agitators to a dangerous extent.

I several times heard the Senussi question discussed in Egypt. Opinions on its seriousness varied greatly. Some loudly and positively asserted that the threat of a Senussi invasion was only a bugbear, and, like every bugbear, more like its first syllable than its second. But there were others who relapsed into silence or changed the subject whenever it was mentioned. It was, however, certain that with the small force we at that time possessed in the country, an attempt to invade Egypt by the Senussi accompanied, as it was almost certain it would have been, by a rising engineered by them among the natives of the Nile Valley, would have caused a considerable amount of trouble.

The appearance of a Mahdi—if he is not scotched in time—may set a whole country in a ferment. Not infrequently some local religious celebrity will proclaim himself the Mahdi and gain perhaps a few followers; but his career is usually shortlived. Occasionally, however, one arrives on the scene, who presents a serious problem—such, for instance, as the well-known Mahdi of the Sudan, and the lesser known, but more formidable, Mahdi of the Senussi sect.

The latter, though he seems to have been a capable fellow, was a theatrical mountebank, who preferred to surround himself with an atmosphere of mystery; as it was this mysterious element that complicated the situation, some explanation of it is necessary.

Sidi Mohammed Ben Ali Senussi, the founder of the Senussi dervishes, while travelling, in 1830, from Morocco to Mecca, divorced his wife, Menna, who had proved unfruitful, with the result that, being wifeless, some natives of Biskra took compassion upon him and presented him with an Arab slave girl. This woman is supposed to have borne him a son—Sidi Ahmed el Biskri—who played a somewhat prominent part later on in the history of the Senussia. By another wife he had a son, Mohammed, whom he declared on his deathbed to be the long-expected Mahdi.

These two half-brothers, Mohammed and Ahmed, are said to have borne a striking resemblance to each other.

An old Senussi that I met in Dakhla, who professed to have seen them both, said that not only were they of the same height and figure, but that even their voices and manner were so much alike that no one could distinguish between them.

There seems to be little doubt that when the Senussi Mahdi did not wish to interview a visitor himself, he sent his double, Sidi Ahmed, to do so instead. This deception was made easy by the fact that the Senussi Mahdi, during the latter part of his life, was a veiled prophet who concealed his face whenever he appeared in public by covering his head with a shawl; it is reported that he never even showed his face to his most intimate followers.

The interviews that he accorded to his visitors were few and difficult to obtain. They were invariably short—the Mahdi himself timing the interview with his watch—and the conversation, so far as he was concerned, consisting of a few questions, followed, if necessary, by a decision; his remarks being made in the low dreamy voice of one who received his inspirations from on high—a method of procedure that could hardly fail to impress, as it was evidently intended to do, the credulous followers who came to see him with his extreme sanctity and importance.

This Mahdi was reported to have died some years prior to my visit to Dakhla, and although news of the happenings in the inaccessible parts of North Africa is apt to be unreliable, there was little doubt that he had.

The native version was that he had gone off into the desert and disappeared; but probably he only followed the example of Sheykh Shadhly, the founder of the great Shadhlia sect, and of several other noted Moslem saints, and went off into the desert to die, when he felt his end approaching.

There was, however, a pretty general feeling in the desert that the last of him had not been seen—an impression that the Senussi endeavoured to keep alive by the vague statement that he was "staying with Allah," and hints that he might at any moment reappear.

There was never much love lost between the Senussia and the Turks. About a year before my visit to the desert, a Turkish official had been sent down to Kufara Oasis, with orders to formally assert the Sultan's authority over the district, and to hoist the Turkish flag. The fanatical inhabitants, however, had hauled down the flag, torn it to ribbons, trampled it under foot, severely beaten the Turkish officer and expelled him from the oasis, so the annexation of any part of the Turkish Empire would have been a scheme well calculated to appeal to the Senussi.

Ahmed el Biskri—the Mahdi's double—was also reported to have died. But nothing would have been easier than for the leading Senussi sheykhs to find someone to personate their veiled prophet on his return from "staying with Allah," and to have used the immense prestige that their puppet would have obtained amongst their credulous followers to increase the influence of the sect, to attract new followers and to work upon their fanaticism. The "reappearance" of the Senussi Mahdi in this way is still a possibility that is worth remembering.

News as to the doings of the leaders amongst the Senussia living in the wilds of the Libyan Desert has always been very difficult to obtain; but at that time they were reported in Dakhla to be somewhere in the neighbourhood of Tibesti, which lay to the south-west of Dakhla Oasis, in the direction of the road we had been following, and it seemed likely, if they were really contemplating a descent upon Egypt, that they might attempt, if water existed upon this road, to make their way along it into Dakhla, and so on to the Nile Valley.

With these considerations in view, I decided to make another trip into the desert before returning to Egypt, to see if we could not manage to reach the well, or oasis, to which the road ran, and to ascertain if the road we had found was feasible for a large body of men.

I sent a note to one of the British officials I had met in Cairo to let the authorities have news of the rumoured invasion, for what it was worth, and set to work to prepare for the journey.

I had not calculated on staying out in the desert so late in the season, so my provisions had almost run out. The few tins of preserved meat that remained had all suffered considerably from the heat and were not fit for use. I had, however, still a few tins of sardines, which in spite of their pronounced tinniness were still quite edible, and a number of emergency rations, which had not suffered in the least from the heat. These with a large skin of Arab flour and a few pounds of mulberry jam, which Dahab made from some fruit that the good people of Rashida sent me, provided ample food for another journey.

After a few more days spent in feeding up the camels and restoring them to a suitable condition for a long desert journey during the hot weather, Qway thoroughly inspected the beasts, dug his thumb into their quarters to test the consistency of their flesh, expressed himself satisfied with the distended state of their tummies, buttered the red camel again for mange, and then, as he declared the beasts to be in first-rate condition, we prepared to start.

CHAPTER X

THE discovery of the five green bushes that we had made on our last journey, insignificant as it may appear, proved of the greatest value to us.

I calculated that by the time we reached the bushes we should have about consumed a camel-load of water and grain; so by taking with us just sufficient firewood to last us till we reached them, and then, loading up the unloaded camel with fuel from the bushes, we should be able to devote yet another camel to the water and grain—so on this journey we had three extra baggage beasts, in addition to my *hagin*, loaded with these indispensable commodities. We hoped in consequence to be able to cover considerably more ground than on our previous attempts.

I had already surveyed the route, and as a second mapping of the road was unnecessary, we were able to travel a great part of the time by night, when the temperature was at its lowest. By rapid marches we were able to reach the pass leading down into Khalil's "Valley of the Mist" on the fifth day.

With hardly an exception, the numerous rocky hills that rose above the plateau were so shaped that it was quite impossible to find any shade under them during the middle of the day, so we were obliged to rig up such shelter as we could by stretching blankets or empty sacks from one water-tank to another, or by supporting them from any framework that could be rigged up on the spur of the moment. Qway usually tied one end of his blanket on to the pommels of his saddle and then stretched the other end over a tank or two that he placed on end, or else secured it on to his gun, which he fixed up as a kind of tent pole.

On descending from the plateau into the "Valley of the Mist," we continued in the same line of march. The floor of the depression proved excellent going, consisting as it did of hard smooth sand, containing a sprinkling of rounded pebbles; there was hardly even a ripple to break the evenness of its surface. Here and there a few stones showed up above the sand that covered the remainder of the surface; from these it was clear that we were still on the same Nubian sandstone formation as the plateau. In one place we found a huge slab of the stone propped up to form an *'alem*, and here and there we came across white pulverised bones, that from their size must have belonged to some camel that in the distant past had died in that part of the desert, all showing that we were still on the line of the road we had been following.

OLD 'ALEM, "VALLEY OF THE MIST."

Soon after descending into the depression we sighted a double peaked hill almost straight ahead of us that, as it stood completely alone in the midst of the level sandy plain, promised to give a wide view from its summit. On sighting the hill, I suggested to Qway, who was riding alongside of me, that it might be a good plan to send Abd er Rahman to climb to the top, to see if anything were to be seen.

Qway looked at the hill doubtfully for a moment. "I think that hill is a long way off," he said. "We shall not reach it before noon."

But distances on these level plains, where there are no natural features with which the size of an object can be compared, are often extraordinarily deceptive—even Qway with all his experience was often taken in by them. We had not reached that hill by noon, and though we continued our march for two hours in the afternoon, at the end of the day it appeared to be no nearer—if anything it looked farther off than it had done in the morning. As there was nothing whatever to survey, we set off again at half-past eleven that night, and continued our journey towards the hill till four next morning.

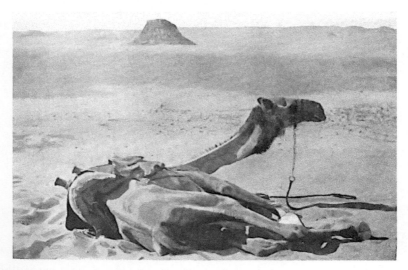

Rather Thin.

Long journeys in the hot weather on a short water supply are very exhausting to the camels; the camel drivers did not consider this one to be in a very bad condition. (p. 181).

But at dawn the hill appeared to be no nearer, and as we continued our march it seemed actually to recede and became noticeably smaller.

Qway was completely puzzled by it, and declared that it must be an *afrit*. As we continued to advance, however, it suddenly appeared to come nearer; then after a time it receded again.

Qway seemed seriously to imagine there was something supernatural about it. The men, too, evidently began to think that they had got into a haunted part of the desert, for they stopped their usual chaffing and singing and trudged along in stolid silence. It certainly was rather uncanny.

It was an unusually bad piece of desert. The scorching noontide sun caused the whole horizon to dance with mirage, and it was impossible to tell where the horizon ended and the sky began—they seemed to merge gradually into each other—strips of the desert hanging some degrees above the horizon in the sky, while large patches of sky were brought down below the horizon, producing the appearance of sheets of water—the *Bahr esh Shaytan*, or "devil's lake," of the natives.

But that hill was no mirage. We reached it at noon on the third day after we had sighted it, and it proved to be about four hundred and twenty feet high above the plain, and not an optical illusion. On account of the peculiar way in which it seemed first to recede as we approached it, and then to leap suddenly towards us, only to recede again, the men gave it the name of the "Jebel Temelli Bayed"—"the ever distant hill"—which they afterwards abbreviated to Jebel el Bayed. I was for a long time puzzled by the way in which it seemed to alter its position as it was approached; but came to the conclusion that this effect was produced by the fact that the road, by which we were travelling over the desert, though apparently of a dead level, was in reality slightly undulating, while the hill itself was of a shape that merged very gradually into the surrounding desert.

Consequently, while standing in a position such as A (Fig. 2), on the top of one of the undulations, we were able to see over the next ridge, E, down to the line A, B (Fig. 1 and 2) almost to the foot of the hill. When, however, we got into a trough between two of the undulations, as at C, we could only see the portion of the hill showing above the line C, D (Figs. 1 and 2), and it consequently appeared to be much smaller, and so more distant, than when seen from A. But on reaching the top of the ridge E, the whole hill down to its base came into view, rapidly increasing in size, and so appearing to leap forward, as we ascended the slope from C to E.

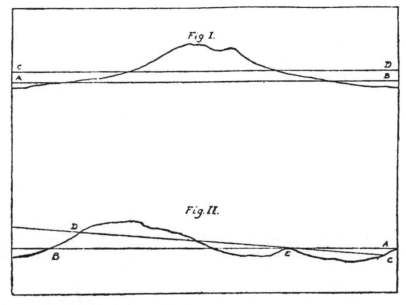

DIAGRAM OF JEBEL EL BAYED.

I explained this view to Qway, who at once accepted it as correct, and was evidently much relieved, for, as he half laughingly admitted, he was beginning to believe that the hill had been enchanted, and did not like having anything to do with it.

From the top of the hill a very wide view was obtainable. Towards the north, the pass by which we had descended from the plateau, was invisible, owing to a rise in the intervening ground; but farther to the west, the southern cliff of the plateau was visible and the surface of the plateau itself in this direction could also be seen, showing that it sloped fairly sharply towards the south; but this part of it seemed to be much less thickly studded with hills than the portions over which we had travelled.

Towards the north-west I saw a line of sand dunes running over the tableland, and the point where they came over the scarp, and their continuation on the floor of the depression could also be seen through my glass. They evidently passed some little distance to the west of us.

The cliff of the plateau became much lower towards the west, and looked as though it were going to die out altogether, and the tableland to become gradually merged into the floor of the depression; but the view in this direction was cut off by a long range of hills, with a very jagged outline, that ran from north to south from the neighbourhood of the scarp, and hid most of the view of the horizon between north-west and south-west.

South of this range of hills was a vast plain of open sandy desert, falling towards the west, and so far as we could see containing no sand dunes, but here and there a single low rocky hill.

Right ahead of us to the south-west, standing alone in this sandy plain, about two days' journey away, was a very conspicuous hill, or cluster of hills, with a jagged skyline. This broken outline, and that of the range of hills to the west, may possibly indicate a change in the geological formation. The hills of Nubian sandstone to be seen on the plateau and in the surrounding desert were, with a few exceptions, all of certain definite types—flat topped, domed or conical—and the irregular skyline was only rarely to be seen in the Nubian sandstone formation.

The desert remained of the same monotonous level, sandy nature all round from south through east to nearly north, though on this side of our position the isolated rocky hills appeared to be rather more plentiful. It was an extraordinarily featureless landscape. From our exalted position we must have been able to see without difficulty for well over fifty miles in almost all directions, but there was hardly anything to go down on a map. I took a few bearings, and jotted them down and minutely examined the rest of the landscape through my glasses to see if there was anything to note. In about five minutes I had collected all the available material for mapping about ten thousand square miles of desert, and left the greater part of it blank—there was practically nothing to record.

When I had finished, Qway borrowed my glass and gazed through it for some time, declaring that it was useless to look for water anywhere near in that part of the desert as it all lay at a very high level, adding that we were getting near the country of the Bedayat, and had better return to Mut.

It was clear that what he said was right. There was no chance of finding water for another three days, and we had not got sufficient supplies with us to go so far, so, very reluctantly, I climbed down from the hill and prepared for our return journey.

Before starting, I had a look round our camp. Close to the foot of the hill I found an *'alem* and one of the low semicircular walls of loose stone that the *bedawin* erect at their halting places as wind shelters; so if any further proof was necessary, that we were still on the line of the road we had been following, these relics of a bygone traffic appeared to settle the point conclusively.

One's beasts during a hot weather journey in the desert require rather careful management. We left Mut on the 3rd of May. On the 8th we gave the camels a drink, and afterwards I sent Abd er Rahman back to Mut with all the empty tanks, telling him to fill them up and return again along our tracks to meet us on our homeward journey. In the event of his not meeting us, he was to leave the tanks behind him and return at once to Mut to await our arrival, taking with him only just enough water for himself for the return journey. The latter instructions were designed to provide for the contingency of our finding water out in the desert and continuing our journey.

We reached Jebel el Bayed on the 12th May, and, as the camels' drink on the 8th had not been nearly enough to satisfy them, the poor beasts were already showing obvious signs of want of water. Even as far back as the 9th, two of them had left part of their feeds uneaten; on the 10th all of them had done so, and two of them had refused their food altogether—a very bad sign. Qway had then wanted me to return; but in spite of their obvious thirst, the camels seemed to be going strongly, and I had made up my mind to see what was to be seen from the top of that hill, before returning, even if we had to run for it afterwards; so, strongly against his advice, and in defiance of his statement that I should lose two or three of the beasts and should not be able to get back if I went on, I had risked it.

OLD WIND SHELTER, "VALLEY OF THE MIST."

But it was clear that the camels were at their last gasp for want of water, and the two weaker ones could hardly even stand. There was only one way of getting those beasts back to Dakhla, and that was to keep just enough water in the tanks to take the men back to our rendezvous with Abd er Rahman, and to give the camels all the rest. This had the double advantage of not only quenching their thirst, but also of lightening considerably the loads that the poor brutes had to carry; but it spelt disaster if Abd er Rahman failed to turn up.

In travelling in the desert during the hot weather, when the whole caravan was on a limited water ration, I usually took the occasion of watering the beasts to have a bath. The water was poured into a folding canvas arrangement, in which—without using any soap—I performed my ablutions, and the camels were allowed to drink out of it afterwards. As a camel is not a fastidious beast in his diet, the arrangement worked very well. But on this occasion I was deprived of my wash, as, owing to the necessity of reducing the weight of the baggage, I had been obliged to leave the bath behind in Mut.

The difficulty of keeping oneself properly clean on a limited water supply constituted perhaps the greatest trial in a desert journey. The baths I obtained when the camels drank were a great luxury, but my washing in between their drinks was of the scantiest possible description. The method that I found made the water go farthest was to scrub myself clean with the moistened corner of a towel and rub myself vigorously with the drier part of it afterwards. Sometimes the supply was insufficient for even this economical method. I then usually retired behind a rock, stripped and rolled in the sand like a camel. This, though not so cleansing as the damp towel method, was distinctly refreshing.

We got what rest we could during the early part of the evening, and got off about two in the morning, marched throughout the night until we halted for the midday rest. We were off again at five in the evening and marched, with only one halt near midnight, to eat a meal, till nine o'clock on the following morning, by which time we had reached the top of the Bab es Sabah. We had then had enough of it and camped till sunset, when we resumed our journey and marched throughout the night till dawn.

The stars in the clear desert atmosphere shine with a brilliance altogether unknown in our more northerly latitudes. The Milky Way appears as a filmy cloud, and is so distinct that, when first I saw it in the desert, I took it to be one. We were practically on the line of the tropic of Cancer, and, in that southerly latitude, many stars appeared that never show above the horizon in England, conspicuous among them being that rather overrated constellation the Southern Cross.

Wasm, or Brand, of the Senussia.

Each Arab tribe has its own camel brand. The Wasm of the Senussi Dervishes is the word "Allah" branded on the neck. (p. 24).

Breadmaking in the Desert.

The *bedawin* roll their dough into a thin cake and toast it on an iron plate. (p. 207).

Sieving the Baby.

This baby is being shaken in a sieve, containing grain, etc., while a woman beats with a pestle on a mortar, to ensure that he shall not starve when he grows up or be afraid of noise, and shall become a fast runner. (p. 249.)

The *bedawin* Arabs, owing to their making so much use of the stars as guides during their night journeys, know them all, and have names, and often stories, to tell concerning them. The Pole Star, the one that they use most as a guide, is known as the Jidi, or he-goat, which the stars of the Great Bear—the Banat Nash, or daughters of Nash, are trying to steal, being prevented from doing so by the two *ghaffirs* (watchmen), which are known to us also—perhaps from this same Arab legend that has been forgotten—as the "guardians" of the Pole Star. In some parts the Great and Little Bear are known as the she-camel and her foal. The Pleiades are called "the daughters of the night." Orion is a hunter with his belt and sword, who is followed by his dog (*canis major*), and is chasing a *bagar el wahash* (wild bull), i.e. the constellation of Taurus. Much of our astronomy originally came, I believe, from the Arabs, and many of the stars are still called by their Arabic names, such for instance as Altair, the bird, the name by which it is still known to the *bedawin*.

Shooting stars, which in the desert often blaze out with a brilliance difficult to realise by dwellers in a misty climate like England, are believed by Moslems to be arrows shot by the angels at the evil spirits to drive them away when they steal up to eavesdrop at the gate of heaven.

There are always certain events in a journey that impress themselves more indelibly on one's memory than those perhaps of greater consequence, and that hurried return to the plateau was one of them.

Qway, as usual, rode alone fifty yards ahead of the caravan. I rode behind with the rest of the men, dozing occasionally in my saddle, and, in between, turning over in my mind some rather knotty problems—whether the Senussi were really coming; whether we were likely to run into them before reaching Mut; whether an oasis was to be seen from the top of that farthest hill, and, most frequently of all, whether we should meet Abd er Rahman.

Occasionally cold shivers would chase each other up and down my back when the idea occurred to me that perhaps the camels I had sent with him might go lame, or that something else might happen to stop him from coming out with the water that we so badly needed.

To tell the truth, I was distinctly doubtful whether the caravan would hold out until we reached him; for in pushing out so far with such a limited amount of water at the worst season of the year, and in sending him back single-handed to bring out fresh supplies, I knew I had broken the first rules in desert travelling, by running a serious risk without water supply.

A journey on a fine night in the desert is always an experience to remember, and the almost perfect silence in which we marched made it more impressive than usual. Hardly a sound was to be heard beyond the gentle shuffling of the camels' feet on the smooth sand, the soft clinking of their chain bridles, the occasional creak of a rope against the baggage, and the hollow splashing of the water to and fro in the half empty tanks. Now and then, when the camels slackened their pace, Musa would shout out to them, his voice breaking the silence with startling suddenness, or he would break into one of the wild shrill songs that the camel drivers sometimes sing to their charges, and the beasts would at once quicken their pace.

A long night march seems interminable. The slow, monotonous stride of the camels, regular as the beat of a pendulum, produces an almost mesmeric effect as one plods along, mile after mile, hour after hour, beside them over the dreary waste of starlit desert.

The most trying part of a night march is the period just before dawn. Then one's vitality is at its lowest, and one feels most the fatigue of the long night's journey. A great silence falls over the caravan at these times. The whole desert seems dead and unutterably dull and dreary, and nothing at all seems in the least worth while. As the dawn approaches, the desert appears to stir in its sleep. A slight freshness comes into the air. A thin breeze—the dawn wind—springs up from the limitless waste, steals softly whispering over the sands and passes sighing into the distance. The false dawn creeps up into the sky, and then, with a suddenness that is almost startling, the sun springs up above the horizon, the elongated shadows of the long line of camels appear as "purple patches" on the level sand of the desert, like those puzzle writings that have to be looked at edgeways before they can be read, and one realises all of a sudden that another scorching day has dawned at last.

CHAPTER XI

TWO days after leaving the pass on to the plateau we reached our rendezvous with Abd er Rahman, where to our intense relief we found him waiting for us.

We had all, I think, been dreading that something might happen to prevent him from bringing out our indispensable water supply. To me, at any rate, the possibility that he might fail us had been something of a nightmare—when one is feeling a bit run down by the hot weather and unsuitable food, problems of this description are apt to assume quite alarming proportions, especially in the long night marches in the hour or two before the dawn.

To make quite sure of our water supply, I sent Abd er Rahman back again to Mut with all the empty tanks, telling him to come out again to meet us as soon as possible.

Our supplies of all descriptions were running short. Our firewood was almost completely consumed, our last match had been struck and, as my flint and steel were lost, getting a light was a matter of considerable difficulty. A fire was not only a necessity for the men to cook their bread in, but the whole caravan—with the exception of Qway—were confirmed smokers, and if a native is deprived of his tobacco he becomes discontented at once.

Musa had solved the difficulty of getting a light the evening before by tearing a piece of rag from his cotton clothing, rubbing it in gunpowder, and then firing it from his gun. Qway rushed forward, picked it up still smouldering, put it into a handful of dried grass which he had brought with him, fanned it into a flame, and by that means succeeded in lighting a fire from the last of our fuel.

The weather was very hot in the middle of the day, and I was considerably amused at the expedients that the men adopted to mitigate their discomfort. In the morning and afternoon, during the hot hours, they all tried to walk as close as they could to the camels, so as to be in their shadows. But when it became nearly noon, and the sun was almost vertically overhead, they threw the tails of their long shirts over their heads, which not only acted to some extent as a protection to their necks and spines, but also, by deflecting the wind, caused a draught to blow down their backs.

The men, hungry and surly, tramped along in silence for two or three hours. Then Qway, who as usual was riding ahead of the caravan, suddenly made his camel kneel, sprang to the ground and sang out to the others to join him. I called out to know what was the matter.

ABD ER RAHMAN'S WIND SCOOP.

"Tahl," he shouted, *"Tahl ya farah. Allah akbar. Allah kerim. El hamdl'illah. Barr."* ("Come, come. Oh, joy! Allah is most great. Allah is merciful. Praise be to Allah. Manure!")

We had reached an old camping ground of ours on one of our former trips, and the ground was plentifully strewn with the camel droppings, that in the great heat had become thoroughly desiccated, making excellent fuel.

Though it was still early in the day, we unloaded the camels, and Khalil started to make a plentiful supply of dough. With the help of the last handful of dried grass, Musa and his gun produced the necessary blaze, and in half an hour the bread was being baked over a hot fire of *barr*. In the evening we reached the bushes, and the fuel difficulty was solved.

Our water was again at its lowest ebb. We had still a long day's journey to make before meeting Abd er Rahman again, and had barely enough water for the purpose. We had watered the camels three times since leaving Mut, sixteen days before, but the total amount that we had been able to give them was far below their requirements.

But Abd er Rahman came in during the course of the evening. He was greatly perturbed to see the state to which the beasts that had remained with us had been reduced. We held a consultation with Qway, and concluded that the only possible way to ensure our being able to get them back again to the oasis was to give them all the water we could possibly spare, keeping only just enough for ourselves, and then to get back again as soon as possible, loading most of the baggage on to the camels that Abd er Rahman had brought with him from Mut, who having drunk their fill in the oasis were in fairly strong condition.

Early in the morning, when the contents of the tanks had had time to cool down, we watered the poor brutes and then, having allowed them an hour to settle their drink, packed up and moved off towards the oasis.

Not long after our start some of the baggage became disarranged, and we had to halt to adjust it. Khalil took the opportunity to sit down and declare that he was tired and had "bristers" on his feet, and could go no farther unless he was allowed to ride, adding that he was "not as these Arabs" and had been "delicutly nurchered!"

As it was less than an hour since we had left the camp, it was quite impossible that he could have been tired, and as for his blisters, when examined they proved to consist of a single small "brister" on his instep, which, as we were travelling over smooth sand and he, like all the rest of us, was walking barefoot, could not have caused him the slightest inconvenience.

I pointed this out to him and told him that if he stayed behind and left the caravan he would be certain to die of thirst.

"Never mind," he replied heroically. "Never mind. I will stay behind and die. I cannot walk any more. I am tired. You go on, sir, and save yourselves. I will stay here and die in the desert."

We had had many scenes of this kind with Khalil, and the *bedawin* never failed to enjoy them thoroughly.

"What is he saying?" asked Qway.

I translated as well as I could.

"*Malaysh*" ("it's of no consequence"), replied Qway calmly. "Let him stay behind and die if he wants to. Whack the camels, Abd er Rahman, and let's go. We can't wait. We are in the desert, and short of water."

"I shall die," sobbed Khalil.

"*Malaysh*," repeated Qway, without even troubling to look back at him.

I felt much inclined to tickle the aggravating brute up with my *kurbaj*, but it was against my principles to beat a native, so we went on and left him sitting alone in the desert.

"My wife will be a widow," screamed Khalil after us—though how he expected that contingency to appeal to our sympathies was not quite clear. Musa shouted back some ribald remarks about the lady in question, and the caravan proceeded cheerfully—not to say uproariously—upon its way.

After we had gone some distance our road dipped down to a lower level, and we lost sight of Khalil for a while. I looked back just before we got out of sight, and saw him sitting exactly where we had left him. We travelled a considerable distance before a rise in the ground over which our road ran enabled us to see him again. On looking back through my glasses, I could just distinguish him sitting still where we had left him. I quite expected that by the time we had gone a few hundred yards—or at any rate as soon as we were out of sight—that Khalil would have got up and followed us. But the *fellahin* of Egypt are a queer-tempered race, who when they cannot get exactly what they want, will sometimes fall into a fit of suicidal sulks that is rather difficult to deal with. As Khalil appeared to have got into this sulky frame of mind I began to fear that he really intended to carry out his threat and to stay where he was until he either died of thirst, or had been so far left behind by the caravan that he would be unable to rejoin us, which would have led to the same result.

Qway, when I asked him how long it would take for us to reach the oasis, was most positive in saying that it would be all that we could do to get across the dunes before sunset the next day. The sand belt, though easy enough to cross in daylight, when we could see where we were going, would have presented a very serious obstacle in the dark. With the possibility of another day of scorching *simum* or, worse still, a violent sandstorm in our teeth, before we reached Dakhla, a delay that would cause us to camp the next night on the wrong side of the dunes, and so entail another twelve hours in the desert before reaching water, might have had very serious consequences.

"If we don't cross the sand to-morrow," said Qway impressively, "we may not reach Mut at all. Look at the camels. Look at our tanks. They are nearly empty. We must go on. We can't wait."

I couldn't risk sacrificing the whole caravan for the sake of one malingerer; so I told Abd er Rahman to whack up the camels, and we left the "delicutly nurchered" Khalil to die in the desert.

Soon afterwards we lost sight of him altogether. We had started early in the morning and we went on throughout the day, with hardly a halt, till eight o'clock at night, when we were compelled to stop in order to rest the camels. We saw nothing more of Khalil and gave him up for lost. To give him a last chance we lighted a big fire and then composed ourselves to sleep as well as we could, on a wholly insufficient allowance of water.

Towards morning Khalil staggered into the camp amid the jeers and curses of the men, croaked a request for water and, having drunk, flung himself down to sleep, too dead beat even to eat.

That little episode cured Khalil of malingering, and he gave no further trouble on our journey to Mut. It just shows what a little tact will do in dealing with a native. Many brutal fellows would have beaten the poor man!

The next day luckily proved fairly cool, and we made better progress than we expected. We consequently struck the dune belt just after noon and, as we seemed to have found a low part of it, by Qway's advice I decided to tackle it at that point.

But in coming to this decision I had overlooked a most important factor in the situation—the light. Curious as it may seem, dunes are sometimes almost as difficult to cross in the blazing sunshine at noon as they are in the dark. The intense glare at this time of day makes the almost white sand of which they are composed most painful to look at, and the total absence of any shade prevents their shape being seen and makes even the ripples practically invisible.

In consequence of this state of affairs, Qway, while riding ahead of the caravan to show the way, blundered without seeing where he was going, off the flat top of a dune on to the steep face below, was thrown, and he and his *hagin* only just escaped rolling down to the bottom, a fall of some thirty feet. After that, until we reached the farther side of the belt, he remained on foot, dragging his *hagin* behind him. Once across the dunes the rest of the journey was easy enough.

The news of affairs in Europe that we heard in Dakhla on our return was simply heartbreaking. The revolution in Turkey that had promised to be rather a big thing, had fizzled out entirely. The Sultan Abdul Hamid—"Abdul the Damned"—it is true had been deposed; but his brother, Mohammed V, had been made ruler in his stead, and was firmly seated on the rickety Turkish throne. The disturbance had quieted down in Turkey; there was no chance of there being a republic, and so the threatened invasion of Egypt by the Senussi, was not in the least likely to come off.

All the same, we felt fairly pleased with ourselves, for we had been for eighteen days in the desert away from water, with only seven camels, in the most trying time of the year, and had got back again without losing a single beast. But anyone who feels inclined to repeat this picnic is advised to take enough water and suitable food.

The Gubary road by which we travelled to Kharga followed the foot of the cliff that forms the southern boundary of the plateau upon which 'Ain Amur lies. It was very featureless and uninteresting. But though it contained no natural features of any importance, the *bedawin* have a number of landmarks along it to which they have given names and by which they divide the road up into various stages. It is curious to see how the necessity for naming places arises as soon as a district becomes frequented.

These little landmarks are often shown in maps in a very misleading way. One of those on the Gubary road is known as Bu el Agul. There is another Bu el Agul, or Abu el Agul, as it is sometimes called, on the Derb et Tawil, or "long road," that runs from the Nile Valley, near Assiut, across the desert to Dakhla Oasis. I have often seen this place marked on maps in an atlas, the name being printed in the same type as that used for big mountains, or villages in the Nile Valley, and there was nothing whatever in the way in which it was shown on these maps to indicate its unimportance.

Now Bu el Agul is only a grave—what is more, it is not even a real grave, it is a bogus one. The commonest form of a native nickname is to christen a man the father of the thing for which he is best known among them. I was myself at one time known as "Abu Zerzura," the "Father of Zerzura," because I was supposed to be looking for that oasis, and later on as "Abu Ramal," "the father of sand," because I spent so much time among the dunes.

Bu el Agul means the "father of hobbles." One of the greatest risks that an inexperienced Arab runs, when travelling alone in the desert, is that of allowing his camel to break loose and escape during the night. Then, unless he be near a well, having no beast to carry his water-skin, his fate is probably sealed. Many lives have been lost in this way.

With tragedies of this description constantly before their minds, the desert guides, as a reminder to their less experienced brethren to secure their beasts properly at night, have made an imitation grave about half-way along each of the desert roads. This grave is supposed to represent the last resting-place of the "father of hobbles," who has lost his life owing to his not having tied up his camel securely at night. It is the custom of every traveller, who uses the road, to throw on to the "grave" as he passes it, a worn-out hobble or water-skin, or part of a broken water vessel, with the result that in time a considerable pile accumulates.

It was the end of June by the time we reached Kharga again. Anyone attempting to work in the desert at any distance away from water after March is severely handicapped by the high temperature. I had already experienced nearly three months of these conditions, and the prospect of doing any good in the desert during the remainder of the hot weather was so remote that I returned to England for the remainder of the summer.

CHAPTER XII

MY first season's work in the desert had been sufficiently successful to warrant a second attempt, as I had carried out one of the objects on my programme by managing to cross the dune-field; so I determined to follow it up by another journey. The main piece of work that I planned for my second year was to push as far as possible along the old road to the southwest of Dakhla, that we had already followed for about one hundred and fifty miles. Before starting I heard rumours of a place that had not previously been reported called Owanat, that lay upon this road and was apparently the first point to which it went. But I was able to gather little information on the subject. I could not even hear whether it was inhabited or deserted. I was not even sure whether water was to be found there.

The journey to this place seemed likely to be of great length before water could be reached, and as the ultimate destination of the road was quite uncertain, and nothing was known of the part into which it led, the possibility of getting into an actively hostile district had to be considered, and arrangements to be made to make sure of our retreat into Egypt, in the event of our camels being taken from us and our finding it necessary to make the return journey on foot.

The distance we should have to travel from Dakhla Oasis, along the road, before we found water or reached an oasis could not, I imagined, be more than fifteen days' journey at the most. I hoped, if we managed to cover this distance and no other difficulties arose, that we should be able to push on still farther, and eventually get right across the desert into the French Sudan, where the authorities had been warned to look out for me and to give me any assistance they could.

This old road from its size had at one time evidently been one of the main caravan routes across the desert. The Senussi, it was known, paid considerable attention to the improvement of the desert roads, and, from what the natives told me, under their able management, Kufara Oasis had become a focus to which most of the caravan routes of this part of the desert converged.

This road must always have been a difficult one, owing to the long waterless stretch that had to be crossed before the first oasis could be reached. So it seemed likely that it had been abandoned in consequence of another road to Kufara having been made easier by sinking of new wells.

My main object in this journey was to see if this route was still usable for caravans or, if not, whether it could not be made so by means of new wells, or by improving the road at difficult points.

A road running up from Wanjunga to Dakhla Oasis would have cut right across all the caravan routes, leading up to Kufara from the Bedayat country and the Eastern Sudan, and so might have diverted into Egypt a great deal of the traffic then going to Kufara and Tripoli. In addition some of the trade carried by the great north and south road, from the Central Sudan through Tikeru to Kufara, might also have been brought into Dakhla by reopening this old route. As the railway from the Nile Valley into Kharga could easily have been extended into Dakhla, that oasis might have supplanted Kufara as the main caravan centre of the Libyan Desert, and a comparatively large entrepôt trade might have been developed there, the merchandise being distributed by means of the railway into Egypt.

The total value of the goods carried across this district by caravan is not great; but still the trade is of sufficient importance to make it worth while to attempt to secure it, especially as, if that were done, it would give a considerable hold over the inaccessible tribes of the interior, and at the same time be a severe blow to the Senussi, who for some time had threatened to become rather a nuisance.

To meet the requirements of the long fifteen days' journey to Owanat from Dakhla, or rather of our return in the event of our having to beat a hurried retreat on foot, I had thirty small tanks made of galvanised iron. These were placed in wooden boxes, a couple being in each box, and packed round with straw to keep the water cool and prevent them from shaking about in their cases.

Each pair of tanks contained enough water for the men and myself for one day, with a slight margin over to allow for contingencies. During the journey, one of these boxes could be left at the end of every day's march, with sufficient food to carry us on to the next depot, in the event of our finding it necessary to retrace our steps. With a pair of tanks in each box, I felt as certain as it was possible to be that, even if one of them should leak and lose the whole of its contents, there would still be sufficient water in the second tank to last us till we reached the next depot. Even if all our *zemzemias* and *gurbas* had been lost, these tanks, even when full, were of a weight that could easily have been carried by a man during the day's march. When empty they could be thrown away.

I went up to Assiut to get together a caravan for the journey, engaged a brother of Abd er Rahman's, named Ibrahim, and also secured Dahab for the journey. Qway and Abd er Rahman joined me in Assiut, putting up at a picturesque old *khan* in the native town, and thus our party became complete. The attempts I had made to find a guide who knew the parts of the desert beyond the Senussi border had again proved fruitless.

I hesitated at first to take Ibrahim into the desert partly because—like many young Sudanese—I found him rather a handful, who required a good deal of licking into shape, but chiefly because he had not had much experience with camels, owing to his having acted for some time as a domestic servant in Kharga Oasis. What finally decided me to take him was one of those small straws that so often tell one the way of the wind when dealing with natives.

Once, while loading a camel, preparatory to moving camp, the baggage began to slip off his back and Ibrahim, as is usual with *bedawin* in the circumstances, immediately invoked the aid of his patron saint by singing out, "Ya! Sidi Abd es Salem."

The saint that a native calls upon in these cases is nearly always the one that founded the dervish Order to which he belongs, and this Abd es Salem ben Mashish—to give him his full name—was the founder of the Mashishia dervishes and is perhaps still better known to Moslems as the religious instructor of Sheykh Shadhly, one of the most famous of all Mohammedan divines.

OLD KHAN IN ASSIUT.

The cardinal principle of the Mashishia is to abstain entirely from politics—a most useful character to have in a servant when going into the country of the Senussi. The same principle was adopted by the Shadhlia order and nearly all its numerous branches, and also by a set of dervishes which split from the Mashishia, that is known as the Madania—the old Madania, not the new Madania, which is of a very different character.

Ibrahim's brother, Abd er Rahman, used to invoke Abd el Qader el Jilany, the founder of the great Qadria order of dervishes, the followers of which, as a rule, are about the least fanatical of Moslems.

Qway, though he made great protestations of keenness, I soon found to be obstructing my preparations, and he developed signs of dishonesty that I had not noticed in him before. What was worse, I found him secretly communicating with a member of the Senussi *zawia* in Qasr Dakhla, who, for some unexplained reason, had come to Assiut, and who seemed to be in frequent communication with him. This all pointed to some underhand dealing with the Senussi, who, until they were brought to their senses by being well beaten in the great war, always opposed any attempt to enter their country—usually by tampering with a traveller's guides.

I concluded that I had better keep a closer watch upon the conduct of my guide than I had done before.

Having finished all arrangements in Assiut and dispatched the caravan by road to Kharga, I set out myself by train.

At Qara Station on the Western Oasis line, I found Nimr, Sheykh Suleyman's brother. He brought up to me a jet black Sudani, about six feet three in height, who was so excessively lightly built that he could hardly have weighed more than eight stone. He answered to the name of "Abdullah abu Reesha"—"Abdulla the father of feathers," a nickname given to him on account of his extreme thinness. He had, however, the reputation of being one of the best guides in the desert, and was always in request whenever a caravan went down to collect natron from Bir Natrun, where there was always a very fair chance of a scrap with the Bedayat. Nimr suggested that I should take him as a guide, and appeared to be greatly disappointed when I told him I had already engaged Qway. I promised, however, to bear him in mind, and, if I wanted another guide at any time, to write and ask Sheykh Suleyman to send him.

Nimr told me the rather unwelcome news that the *bedawin*, who had been pasturing their camels in Dakhla Oasis, were all scuttling back again with their beasts to the safety of the Nile Valley, as there was a report that a famous hashish runner and brigand, known as 'Abdul 'Ati, was coming in to raid the oasis. As I had counted on being able to hire some camels off these

Arabs in the oasis, to supplement my own caravan when starting off on our fifteen days' journey, this threatened raid was rather a nuisance and seemed likely somewhat to upset my plans.

This 'Abdul 'Ati was a well-known character in the desert, and if half the reports concerning him were true, he must have been a most formidable personage. He was rather badly wanted by the Frontier Guard (Camel Corps), as one of his principal occupations was that of smuggling hashish (Indian hemp), at which he had proved himself most successful. When business of this kind was slack, he occasionally indulged in a little brigandage, presumably just to keep his hand in.

Ibrahim, had the usual admiration for an outlaw common to youths of his age all over the world, and 'Abdul 'Ati was his idol, and he was a born hero-worshipper. He declared that he was a dead shot, and owned a rifle that carried two hours' journey of a caravan, i.e. about five miles, and that he had no fear of anyone—not even of the Camel Corps.

When next I heard of 'Abdul 'Ati, he was very busy in Tripoli fighting against the Italians, and apparently making very good indeed. The Camel Corps shot him eventually.

My caravan reached Kharga a day or two after my arrival, having come across the desert from Assiut by a road that enters the oasis at its northern end.

In Kharga I met Sheykh Suleyman, and, as I was camped not far from his tent, rode over and spent an evening with him. Qway, of course, accompanied me in hopes of a free meal, but was most frigidly received by the sheykh, who treated him in the most contemptuous manner. We had supper, consisting of bread and treacle and hard boiled eggs, followed by coffee and cigarettes. After which we sat for a time and talked.

"You had better take me as a guide instead of Qway," suddenly suggested Sheykh Suleyman.

Qway looked quickly up, evidently greatly annoyed, and the social atmosphere became distinctly electric.

I explained that I could not well do that as I had found Qway an excellent guide the year before, and had already signed an agreement to take him on again for the season. Qway rather hotly added some expostulation that I could not quite catch; but the gist of it apparently was that Sheykh Suleyman was not quite playing the game.

The sheykh laughed. "*Maleysh*" (never mind), he said, "if you want another guide, write me a letter, and I will send Abdulla abu Reesha. He's a good man—better than Qway."

Qway commenced a heated reply, only to be laughed at by Sheykh Suleyman. As the interview threatened to become distinctly stormy, I took the earliest opportunity of returning to camp.

The sheykh insisted on providing my breakfast the next morning. Qway, for once, effaced himself, while breakfast and the subsequent tea were in progress. He seemed to have seen as much of Sheykh Suleyman as he wanted for the moment.

We got off at about ten in the morning, and after a short march pitched our camp early in the day at Qasr Lebakha, a small square mud-built keep on a stone foundation, having circular towers at the four corners, all in a fairly good state of preservation. The walls at the top of the tower were built double, with a kind of parapet walk round the top, which may originally have been a mural passage of which the roof had fallen in.

From Qasr Lebakha we went on to 'Ain Um Debadib. Our road lay almost due west, parallel to the cliff of the plateau on our right, and turned out to be anything but a good one, being both hilly and very heavy going owing to the drift sand. The camels, too, gave a lot of trouble.

The caravan, as a whole, turned out to be the worst I ever owned. There was, however, one exception. He was an enormously powerful brute from the Sudan, that it seemed almost impossible to overburden. The proverbial "last straw" that would have broken that camel's back could not, I believe, have been grown. But like other powerful camels, he was always trying to bite the other beasts and was a confirmed "man-eater."

'Ain Um Debadib is a considerably larger place than Qasr Lebakha. At the time of my visit it was inhabited by two men and their families, natives of Kharga village, to which they occasionally returned, leaving this little oasis to look after itself. Like Qasr Lebakha, the place was originally defended by a castle, also apparently of Roman date. An old road runs north-west from 'Ain Um Debadib, which leads over the cliff to the north of the oasis by what appears from below to be a difficult pass. I intended at some later date to come back and try to find this place; but unfortunately the opportunity did not occur. The Spaniards have a proverb to the effect that hell is not only paved with good intentions, but is also roofed with lost opportunities, and probably, in omitting to find out what lay beyond that cliff, I added a slate to the infernal regions, for I think it extremely likely that a depression lay on the other side of it containing the well of 'Ain Hamur—not to be confused with 'Ain Amur—or possibly a place called 'Ain Embarres.

CHAPTER XIII

WE reached Dakhla Oasis on 23rd January, and stayed for a day in the scrub-covered area, through which the road runs before entering the inhabited portion of the oasis, on the chance of getting a shot at gazelle. While camped here the *'omda* of Tenida, the nearest village, who was notorious throughout the oasis for his meanness, sent down over night a *ghaffir* (night watchman) after dark, to spy out who we were, and, having made sure of our identity, carefully got himself out of the way, in order to avoid having to invite us in to a meal, according to the hospitable custom of the oasis!

As gazelle-hunting, owing to some confounded *bedawin*, who were camping in the neighbourhood and wandering all over the place, seemed likely to prove a waste of energy, I moved on the following day to the village of Belat.

Very little barley is grown in the oasis beyond that required for the use of the inhabitants; but as I heard that the *'omda* had a large store of it that he had been unsuccessfully trying to sell, I endeavoured to buy some off him.

But unfortunately he "followed the Skeykh," and Qway continuing his obstructive tactics of Assiut, secretly got hold of him, with the result that, when I approached him on the subject, the *'omda* declared that there was not a grain left in the village—"not one."

A distinctly stormy scene followed, which ended in the *'omda* caving in and producing about a quarter of a ton of the absent grain, which I bought off him at an exorbitant price.

After this I gave him a thorough good dressing down, and then graciously forgave him and we drowned our enmity in the usual tea. I was not altogether dissatisfied with the transaction, for I felt that I had read the *'omda* a lesson that he would not forget for some time. In this, however, as events turned out, I was to be grievously disappointed—my troubles with regard to the camels' fodder had only just begun.

On our arrival in Mut, I went at once to the post office for letters, and finding that the upper story of the place was vacant, arranged to rent it during my stay in the oasis. It proved to be far better quarters than the old gloomy, scorpion-haunted store, and I found no reason to regret the change.

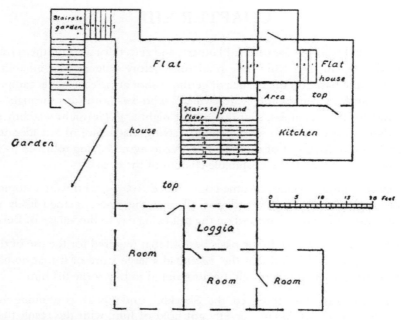

UPPER FLOOR OF POST OFFICE.

The man who tended the garden of the post office was quite a local celebrity. He was no other than the blind drummer who officiated in the band, when there was a wedding in the district. He was also the town crier, and I frequently met him in the streets, where, after beating a roll on his drum to attract attention, he would call out the news that he was engaged to spread.

Curiously, considering that he was totally blind, he had the reputation of being the best grower of vegetables in the neighbourhood, and his services as gardener were in great request in consequence. He was passionately fond of flowers, and was almost invariably seen with a rose, or a sprig of fruit blossom in his hand, which, as he made his way about the streets, he continually smelt. Once, when I happened to meet him, the supply of flowers must have run short, for he was inhaling, with evident gusto, the delicious perfume of an onion!

His sense of locality must have been wonderful, for he made his way about the streets almost as easily as though in full possession of perfect eyesight. Plants of all kinds seemed to be an obsession with him. He would squat down by the side of a bed of young vegetables he had planted, feel for the plants by running his hands rapidly over the soil, and, having found one, would tenderly finger it to see how it was growing. He would in this way rapidly examine each individual plant in the bed, and occasionally comment on the growth of some particular plant since he had last handled it. The loss of his eyesight had evidently greatly quickened his other faculties, for he could find any plant he wished without difficulty, and seemed to have a perfect recollection of the state in which he had last left them, never, I was told, making any mistake in their identity. The gratified smile that lighted up his blind, patient face, when his charges were doing well was quite pathetic.

While staying in the post office my camels were accommodated about a hundred yards away, in an open space under the lea of the high mud-built wall that surrounds the town, close to where a break had been made in it to allow free passage to the cultivation beyond. The choice of this site for the camping ground of the camels turned out to be unfortunate, for the locality was haunted. A man, it was said, had been killed near there while felling a tree, and his ghost—or as some said a *ghul*—frequently appeared there.

A night or two after our arrival, Ibrahim, who was sleeping there alone with the camels, came up to my room, just as I was getting into bed, and announced that he was not a bit afraid—and he did not seem in the least perturbed—but an *afrit* kept throwing clods of earth at the camels, which prevented them from sleeping, so he thought he had better come and tell me about it.

The clods came from over the wall, and several times he had rushed round the corner, through the gap, to try and see the *afrit* who was throwing them, but he had been unable to do so, so he wanted me to come down and attend to him.

BLIND TOWN CRIER, MUT.

It is not often that one gets the chance of interviewing a real ghost, so taking a candle and my revolver, I went down to the camel yard. Ibrahim showed me a pile of clods that had been thrown that he had collected—there must at least have been a dozen of them—and showed me the direction from which they had come.

It certainly was rather uncanny. On the other side of the wall was a flat open space, and there was nowhere within stone's throw where any human being could possibly have hidden. I waited for some time to see if any more clods would be thrown; but as none came, I told Ibrahim in a loud voice to shoot any *afrit* he saw and gave him my revolver, and then in a lower tone told him that he was on no account to shoot at all, but that if anyone came he might threaten to do so.

Ibrahim was perfectly satisfied. It was not so much the possession of the revolver that reassured him as the fact that it was made of iron, and *afrits*, as of course is well known, are afraid of iron!

No more clods were thrown that night; but they began again on the following evening, and still Ibrahim was unable to see the culprit. The thing was becoming a nuisance and it had to be stopped. It was of no use going to the native officials; they would have been just as ready to believe in the *afrit* or *ghul* yarn as any of the natives of the oasis, so I decided to tackle the question myself.

Dahab, carrying a pot of whitewash and a brush, and I, with a sextant and the nautical almanac, repaired to the scene of the haunting in the afternoon. I wrote "Solomon" and "iron" in Arabic on the wall, drew two human eyes squinting diabolically, a little devil and the diagram of the configuration of Jupiter's Satellites, taken from the nautical almanac—an extremely cabalistic-looking design. I then waved the sextant about and finally touched each of the marks I had drawn on the wall with it in turn.

By this time a small crowd had collected, and were watching the proceedings with considerable interest. A six-inch sextant, fitted with Reeve's artificial horizon, is as awe-inspiring an instrument as any magician could show.

I told Dahab to explain to the crowd that I had just put a *tulsim* (talisman) on the wall, and that if it were an *afrit* that had been throwing the clods, the words, "Solomon" and "iron," acting in conjunction with Jupiter's Satellites, would certainly do for him completely. But if it were a human being who had been throwing the clods, the little devil and the eyes would get to work upon him at once.

The devil I explained was a particularly malignant little English imp that I had under my control, and if anyone threw any more clods at my camels, I had so arranged things, that the devil in the form of this tiny little black imp would crawl up his nostrils while he slept, and would stick the forked end of his tail into his brain and keep waggling it about, causing him the greatest suffering, until in a few years' time he went mad. Then it would stamp with red-hot feet on the backs of his eyeballs till they fell out; after which the culprit would die in horrible agony.

Dahab, on the way back, said he thought my *tulsim* looked a very good one, but he did not at all believe in the *afrit* theory.

"*Afrit*," he said in his funny English. "Never. Ibrahim he very fine man and women in Dakhla all bad, very bad, like pitch. One women he want speak Ibrahim." This was very likely the size of it.

But I laid the ghost anyway. No more clods were thrown at my camels.

CHAPTER XIV

THERE had been a complete change in the officials of the oasis since we had last been there. The new doctor—Wissa by name—came round to call the day after my arrival. He was a Copt.

He belonged to a rich family, owning large landed estates in the neighbourhood of Assiut.

He spoke English almost perfectly, for like so many Egyptians he was a born linguist. He was, I believe, almost equally at home with French and German. His people being very well-to-do had given him an excellent education, part of which he had received in England and other European countries.

Like all the Egyptians who have been educated in Europe, he was an interesting mixture of East and West—and a very curious compound it was. He talked most learnedly on the subject of medicine, and appeared to have especially studied such local diseases as "dengue" and "bilharsia." Whenever I allowed him to do so, he gave me most racy accounts of his life as a medical student in Europe.

But he was an ardent treasure seeker, and his favourite topic of conversation was occultism and magic, in all of which he had the native Egyptian's profound belief. He, the Senussi sheykh, Ahmed el Mawhub, and the *'omda* of Rashida, had formed a sort of partnership to search for treasure, agreeing to divide equally between them anything that they found.

He told me a good deal about the Mawhub family of the Senussi *zawia* at Qasr Dakhl. He said they were entirely neglecting their religious work in order to make money, and had then only got five pupils left in the *zawia* at Qasr Dakhl, where formerly they had had great numbers. Old Sheykh Mohammed el Mawhub, who was well over seventy, had just started, he said, for Kufara with one servant and three men, who had been sent from that oasis to fetch him.

Wissa professed to have collected information from some unknown source of treasure that was hidden in many places in or near the oasis. One place in which he said it was to be found was in a stone temple eighteen hours' journey to the west of the village of Gedida. I afterwards met a native who said he had ridden out and found this place, so probably it exists—the temple, not the treasure. He was clearly badly bitten with the treasure-seeking mania.

He was, of course, the possessor of a "book of treasure." In the triangle between Mut, Masara and Ezbet Sheykh Mufta there is, he said, an old brick building on a white stone foundation covered by a dome, known as the Der el Arais—I saw this place afterwards. In it, under the dome, the book said, is a staircase with seven flights of steps, at the bottom of which is a passage seven cubits long. At the end of the passage is a monk—painted, Wissa thought, on the wall. The book said that there is an iron ring let into the floor near his feet, and that by pulling the ring a door would be caused to appear—this Wissa concluded to be a trap-door. Below is a flight of steps, which the book said must be descended without fear. At the bottom of the stair is a small chamber in which a king is buried.

The king has a gold ring with a stone in it on his finger. This is a magic ring, and if it is immersed in water, which is then given to a sick person, he will at once be cured, no matter what the nature of his malady may be. In the chamber there is also a clock that goes for ever, and in addition a *sagia* (wheel for raising water) that contains the secret of Zerzura.

After I had got to know him better, he one day suggested that "as I was looking for Zerzura," we should join together to search for the Der el Arais. He offered to let me keep the wonderful clock and *sagia*, and any treasure we might find, if I would only let him have the ring. With the help of that magic ring he felt certain that he would become the greatest doctor in the world—yet this was a man who had taken a diploma at the Qasr el 'Aini Hospital, spent a year at St. Thomas's, six months at the Rotunda, and another six studying medicine between Paris and Geneva—and he wanted to cure his patients with a magic ring!

On leaving Dakhla, as he was an unusually capable native doctor, he was appointed to Luxor. Here he got into trouble. His sister contracted plague, and Wissa, without notifying the authorities, as he should have done, took her into his house, where he seems to have neglected the most elementary sanitary precautions. The last I heard of him he was, perhaps naturally, again in disgrace, and was on his way to take up an appointment at Sollum, where delinquents of his kind are sent when there is no room for them in the oases.

All this just shows what inestimable benefits an unusually intelligent native will reap from a highly expensive European education!

I had several times noticed in Mut a man dressed like a Tripolitan Arab in a long woollen blanket, but had never been able to get a good look at him, as he always avoided meeting me. On one occasion, when he saw me approaching, he even turned back and slunk round a corner to get out of my way.

Meeting Wissa one day, I asked him if he knew this Maghrabi Arab. He replied that he was not really an Arab at all, but a native of Smint, in Dakhla, and that he was a local magician he had often spoken to me about, who only wore the Tripolitan dress for effect, as the Western Arabs are noted as being the best sorcerers.

This man was a member of the Senussi—or as it was usually expressed "he followed the Sheykh." I found that he was staying with Shekyh Senussi, the Clerk in Mut, and by a curious coincidence Qway also happened to be living in the same house.

I gathered that Qway was in the position of an honoured guest, for nearly every time I saw him he dilated upon Sheykh Senussi's kindness to him. At times he became almost sentimental on the subject, declaring that he was like a brother to him. The reason for Qway's affection evidently being that his camel, of which he was so proud, was being fed on the fat of the land and that he apparently was getting unlimited tea. This rapprochement between Qway and the Senussi, added to the rather secretive manner in which it was going on, made me suspect that this lavish hospitality had some ulterior object, though it was difficult to see what they were planning.

There were signs, too, that the Senussi were endeavouring to get round my other men, for when I went one morning to look at the camels, I saw an unpleasant-looking, pock-marked Arab skulking about in the yard to which Abd er Rahman had moved them to protect them from the wind—or the *afrit*. He kept dodging about behind the beasts and making for the entrance to the yard, evidently trying to avoid being seen. When I called him up and spoke to him, he told me he had come from "the north," and tried to give the impression that he had recently left Assiut.

But on questioning Abd er Rahman about him afterwards I found that he was one of Sheykh Ahmed's men, who had come down from his *ezba* in charge of two camels on some mysterious errand, the nature of which was not quite clear. Abd er Rahman, when I told him that he looked a disreputable scoundrel, was loud in his praise.

I managed to elicit one useful piece of information from him, as he told me that, owing to most of the camels belonging to the Senussi having gone with old Mawhub, on his journey to Kufara, they only had three left in the oasis. This was rather welcome news, as I was afraid that they might go out and tamper with the depots I was intending to make in the desert.

CHAPTER XV

AS soon as the camels had been got into good condition I sent Qway, Abd er Rahman and Ibrahim off with the caravan loaded with grain, which the two Sudanese were to deposit at Jebel el Bayed, the hill we had reached at the end of our last journey the season before.

Ibrahim had not been with me at all the previous season and, as Abd er Rahman had never even been within sight of the hill, as I had sent him back to Mut to bring out more water on the journey on which I reached it, I arranged that Qway should ride with them as far as the edge of the plateau, where he was to give Abd er Rahman directions to take him to Jebel el Bayed. Here, however, he was to leave the caravan and to ride west along the tableland and come back and report what he had seen.

Abd er Rahman, following the directions given him by Qway, easily found Jebel el Bayed, and left the grain to form the depot in the neighbourhood. Qway himself rejoined the caravan on their way back just before reaching Mut, so they all returned together.

Qway, of course, had done practically nothing. It was difficult to see the best way of dealing with him. I could, of course, have discharged him, but drastic remedies are seldom the best, and to have done so would only have had the effect of playing straight into the hands of the Senussi, as he was a magnificent guide and they would have at once gained him as a wholehearted recruit. As he unfortunately knew the whole of my plans, the better scheme seemed to be to keep him with me and to tie him up in such a way that he could do no harm. In the circumstances I thought it best to send Sheykh Suleyman a letter, asking him to let me have Abdulla and the best *hagin* he could find. This, at any rate, would ensure my having a guide if Qway went wrong; and I hoped by stirring up a little friction between him and Abdulla to make the latter keep an eye upon his actions.

Soon after the return of the caravan the *mamur* left and I went round to see him off. On the way I looked into the enclosure where the camels were housed, and again caught Sheykh Ahmed's pock-marked camel-man hobnobbing with my men, and saw that he was stabling his two camels in the neighbouring yard.

On reaching the *mamur's* house I found him in a great state of excitement. The post *hagan*, with whom he was going to travel, had omitted, or forgotten, to bring any camels for his baggage. The *mamur* was in a terrible state about this, saying that he might have to send in to the Nile Valley for beasts before he could leave, and that he was due there himself in six days.

This was an opportunity too good to be lost. I told him there were two unusually fine camels in the yard next to my caravan, and suggested that as a

Government official going back to the Nile on duty, he had the power to commandeer them and their drivers, and suggested that he should do so. No petty native official can resist the temptation to commandeer anything he has a right to in his district—it is a relic of the old corrupt Turkish rule. The *mamur* jumped at the idea and departed shortly after with a very sulky camel driver and two of the finest camels owned by the Senussi. It was with great relief that I saw the last of that pock-marked brute and his beasts, for their departure left the Senussi with only one camel until in about a month's time, when old Mawhub was due to return from Kufara. I went back to my rooms feeling I had done a good morning's work, and effectually prevented the Senussi from getting at the depot I was making near Jebel el Bayed.

Abdulla, whom I had asked Sheykh Suleyman to send, did not turn up on the day I had expected; but a day or two afterwards Nimr, Sheykh Suleyman's brother, arrived in Mut on some business and came round to see me. Gorgeously arrayed with a revolver and silver-mounted sword, he looked a typical *bedawi*—he certainly behaved as one. He drank about a gallon of tea, ate half a pound of Turkish Delight and the best part of a cake that Dahab had made, and topped up, when I handed him a cigarette box for him to take one, by taking a handful. He then left, declaring that he was very *mabsut* (pleased) with me and promising to send Abdulla along as soon as he could, and to see that he had a good *hagin*. As he went downstairs he turned round, looking much amused, and asked how I was getting on with Qway!

While dressing one morning I heard Qway below greeting some old friend of his in the most cordial and affectionate manner; then I heard him bring him upstairs and, looking through the window, saw that Abdulla had arrived at last. Qway tapped at the door and, hardly waiting for me to answer, entered, beaming with satisfaction and apparently highly delighted at the new arrival—he was an admirable actor.

Abdulla looked taller and more "feathery" than ever. With a native-made straw hat on the back of his head and his slender waist tightly girthed up with a leather strap, he looked almost girlish in his slimness. But there was nothing very feminine about Abdulla—he was wiry to the last degree.

He carried an excellent double-barrelled hammer, ejector gun, broken in the small of the stock it is true, but with the fracture bound round and round with tin plates and strongly lashed with wire. His saddlery was irreproachable and hung round with the usual earthenware jars and leather bags for his food supply.

His *hagin* was a powerful old male and looked up to any amount of hard work. I told him to get up on his camel and show me his paces. Abdulla swung one of his legs, which looked about four feet long, over the cantle of his saddle and seated himself at once straight in the seat. He kicked his camel in the ribs and at once got him into a trot. The pace at which he made that beast move was something of a revelation and augured well for his capacity as a scout. He was certainly a very fine rider.

But when I made him take off the saddle I found, as is so often the case with *bedawin* camels, the beast had a sore back. There was a raw, festering place under the saddle on either side of the spine.

As Abdulla had a hard job before him, I had to see his camel put right before he started, so we went off to a new doctor, who had come to take Wissa's place, to buy some iodoform and cotton-wool, and proceeded to doctor the *hagin*. But it was clear that it would take some days to heal.

It made, however, no difference as it turned out. For the caravan was unable to start as four *ardebs*[3] of barley that I had ordered from Belat, never turned up. The barley question was becoming a serious one; but by dint of sending the men round Mut from house to house I managed to buy in small quantities, of a few pounds at a time, an amount that when put together came to about three *ardebs*, with which I had for the moment to be content.

The sores on Abdulla's *hagin* having sufficiently healed, I packed the whole caravan off again into the desert. Abd er Rahman and Ibrahim as before were to carry stores out to the depot at Jebel el Bayed. Abdulla's work was to go on ahead of the caravan, following directions to be given him by Abd er Rahman, as I was afraid Qway might mislead him, till he reached Jebel el Bayed. There he was to climb to the top of the hill, whence he could see the one I had sighted in the distance the season before. This lay in practically the same line from Mut as Jebel el Bayed itself. Having in this way got its bearing, he was to go on to the farther hill, which he was also to climb and make a note of anything that was to be seen from the summit. He was then— provided the country ahead of him was not inhabited—to go on again as far as he could along the same bearing before returning to Dakhla.

I asked Abdulla how far out he thought he would be able to get. In a matter-of-fact tone he said he thought he could go four, or perhaps four and a half, days' journey beyond Jebel el Bayed before he turned back. As he would be alone in a strange desert, I doubted somewhat if he would even reach Jebel el Bayed. But I did not know Abdulla then.

There really was nothing much for Qway to do, but, as I thought it better to send him off into the desert to keep him out of mischief, I told him to ride west again along the plateau.

Qway was rather subdued. Abdulla's arrival had considerably upset him, in spite of his efforts to disguise the fact. He objected strongly to his going on ahead of the caravan to scout, but I declined to alter the arrangement. So to keep Abdulla in his place, Qway, with the usual high-handed manner of the

Arabs, when dealing with Sudanese, collared a water tin of his for his own use. On hearing of this I went round to the camel-yard and gave Abdulla back his tin, and pitched into Qway before all the men. Having thus sown a little discord in the caravan, I told them they had to start in the morning.

I went round again later in the day and found all the Sudanese having their heads shaved by the village barber and being cupped on the back of their necks, preparatory for their journey. The cupping they declared kept the blood from their heads and made them strong!

This operation was performed by the barber, who made three or four cuts at the base of the skull on either side of the spine, to which he applied the wide end of a hollow cow's horn, pressed this into the flesh and then sucked hard at a small hole in the point of the horn, afterwards spitting out the blood he had thus extracted. It seemed an insanitary method.

The Sudanese were all extremely dark. Abd er Rahman and Ibrahim even having black, or rather dark brown, patches on their gums. Their tongues and the palms of their hands, however, showed pink. Abdulla was even darker. He came up to my room the evening after his cupping and declared that he was ill. There was nothing whatever the matter with him, except that he wanted pills and eye-drops because they were to be had for nothing. But I made a pretence of examining him, took his temperature, felt his pulse, and then told him to show me his tongue.

The result of my modest request was rather staggering. He shot out about six inches of black leather, and I saw that not only his tongue was almost black, but also his gums and the palms of his hands as well. He was the most pronounced case of human melanism I ever saw.

Sofut.

Sand erosion producing sharp blades of rock very damaging to the soft feet of a camel. (p. 87).

The Descent into Dakhla Oasis.

This cliff was several hundred feet in height, but the sand drifted against it and made the descent easy. (p. 36).

A Made Road.

Made roads are practically unknown in the desert. This one was notched out of the side of the slope and led to the site of an unknown oasis, where treasure was said to be hidden. (p. 205).

CHAPTER XVI

THE caravan, with Abd er Rahman and Ibrahim, returned, dead beat, but safe. No less than four of the tanks they had taken out filled with water had leaked and had had to be brought back. They had had to race home by day and night marches all the way. But they had got in all right—we had extraordinary luck in this way.

As Abdulla did not come in till two days later, I began to fear that something had happened to him. He arrived with his camel in an awful state. The sores on his back, which appeared to have healed when he started, had broken out again and were very much worse than when he first reached Mut.

His camel had gone so badly, he said, that he had not been able to do half as much as he would have done if his mount had been in good condition, and he was very vexed about it indeed. He had followed Abd er Rahman's directions and had found Jebel el Bayed without difficulty. He had climbed to the top and seen the second hill beyond. He had then gone on towards it—his camel going very badly indeed—for a day and a half over easy desert, after which he had crossed a belt of dunes that took about an hour to negotiate. Then after another half-day he managed to reach the second hill and had climbed to the top of it. To the south and south-west lay open desert with no dunes, falling towards the west, dotted with hills and stretching away as far as he could see. To the north he had been able to see the cliff on the south of the plateau—the pass down which we had descended into the "Valley of the Mist" being distinctly visible, though it must have been a good hundred and twenty miles away. After this he said he could do no more with such a wretched camel, so he had been obliged to return. He was very apologetic indeed for having done so little.

It never seemed to occur to this simple Sudani that he had made a most remarkable journey. Acting only on directions given him by Abd er Rahman, he had gone off entirely alone, into an absolutely waterless and barren desert, with which he was totally unacquainted, with a very sore-backed camel and riding only on a baggage saddle—his riding saddle had got broken before the start—but he had covered in thirteen days a distance, as the crow flies, of nearly four hundred miles, and more remarkable still had apologised for not having been able to do more! He got some *bakhshish* that surprised him—and greatly disgusted Qway who got none.

The fact that Abdulla saw the pass into the "Valley of the Mist" from the top of the hill he reached—Jebel Abdulla as the men called it—shows that the hill was of considerable height, for it, Jebel el Bayed and the pass, lay in practically a straight line, and the desert there was very level. The summit of the pass was about 1700 feet high—the cliff itself being about 250 feet. But it could not be seen from the top of Jebel el Bayed, which was 2150 feet, owing to a low intervening rise in the ground. A simple diagram will show that, as it was visible over this ridge from the top of Jebel Abdulla, the latter must have been at least 2700 feet high.

Qway, of course, though excellently mounted, had done practically nothing. There could be little doubt that he and the Senussi were hand in glove. He was always asking leave to go to places like Hindaw, Smint and Qalamun, where I knew the Senussi had *zawias*, and the Sheykh el Afrit at Smint and Sheykh Senussi, the poet in Mut, were his two intimate friends, and both of them members of the Senussia.

The Senussi had always been a nuisance to travellers wanting to go into their country. It was, however, difficult to see what they could do. They would not, I thought, dare to do anything openly in the oasis and, by getting rid of two out of their three camels I had rather tied them up for the time being, so far as the desert was concerned. So I went on with my preparations for our final journey with a fairly easy mind, making the fatal mistake of underestimating my opponents.

First I engaged the local tinsmith to patch up six tanks that had developed leaks. Then I sent Ibrahim round the town to see if he could not find some more weapons. He returned with a neat little battle axe, a spear and a six-foot gas-pipe gun with a flint-lock. All of which I bought as curiosities.

We then went out and tried the gun. It shot, it is true, a few feet to one side; but little trifles like that are nothing to a *bedawi*. The general opinion of the men was that it was a very good gun indeed. Abdulla said he had been in the camel corps and understood guns, and undertook to put it right. He shut one eye and looked along the barrel, then he rested the muzzle on the ground and stamped about half-way down the barrel to bend it. He repeated this process several times, then handed the gun back to Ibrahim, saying that he thought he had got it straight.

I got up a shooting match between the three Sudanese to test it. The target was a tin of bad meat at eighty yards, and Ibrahim with the flint-lock gun, with his second shot, hit the tin and won the ten piastres that I offered as a prize, beating Abd er Rahman and Abdulla armed with Martini's.

Then I set to work to buy some more barley for our journey and difficulties at once arose. I sent Abd er Rahman and Abdulla with some camels to Belat, but the '*omda* told them he had sold the whole of his grain; though they learnt in the oasis that he had not been able to sell any and still had huge stores of it left.

Abd er Rahman began dropping ponderous hints about Qway, the Senussi, "arrangements" and "intrigue"; but, as usual, declined to be more definite.

Qway, when I told him of the difficulty of procuring grain, was sympathetic, but piously resigned. It was the will of Allah. Certainly the *'omda* of Belat had none left—he knew this as a fact. It would be quite impossible, he said, to carry out my fifteen days' journey with such a small quantity of grain and he thought the only thing for me to do was to abandon the idea of it altogether.

I told him I had no intention of giving the journey up in any circumstances. The only other plan he could think of was to buy the grain from the Senussi at Qasr Dakhl. They had plenty—excellent barley. I mentioned this to Dahab, who was extremely scornful, declaring that they would not sell me any, or if they did, that it would be poisoned, for he said it was well known that the Mawhubs thoroughly understood medicine.

The new *mamur* arrived in due course. The previous one, 'Omar Wahaby, had endeavoured to *ayb* me by not calling till I threatened him. The new one went one better—he sent for me—and had to be badly snubbed in consequence.

The natives of Egypt attach great importance to this kind of thing, and I was glad to see that my treatment of the *mamur* caused a great improvement in the attitude of the inhabitants of Mut towards me, which had been anything but friendly before.

The *mamur* himself must have been considerably impressed. He called and enquired about my men, and asked if I had any complaints to make against them. I told him Qway was working very badly and had got very lazy; so he said he thought, before I started, that he had better speak to them privately. I knew I should hear from my men what happened, so thinking it might have a good effect upon Qway, I sent them round in the afternoon to the *merkaz*.

They returned looking very serious—Abd er Rahman in particular seemed almost awed. I asked him what the *mamur* had said. He told me he had taken down all their names and addresses, and then had told them they must work their best for me, because, though he did not quite know exactly who I was, I was clearly a very important person indeed—all of which shows how very easily a *fellah* is impressed by a little side!—*il faut se faire valoir* in dealing with a native.

The *mamur* afterwards gave me his opinion of my men. His views on Dahab were worth repeating. He told me he had questioned him and come to the conclusion that he was honest, *very* honest—"In fact," he said, "he is almost stupid!"

The barley boycott began to assume rather alarming proportions. The men could hear of no grain anywhere in the oasis, except at Belat, Tenida and the Mawhubs, and it really looked as though I should have to abandon my journey.

I could, of course, have tried to get some grain from Kharga, but it would have taken over a week to fetch. It was doubtful, too, whether I could have got as much as I wanted without going to the Nile Valley for it, and that would have wasted a fortnight at least. I was at my wits' end to know what to do.

The *Deus ex machina* arrived in the form of the police officer—a rather unusual shape for it to take in the oases. He came round one afternoon to call. I was getting very bored with his conversation, when he aroused my interest by saying he was sending some men to get barley for the Government from the Senussi at Qasr Dakhl. From the way in which he was always talking about money and abusing the "avaricious" *'omdas*, I felt pretty sure that he lost no chance of turning an honest piastre; so finding that the price he was going to pay was only seventy piastres the *ardeb*, I told him that I was paying hundred and twenty, and that, if he bought an extra four *ardebs*, I would take them off him at that price—and I omitted to make any suggestion as to what should be done with the balance of the purchase money.

As trading in Government stores is a criminal offence, I felt fairly sure that he would not tell the Senussi for what purpose that extra four *ardebs* was being bought.

The result of this transaction was that, in spite of the barley boycott that the Senussi had engineered against me, I was eventually able to start off again to explore the desert, whose secrets they were so jealously guarding, with my camels literally staggering under the weight of some really magnificent grain, bought, if they had only known it, from the Senussi themselves!

The plan for the journey was as follows: we were to leave Dakhla with every camel in the caravan, including the *hagins*, loaded to their maximum carrying capacity with water-tanks and grain. At the end of every day's march a small depot was to be left, consisting of a pair of the small tanks I had had made for the journey, and sufficient barley for the camels and food for the men for a day's supply. The reduction in the weight of the baggage entailed by the making of these depots, added to that of the water and grain consumed by the caravan on the journey, I calculated would leave two camels free by the time that we reached the five bushes.

Qway and Abdulla, who were to accompany the caravan up to this point, were then to go on ahead of the caravan with their *hagins* loaded with only enough water and grain to take them out to the main depot at Jebel el Bayed. Here they were to renew their supplies, go on for another day together and then separate. Qway was to follow Abdulla's tracks out to the second hill—Jebel Abdulla as the men called it—that the Sudani had reached alone on his scouting journey, and was to go on as much farther as he felt was safe in the same direction, after which he was to retrace his steps until he met the caravan coming out along the same route, bringing out water and supplies for his relief. Abdulla's instructions were to go due south when he parted from Qway for two or, if possible, three days. Then he was to strike off west till he cut Qway's track, which we should be following, and return upon it till he met the caravan, which would then go on along the line of the old road we had found to complete our fifteen days' journey, and, if possible, push on till we had got right across the desert into the French Sudan.

I was not expecting great results from Qway's journey, but he knew too much about our plans and was too useful a man in the desert to make it advisable to leave him behind us in Dakhla, where the Senussi might have made great use of him. Abdulla was well armed, an experienced desert fighter, and, in spite of his "feathery" appearance, was a man with whom it would not be safe to trifle. As there was a considerable amount of friction between him and Qway, owing to the Arab's overbearing attitude towards the Sudanese in general, I had little fear of their combining.

Abdulla, too, had special instructions to keep an eye on Qway, and, as there was not much love lost between them, I felt sure he would do so. While Abdulla was with him on the journey out to the depot, and for a day beyond, Qway, I felt, would be powerless; while if, after parting from him, he turned back to Jebel el Bayed to try and get at the depot, he would have us on top of him, as we should get there before him. When once the caravan had reached the depot we should pick up all the water and grain it contained and take it along with us following his tracks.

I had made him dependent on the caravan, by only giving him about five days' water for his own use, and none at all for his camel. So long as he adhered to his programme he was quite safe, as we could water his camel as soon as he rejoined us. But if he tried to follow some plan of his own, he would at once run short of water and find himself in trouble.

I felt that the precautions I had taken would effectually prevent any attempt at foul play on his part. My whole scheme had been thought out very carefully, and had provided, I thought, for every possible contingency, but "the best laid plans o' mice and men gang aft agley"—especially when dealing with a Senussi guide.

CHAPTER XVII

AT the start everything went well. Qway, it is true, though he did his best to disguise the fact, was evidently greatly put out by my having been able to produce so much barley. But the rest of the men were in excellent spirits. Ibrahim, in particular, with the flint-lock gun slung over his back, was as pleased with himself as any boy would be when carrying his first gun. The camels, in spite of their heavy loads, went so well that on the evening of the second day we reached the bushes.

I found that a well which, without finding a trace of water, I had dug the year before to a depth of thirty feet had silted up to more than half its depth with sand. Here we cut what firewood we wanted, and on the following morning Abdulla and Qway left the caravan and went on ahead towards Jebel el Bayed.

I walked with them for a short distance as they left, to give them final instructions. I told them that we should closely follow their tracks. Having some experience of Qway's sauntering ways when scouting by himself, I told him that he must make his camel put her best leg forward, and that if he did I would give him a big *bakhshish* at the end of the journey.

He at once lost his temper. The camel was his, he said, and he was not going to override her, and he should go at whatever pace he choose. He was not working for me at all, but he was working for Allah. My obvious retort, that in that case there was no necessity for me to pay his wages, did not mend matters in the least, and he went off in a towering rage. The Senussi teach their followers that every moment of a man's life should be devoted to the service of his Creator; consequently, though he may be working for an earthly master, he must first consider his duty towards Allah, as having the first claim upon his services—a Jesuitical argument that obviously puts great power into the hands of the Senussi sheykhs, who claim to be the interpreters of the will of Allah.

Abd er Rahman, who had been watching this little scene from a distance, looked very perturbed when I got back to the caravan. Qway, he said, was feeling *marbut* (tied) and that was very bad, because he was very cunning, and he prophesied that we should have a very difficult journey.

The Arabs are naturally a most undisciplined race, who kick at once at any kind of restraint. They are apt to get quite highfalutin on the subject of their independence, and will tell you that they want to be like the gazelle, at liberty to wander wherever they like, and to be as free as the wind that blows across their desert wastes, and all that kind of thing, and it makes them rather kittle cattle to handle.

Abd er Rahman was right; things began to go wrong almost at once. The first two days after leaving Mut had been cool, but a *simum* sprang up after we left the bushes and the day became stiflingly hot. Towards midday the internal pressure, caused by the expansion of the water and air in one of the tanks, restarted a leak that had been mended, and the water began to trickle out of the hole. We unloaded the camel and turned the tank round, so that the leak was uppermost and the dripping stopped. But soon a leak started in another of the mended tanks, and by the evening the water in most of those I had with me was oozing out from at least one point, and several of them leaked from two or more places.

When a tank had only sprung one leak, we were able to stop the wastage by hanging it with the crack uppermost; but when more than one was present, this was seldom possible. One of the tanks leaked so badly that we took it in turns to hold a tin underneath it, and, in that way, managed to save a considerable amount of water that we poured into a *gurba*.

On arriving in camp, I took the leaks in hand and stopped them with sealing-wax. This loss of water was a serious matter. Every morning I measured out the day's allowance for each man by means of a small tin; in face of the leakage from the tanks, I thought it advisable to cut down the allowance considerably.

This called forth loud protests from Abd er Rahman, who declared that it was quite impossible for him to work in such heat on such a meagre supply.

I endeavoured to pacify him by pointing out that I was not asking him to do anything I was not prepared to do myself, and that, as a Sudani, he belonged to a race that prided themselves on being able to endure the hardships to be encountered in a desert journey. But he only got more excited, saying that he and Ibrahim did more work than I did, as they had to load and unload the camels and walked all day, while I occasionally rode. Dahab, he added, was of no use in the desert, as he was only a cook, and I could do without him, and, as we were short of water, we had better get rid of him. At the end he was fairly shouting at me with rage, and, as he was not in a state to listen to arguments, I walked away from the camp into the desert to give him time to cool down.

A Sudani at heart is a savage, and if a savage thinks he is deprived of the necessaries of life he is very apt to fall back upon primitive methods, and is quite capable of "getting rid" of anyone who stands between him and his water supply. Visions of the ghastly scenes that took place among the survivors of the shipwrecked "Medusa" and "Mignonette," when they ran short of water, and of the terrible fate that overtook the survivors of the disastrous Flatters expedition, during their retreat to Algeria from the central Sahara, came up before my eyes, and, as I saw Abd er Rahman and Ibrahim earnestly consulting together, I felt the situation was not one to be trifled with.

I went back to the camp fully expecting to have to deal with something like a mutiny. I called Abd er Rahman up and told him he was never to speak to me again like that, and if he did I should fine him heavily. I said that we should find plenty of water in the depot at Jebel el Bayed and there was no need at all for any anxiety, but that, owing to the leakage from the tanks, we should have to be careful till we got there. I told him that I should help to load and unload the baggage, and would walk all day to show that the allowance of water was sufficient. As to Dahab, I pointed out that he had worked with him for two seasons in the desert, and that it was very treacherous for him to turn round and want to "get rid" of him directly there was a slight deficiency in the water supply.

Much to my surprise, I found him extremely penitent. He said I could drink all his water supply and Ibrahim's as well if I wanted it; of course he could put up with a small water supply better than I could, he was very strong; and as for Dahab he was an excellent fellow and a friend of his; he had only been angry because he was thirsty. I told him that it was very easy for him to talk, but that I should like to see how much there was at the back of what he said, so I challenged him to see if he could do on less water than I could. A sporting offer of this sort generally appeals to a Sudani or an Arab. He accepted my challenge with a grin.

Ibrahim afterwards apologised for his brother, saying that he had been behaving like a woman.

The sealing-wax I had put on the leaks effectually closed them; but towards noon the increasing heat melted the wax and soon they were leaking as badly as ever; the other tanks, that had held out up to that point, also opened their seams in the heat, and, by the end of the day, *every single tank* that I had was dripping its precious contents on to the ground. Only the small ones that I had made for the depots remained waterproof.

As the sealing-wax proved ineffectual, I scraped it off in the evening, and, since the leaks were all in the seams of the tanks, I plugged them with some gutta-percha tooth stopping that I had fortunately brought with me, wedging it into the seams where they leaked with the blade of a knife. This was apparently unaffected by the heat, and, though it was liable to be loosened by rough usage, was a great improvement on the wax. But the leaks were plugged too late. During the two days while they were open, one tank had become almost entirely empty, and the others had all lost a considerable portion of their contents. Fortunately I had allowed an ample supply of water, most of which was in the depot at Jebel el Bayed, so with the small tanks to fall back on in case of need, we could count on being able to get out about twelve days instead of the fifteen I had arranged for, which I expected would more than take us to Owanat.

We continued our march, leaving a small depot behind us at each camp till we reached the main store. This I found had not been made, as I intended it should be, at the foot of Jebel el Bayed, but a good half-day's journey to its north.

I was greatly relieved to see that the depot appeared to be quite in order; but Abd er Rahman was evidently suspicious, for leaving the unloading of the camels to Ibrahim and Dahab, he went off to the depot and began peering about and searching the neighbourhood for tracks.

Almost at once he returned with a very long face, announcing that a lot of water had been thrown away. I hurried up to the depot, and he pointed out two large patches of sand thickly crusted on the surface, showing that a very large amount of water had been spilt. We examined the depot itself. The sacks of grain were quite untouched, but every one of the large iron tanks was practically empty, with the exception of one which was about half full. The little tanks intended for the small depots did not appear to have been tampered with, perhaps because they would have required some time to empty.

The neighbourhood of the place where the water had been poured was covered with the great square footprints made by Qway's leather sandals, and made it quite clear that it was he who had emptied the tanks. There was no trace of the more rounded sandals worn by Abdulla on that side of the depot.

We followed Qway's footprints for a short distance. About two hundred yards away from the depot they joined on to Abdulla's, the small neat marks of Qway's camel overlaying the bigger prints of Abdulla's *hagin*—showing clearly that Qway had been the last to leave. I then returned with Abd er Rahman to the camp to decide what was best to be done.

The heavy leakage from the tanks we had brought with us, coupled with the large amount of water thrown away by Qway, made it abundantly clear that all chance of carrying out the scheme for which I had been working for two seasons, of getting across the desert to the Sudan, or of even getting as far as Owanat, was completely out of the question. It was a nasty jar, but it was of no use wasting time in grousing about it.

Our own position gave cause for some anxiety. So far as I and the men with me were concerned we were, of course, in no danger at all. Mut, with its water supply, could easily have been reached in about a week—it was only about one hundred and fifty miles away—and we had sufficient water with us and in the depots to take us back there.

As for Qway, I felt he was quite capable of looking after himself, and I did not feel much inclined to bother about him. The difficulty was Abdulla. From his tracks it was clear that he had no hand in emptying the tanks, and I very much doubted whether he knew anything at all about it. Abd er Rahman's explanation of what had occurred was, I felt sure, the correct one. His view was that Abdulla, though "very strong in the meat, was rather feeble in the head," and that Qway had managed to get rid of him on some excuse and had stayed behind to empty the tanks, which he had then put back in their places, hoping perhaps that we should not notice that anything was wrong.

Abdulla, counting on me to bring him out water and provisions, had gone off for a six days' journey, relying on meeting us at the end of that time. After going as far as he could to the south, he was to cut across on to Qway's track and then to ride back along it to meet us. The man had served me well, and in any case I did not feel at all inclined to leave him to die of thirst, as he certainly would, if we did not go out to meet him. Obviously, we should have to follow up Qway's track to relieve him—a course which also held out the alluring prospect of being able to get hold of Qway himself.

But our water was insufficient to enable the whole caravan to go on together, and it was urgently necessary to send back to Dakhla for a further supply. The difficulty was to know whom to send. There was always the risk that Qway might wheel round on us and try to get at our line of depots; and unfortunately he carried a Martini-Henri rifle I had lent him. My first idea was to go back with Dahab myself, as I could have found my way back to Mut without much difficulty, using my compass if necessary—the road was an easy one to follow—and to let the two Sudanese go on to relieve their fellow-tribesman, Abdulla; but this scheme seemed to be rather throwing the worst of the work on them—besides I wanted to go ahead in order to make the survey.

Abd er Rahman, of course, could have found his way back quite easily; but, though he carried a Martini-Henri carbine, he was a vile shot, even at close range, as he funked the kick; moreover, he stood in such awe of Qway that I was afraid, if they met, he would come off second best in the event of a row, even with Dahab to back him up.

Ibrahim, however, cared no more for Qway than he did for an *afrit* that threw clods, or for anyone else. With his flint-lock gun—bent straight by Abdulla—he was a very fair shot; but he was young and had had little experience of desert travelling, and I was very doubtful whether he would be able to find his way. When I questioned him on the subject, however, after a little hesitation and a long consultation with Abd er Rahman, he declared his willingness to try, and his brother said he thought he would be able to do it.

The next morning he set out with Dahab and the two worst camels, carrying all the empty tanks. His instructions were to get back as fast as possible to Mut, refill the tanks, and come out again as quickly as he could with a larger caravan, if he could raise one, and to beg, borrow or steal all the tanks and water-skins he could get hold of in the oasis, and to bring them all back filled with water. I gave him a note to the police officer, telling him what had happened and asking him to help him in any way he could. I gave him my second revolver and Dahab my gun, in case they should fall foul of Qway on the way, and then packed them off, though with considerable misgivings as to the result.

It was curious to see how the discovery that our tanks in the depot had been emptied, in spite of the difficulties that it created, cheered up the men. The feeling of suspense was over. We knew pretty well what we were up against, and everyone, I think, felt braced up by the crisis. Dahab looked a bit serious, but Ibrahim, with a gun over his shoulder, and suddenly promoted to the important post of guide to a caravan, even though it consisted of only two camels and an old Berberine cook, was in the highest spirits. I had impressed on him that the safety of his brother, his tribesman Abdulla and myself, rested entirely on his brawny shoulders, and that he had the chance of a lifetime of earning the much-coveted reputation among the *bedawin* of being a *gada* (sportsman)—and a *gada* Ibrahim meant to be, or die. I had no doubt at all of his intention of seeing the thing through, if he possibly could. I only hoped that he would not lose his way.

Having seen him off from the depot on the way back to Mut, I turned camel driver and, with the remainder of the camels and all the water we could carry, set out with Abd er Rahman to follow up Qway's tracks to relieve Abdulla. Abd er Rahman, too, rose to the occasion and started off gaily singing in excellent spirits. I had told him that I wanted to see whether he or Qway was the better man in the desert, and the little Sudani had quite made up his mind that he was going to come out top-dog.

CHAPTER XVIII

ABD ER RAHMAN was an excellent tracker.

There had been no wind to speak of since Qway had left the depot, and the footprints on the sandy soil were as sharp and distinct as when they were first made. By following Qway's tracks we were able to piece together the history of his journey with no uncertainty; and a very interesting job it proved.

We followed his footprints for three days, and there was mighty little that he did in that time that was not revealed by his tracks—Abd er Rahman even pointed out one place where Qway had spat on the ground while riding on his camel!

We could see where he had walked and led his mount, and where he had mounted again and ridden. We could see where he walked her and where he trotted; where he had curled himself up on the ground beside her and slept at night, and all along his track, at intervals, were the places where he had stopped to pray—the prints of his open hands where he bowed to the ground, and even the mark where he had pressed his forehead on the sand in prostration, were clearly visibly. The Moslem prayers are said at stated hours, and Qway was always extremely regular in his devotions. This prayerful habit of his was of the greatest assistance to us, as it told us the time at which he had passed each point.

Walking on foot he had led his camel behind him, when he left the depot, till he reached Abdulla's trail. He had then mounted and gone forward at a slow shuffling trot. Abdulla also had left the depot on foot, leading his *hagin*, and the tracks of Qway's camel occasionally crossed his spoor and overlaid them, showing that Abdulla and his *hagin* were in front.

Abdulla had continued at a walk until Qway overtook him—as shown by his tracks overlying those of Qway. Knowing the pace at which Qway must have trotted and at which Abdulla would have walked, by noting the time it took us to walk from the depot to where Qway caught Abdulla up, we were able to estimate that Qway could not have left the depot until Abdulla was nearly a mile and a half away, and consequently too far off to see what he was doing.

After Qway joined on to Abdulla, the two men had ridden on together till they reached Jebel el Bayed. Here, however, they had halted and evidently consulted together for some time before separating, as the ground all over a small area at this point was closely trampled. On separating, Abdulla had gone off at a trot, as arranged, towards the south, while Qway had sauntered leisurely along towards the second hill, two days' away to the south-west, or Jebel Abdulla as the men had named it.

We concluded from Qway's tracks, as dated by his praying places, that he must be rather more than a long day's journey ahead of us.

We continued following his trail until the sun began to set, when, as we did not want to overlook any tracks in the dark, we halted for the night. We had got by that time into rather broken ground, cut up into ridges and hills about twenty feet high, at the foot of one of which we camped.

In spite of Abd er Rahman's scandalised protests, I insisted on doing my share of the work in the caravan. I helped him to unload the camels, then, while he was feeding the beasts, I lit the fire and made the tea.

Abd er Rahman returned and made bread, and I opened a small tin of jam, which we shared together. Abd er Rahman then made some coffee, and very well he did it; and after eating some dates I produced a cigarette-case and we sat and smoked over the fire. The result of this informal treatment on my part being that Abd er Rahman became more communicative.

His views were those of a typical *bedawi*. He disapproved highly of the way in which Qway had behaved. If we had been a caravan of *feilahin*, he said, it would not have been so bad, but for a guide to behave in that way to us who knew the *nijem* was, he considered, the last word in treachery. To "know the *nijem*" (stars) by which the Arabs steer at night means to have a knowledge of desert craft, an accomplishment that forms perhaps the strongest possible recommendation to the true *bedawin*.

He told me that when the *mamur* had had them all round to the *merkaz*, and it came to be Qway's turn to be questioned—the very man of whom I had complained—directly he heard his name, he told him he need give him no further details, as he knew all about him, and that he was to be trusted to do his duty; but he apparently omitted to specify what that duty was—the *mamur* was a nationalist.

When I asked if he felt afraid to go on with me after Qway, he laughed, saying that he was quite as clever as he was in the desert, having lived there nearly the whole of his life and had often travelled long distances alone. So long as he had enough water he did not care how far he went, provided I did not want to take him to the Bedayat. He even volunteered to go with me to within sight of their country, in order that I might be able to fix its position, provided he did not see any tracks of theirs before getting there. He was highly elated at having found Qway out, and very full of confidence in his own abilities.

He then began to tell me some of his experiences. Once he had been out in the desert with a single camel, when it had broken down a long way from water. He had tied the camel up, slung a *gurba* on his back, and, leaving his beast behind him, walked into the Nile Valley. He arrived with his *gurba* empty and half dead from thirst, but managed to crawl up to a watercourse, where he drank such an enormous amount that he immediately vomited it all up again. He managed to borrow another camel, with which he had taken water out to the one he had abandoned in the desert. The latter was almost dead on his arrival; but after drinking and resting for a day, had been able to get back to safety.

When Arabs are running short of water, but their camels are still able to travel, he said, they throw all their baggage down in the desert, where no one but the worst of *haramin* (robbers) would touch it, put all their water on to the camels and travel all through the night and cool part of the day, resting in the shade, if there be any, during the hot hours, and resuming their march as soon as it gets cool again in the evening. In this way, occasionally riding their beasts to rest, they can cover forty miles a day quite easily for several consecutive days.

I asked whether he had ever heard of a man, when in difficulties, cutting open his camel to drink the water from his stomach, according to the little tales of my childhood's days. This caused Abd er Rahman considerable amusement. He pointed out that if a caravan were in great straits from thirst, there would not be any water in the stomachs of the camels. But he said he had heard of several cases where a man, reduced to the last extremity, had killed his camel, cut him open and got at the half-digested food in his interior and had wrung the gastric juices out of it and drank them. This fluid, he said, was so indescribably nasty, as to be hardly drinkable, but, though it made a man feel still more thirsty, it enabled him to last about another day without water.

While sitting over the fire with Abd er Rahman I heard a faint sound from the west that sounded like a stone being kicked in the distance. Abd er Rahman, who was, I believe, slightly deaf, was unable to hear anything. I put my ear to the ground and listened for some time, and at last heard the sound again, but apparently from a greater distance than before.

Leaving Abd er Rahman in charge of the camels and taking my rifle, I went off to see if anything was to be seen. The moon was too faint and low at the time for any tracks to be visible. The whole desert was bathed in a faint and ghostly light that made it impossible to see any distance; so after watching for some time, and hearing no further sounds, I returned and lay down for the night about a hundred yards from Abd er Rahman and his camels.

It is curious how easily, in the absolute calm of a desert night, the slightest sound is audible, and how quickly one wakes at the faintest unusual noise. About midnight I started up. The distant sound of a trotting camel approaching the camp was clearly audible, and the camel was being ridden very fast. By that time the moon was high in the heavens, making the surrounding desert visible for a considerable distance, and presently I saw a solitary rider come round the shoulder of the ridge near which we were camped, sending his camel along at a furious pace.

Instantly I heard Abd er Rahman's sharp, threatening challenge and saw him slinging his carbine forward in readiness for an attack. The answer came back in a hoarse exhausted voice and was apparently satisfactory, for the camel man rode into the camp, his camel fell down on his knees, and the man got— or rather fell—off on to the ground.

I sang out to Abd er Rahman to ask who it was. He called back that it was Abdulla and, after bending for a few moments over his prostrate form, came running across to where I lay. Abdulla and his *hagin* were, he said, extremely exhausted; but he had told him that there was no danger and that we could do nothing before daylight and had begun a long statement about Qway having turned back, in the middle of which he had fallen asleep. I went over to the camp to look at him. His long attenuated form was stretched out along the ground, almost where he had dismounted, plunged in the deepest of slumbers; so, as I saw no object in disturbing him, and wanted him to be as fresh as possible on the morrow, I went back to my bed and followed his example, leaving Abd er Rahman to keep watch, till he woke me to take my turn at keeping guard later in the night.

Abdulla, on the following morning, looked hollow-eyed, and, if possible, thinner about the face than ever; but beyond having obviously had a severe fright, he seemed to be little worse for his ride; the Sudanese have wonderful recuperative powers. His *hagin*, however, was terribly tucked up, and he had evidently had to ride him extremely hard; but he was a fine beast, and otherwise did not seem to have suffered much from his exertions, for he was making a most hearty breakfast.

Abdulla's nerves, however, seemed to have been very badly shaken. He spoke in a wild incoherent way, very different from his usual slow, rather drawling, speech. He rambled so much in his account of what had happened, and introduced so many abusive epithets directed at Qway, that at times it was rather difficult to follow him, and Abd er Rahman had to help me out occasionally by explaining his meaning.

Qway, in the depot, had dawdled so over his preparations for leaving the camp that Abdulla, with his eye probably on the *bakhshish* I had promised him, had become impatient at the delay. At the last moment, just before he was ready to start, Qway calmly sat down, lighted a fire and began to make tea. Abdulla expostulated at this delay, but Qway assured him that there was no immediate hurry, told him that as soon as he had finished his tea and filled his *gurba*, he would start, and suggested that he had better go on before him and that he would follow and catch him up.

After he had gone some distance, Abdulla looked back and saw Qway hauling the tanks about, which struck him at the time as a rather unnecessary performance; but as Qway explained, when he overtook him, that he had only been rearranging the depot and placing the sacks of barley so as more effectually to shade the tanks, his suspicions had been lulled. Just before they separated, Qway had told him that he intended to get out as far as he could, so as to earn a very big *bakhshish*, and he hoped to go three and a half days more before he turned back. He advised Abdulla to do the same.

For most of the first day after leaving Qway, Abdulla kept turning things very slowly over in his "feeble head," and, towards the end of the second day, it began to occur to him that Qway's long delay in the depot was rather suspicious; so before proceeding any farther along his route, he thought it advisable to ride across and have a look at the old track he had made himself on his previous journey, to make sure that Qway was keeping to his share of the arrangement, by following it towards Jebel Abdulla.

On reaching his track he saw no sign of Qway having passed that way, so becoming seriously uneasy, he rode back along it hoping to meet him. At a distance of only about a day from Jebel el Bayed he found the place where Qway had turned back, which as he had told him he intended to go for another two and a half days farther, convinced him that something was very seriously wrong. He then apparently became panic-stricken and came tearing back along his tracks to make sure that we were coming out to meet him and that the depot had not been interfered with.

Qway, he said, had returned along his tracks for some distance, until he had got within sight of Jebel el Bayed, when he had turned off towards the western side of the hill, apparently with the object of avoiding the caravan, which according to the arrangement, he knew would be following Abdulla's track on its eastern side.

It struck me that as Qway's track lay to the west of our camp, the sounds I had heard during the preceding evening from that direction had probably been caused by him as he rode past us in the dark, so I sent Abd er Rahman off to see if he could find anything, while Abdulla and I packed up and loaded the camels.

Abd er Rahman returned in great glee to announce that I had been right in my conjecture, and that he had found Qway's track; so we started out to follow it. To the west of the camp was a ridge of ground that lay between our position and Qway's footprints, and this may perhaps have prevented my seeing him, and certainly would have made it impossible for him to see either us or our fire.

Qway had passed us at a considerable distance, for it took us twenty-one minutes to reach his trail, which shows the extraordinary way in which even the slightest sounds carry in the desert on a still night.

As we followed his track we discussed the position. It was clear that, as Qway, when he left the depot, only had five days' water in the two small tanks I had given him, he would be forced before long to renew his supply from our tanks, as he had already been three days away from the depot.

Abd er Rahman, instead of making our depot at Jebel el Bayed, as I had told him to do, on account of it being such a conspicuous landmark, had, fortunately as it turned out, made it about half a day to the north of the hill, in the middle of a very flat desert with no landmark of any kind in the neighbourhood. When the tanks and grain sacks composing the depot were all piled up they made a heap only about three feet high and, as the sacks, which had been laid on the top of the tanks to keep off the sun, were almost the colour of their sandy surroundings, our little store of water and grain was quite invisible, except at a very short distance to anyone not blessed with perfect sight, and Qway was rather deficient in this respect. He would consequently experience very great difficulty in finding that depot, unless he struck our tracks.

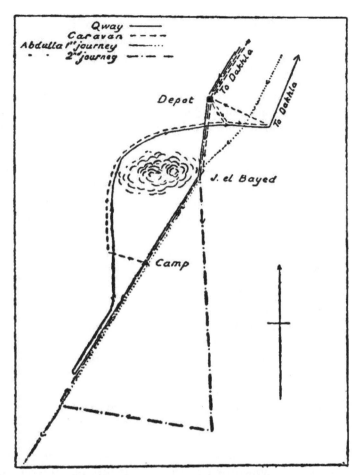

SKETCH PLAN OF TRACK ROUND JEBEL EL BAYED.

As we continued to follow his footprints, it became clear that this was what he was aiming at, for his route, that at first had been running nearly due north, gradually circled round Jebel el Bayed till it ran almost towards the east, evidently with the intention of cutting the tracks that we had made the day before. His trail went steadily on, circling round the great black hill behind us without a single halt to break the monotony of the journey.

We had been following his spoor for about three hours and a half when we reached the point where his trail met and crossed the one that we had made ourselves and, as Qway had not hesitated for a moment, it was clear that in the uncertain moonlight he had passed it unnoticed.

As we continued to follow his tracks, presently it became evident that he had been considerably perplexed. Several times he had halted to look round him from the top of some slight rise in the ground, and had then ridden on again in the same easterly direction and repeated the process.

Abd er Rahman, on seeing these tracks, was beside himself with delight. He slapped his thigh and burst out laughing, exclaiming that Qway was lost, and "Praise be to Allah" had only got five days' water supply. Abdulla, if anything, seemed even more pleased.

After a time Qway apparently concluded that he would wait till daylight before proceeding any farther, for we found the place where he had lain down to sleep. That he had started off again before dawn was clear from the fact that he had not prayed where he slept, but nearly an hour's journey farther on.

We followed him for a little farther, but as the afternoon was then far spent, I thought it best to return to the depot for the night, in case Qway should get there before us.

Frequently when out in the desert I had occasion to send Qway, or one of the men away from the caravan, to climb a hill to see if anything was to be seen from the summit, to scout ahead of the caravan, or for some other purpose, and as there was always a risk that the absentee might not get back to the caravan by dark I had a standing arrangement that if anyone got lost from this cause I would send up a rocket half an hour after sunset, and a second one a quarter of an hour later, to enable him to find the camp. These two rockets were accordingly fired from the depot and, moreover, as it was an absolutely windless night, a candle was lighted and left burning on the top of a pile of stones to attract his attention in the dark, if he were anywhere in the neighbourhood. I hoped by this means to induce him to come in and give himself up, in preference to risking a possible death by thirst—but he never materialised.

In the morning we set out again to follow his track. I could not exactly leave him to die of thirst, if he had really got lost, and I also wanted to know what he was doing. As the camels were getting into a very poor condition, owing to the hard work they had had and the short water allowance I had put them on, we left all the baggage in the depot, and took them along with us, carrying only sufficient water for our own use during the day.

We picked up Qway's trail where we had left it and, after following it for some distance, found where he had reached the old faint footprints left by Abdulla on his first journey, when he had ridden out alone to Jebel Abdulla. They had clearly puzzled him extremely. He dismounted and stood for some time examining the track and scanning the surrounding desert, as was clear from the number of footprints he had left at the place and the number of directions in which they pointed.

After a considerable amount of hesitation, he again set off in the same easterly direction he had been previously following, probably still hoping to find the tracks of the caravan that he had crossed in the moonlight without seeing.

I wanted Abdulla to get on his *hagin* and follow his tracks at a trot, hoping that in that level country, as Qway was only travelling at a walk, he would be able to overtake him sufficiently to sight him from a distance. But he had not recovered his nerve from the fright he had experienced and flatly refused to leave us, so we continued to follow the tracks together.

After riding for some distance farther, Qway had again climbed to the crest of a low ridge. Here he had stood for some time, his footprints pointing in all directions, endeavouring to pick up the bearings of the depot and the route that he had followed when he had left it.

But that bit of desert might have been especially made for the purpose of confusing an erring guide. As far as could be seen in all directions stretched a practically level expanse of sandy soil, showing no landmark to guide him, except where the great black bulk of Jebel el Bayed heaved itself up from the monotonous surface. We could tell from his tracks that he had reached that point not much before midday, when, at that time of the year, the sun was almost directly overhead, and consequently of little use to indicate the points of the compass. From where he had stood, Jebel el Bayed itself would have been of little use to guide him, for though the hill had two summits lying roughly east and west of each other, the western one was from that point hidden by the eastern, which was of such a rounded form that it looked almost exactly the same shape from all angles on its eastern side.

Qway at last had evidently given up the problem. He had remounted his camel, ridden round a circle a hundred yards or so in diameter in a final attempt to pick up his bearings, and then had made off at a sharp trot towards the north. Abd er Rahman was in ecstasies.

"Qway's lost. Qway's lost." He turned grinning delightedly to me. "I told you I was a better guide than Qway." Then he suddenly grew solemn. Much as he hated the overbearing Arab, he had worked with him for two seasons, and, as he had said, there is a bond of union between those who "know the *nijem*." "He will die. It is certain he will die. He only had five days' water, and it is four days since he left the depot. He is not going where the water is, but he is making for the 'Valley of the Rat.' It is certain he will die of thirst. His camel has had no water for four days."

Abdulla took a more hard-hearted view, and after the way in which Qway had treated him, he could hardly be blamed. "Let the cursed Arab die," said the Sudani. "The son of a dog is only a traitor."

We followed Qway's footprints for a short distance. But he had been travelling very fast, and it was obvious that we should never catch him up. He was off on a non-stop run to Mut, and as our own water supply was by no means too plentiful, I thought we had better follow his example; so I told Abdulla to take us back to the depot. It was then about noon.

Abdulla looked at Jebel el Bayed, glanced at the sun and looked round the horizon, scratched his cheek in perplexity, and said he did not know where the depot was, but he thought it must be *there*—he pointed somewhere towards the north-west. Abd er Rahman, however, was emphatic in saying that that was not the right direction, and indicated a point about west as being its position.

After some discussion, as they were unable to agree, Abd er Rahman turned to me and asked me to look at my compass to decide the direction in which we were to go. Unfortunately, I had left the compass in camp and had not been making a traverse of Qway's tracks, as I had done on the previous day. We had all been too keen on reading Qway's spoor to pay much attention to the changes in its direction, and so found ourselves in the same dilemma as Qway.

It was a furiously hot still day, and the sun shining almost perpendicularly down made the whole horizon dance with mirage, producing the impression that we were standing on a low sand bank in a vast sheet of water, whose distant shores flickered continuously in the heat haze—a veritable "devil's sea" as the natives call it.

I had only the vaguest idea as to where the depot lay, but as I had to decide in which direction to go, I told them I felt quite certain that it stood west north-west—about half-way between the two bearings pointed out by the men. It was a mere guess, based on the assumption that they were neither of them very far wrong, but that their errors lay on either side of the true direction. As luck would have it, I was much nearer right than either of the others, a fact that greatly increased their respect for my knowledge of the *nijem*!

After marching for a couple of hours or so, Abd er Rahman peered for a moment into the distance and announced that he saw the depot ahead of us. Neither Abdulla nor I could see anything. After some difficulty, however, I managed to identify the object to which Abd er Rahman was pointing, but all I could make out was an indistinct and shapeless blur, dancing and continually changing its shape in the mirage. Abd er Rahman, however, was most positive that it was the goal for which we were making, and, as I knew his extraordinary powers for identifying objects in similar circumstances, we made towards it and found that he had been correct.

We rested in the depot until sunset. Just before starting, it struck us that possibly we might pass Ibrahim and Dahab on the road. The arrangement I had made with them was that, if they failed to see us before reaching the depot, they were to leave as much water there as they could and return at once to Mut. But I wanted to arrange some means by which they should know where we had gone in the event of their reaching the depot. A letter was the obvious method, but Dahab was the only man in the caravan who could read or write, and I was doubtful whether he would come out again, as I had told him not to do so if he got at all knocked up on the journey back to Mut. Ibrahim, of course, was wholly illiterate, like the other two Sudanese, so it was difficult to see how I could communicate with him, if he came out alone. Abd er Rahman, however, was quite equal to the emergency. He told me that he would write Ibrahim a "letter" that he would understand, and, taking a stick scratched his *wasm* (tribe mark) deeply into the soil, and then drew a line from it in the direction of Dakhla, the "letter" when finished being as follows: ☙, the mark ♦ being his *wasm*. This letter, Abd er Rahman said, meant, "I, belonging to the tribe who use this *wasm*, have gone in the direction of the line I have drawn from it." This important communication having been completed, we set out on our return journey.

CHAPTER XIX

WE travelled after the manner described by Abd er Rahman as that of the Arabs when in difficulties in the desert. We rested, that is, in the middle of the day, marching throughout the morning and through most of the night.

At our last noon halt before reaching the bushes I overhauled the caravan. With the exception of the one big camel the whole of the beasts by this time were in a deplorable condition. My *hagin* was so weak that he was unable even to carry my *hurj*. Another brute that Abd er Rahman called the "rather *meskin*" (feeble) camel, was very emaciated; while one that he called *the meskin* beast, par excellence, was so excessively attenuated, that, in the photograph I took of him, only the desert appeared!

It was the big camel that pulled us through. The loads of the *meskin* and the "rather *meskin*" camels were both put on to his back, in addition to his ordinary burden, and my *hurj* was added to the pile. Moreover, whenever any of us wanted a lift we rode him—and he seemed to like it!

Ibrahim was two days overdue, and, as nothing had been seen of him, I was beginning to feel rather anxious and to fear he had passed us in the dark without our seeing him. During one noon halt, however, Abdulla, who was still rather jumpy, raised the alarm of *haramin* (robbers). We immediately collected our ironmongery and turned out to receive them. But to our great relief we found it was only Ibrahim approaching with three camels and another man.

Dahab and one of my camels, we found, had knocked up on the journey to Mut and had had to be left behind. It had taken Ibrahim two days to get more beasts and someone to fill Dahab's place. The new-comer was an elderly Sudani, who had been at Qasr Dakhl with two camels on Ibrahim's arrival at Mut. He went by the name of Abeh Abdulla.

I was considerably prejudiced in his favour by hearing him invoke the aid of a certain "Sidi Mahmed," or Mahmed ben Abd er Rahman Bu Zian, to give him his full name, the founder of the Ziania dervishes, a branch of the great Shadhlia order, that plays the rôle of protector of travellers. It is, I believe, better known in north-west Africa than on the Egyptian side. In the Western Sahara "Sidi Bu Zian," as he is sometimes called, may almost be termed the patron saint of wayfarers in the desert.

Abdulla, when he got into difficulties, used to invoke a certain "Sidi Abd el Jaud," whose identity I was never able to discover.

Ibrahim had done his job splendidly. During the two days in Mut, he had had the leaking tanks repaired and had borrowed some others from the native officials. He had brought them all out filled to the brim. We watered all the camels, and, when we had given them time to absorb their drink, made a fresh start for the bushes.

When we reached Mut it was evening, and I walked to my lodgings through the quaint old town, stumbling over the uneven surface of the tunnelled street, whose darkness in the gathering dusk was only broken here and there by a gleam of firelight, through some half-opened door. The familiar smell of wood fires, whose smoke hung heavily in the streets, the scraping drone of the small hand-mills that the women were using to grind their flour, and the monotonous thudding as they pounded their rice inside their houses, had a wonderful effect in making me feel at home.

Soon after my arrival the usual boring deputation of the Government officials turned up to felicitate me in conventional terms on my safe return. After thanking them for the loan of the tanks, I asked the *mamur* whether anything had been heard of Qway. He professed to a total ignorance on the subject and wanted to have full details of what he had been doing. I gave him an account of Qway's conduct as shown by his tracks and the empty tanks and asked, as he had nearly done for Abdulla, that he should be immediately arrested.

The *mamur* hesitated for a moment, then burst out with a passionate "Never! Qway is a *gada*" (sportsman). I pointed out the *gada* had, at any rate, walked off with a rifle and telescope of mine, and that I felt certain he had come into the oasis and was hiding. The *mamur* did not think he was hiding, but that he would turn up as soon as he heard I had got back—and anyway he declined to send out men to look for him or to have him arrested. I insisted that it was his duty both to find and arrest him, and, after a considerable amount of pressing, he at length gave way to the extent of promising, if Qway did not turn up, to send *a* man to look for him "the day after to-morrow."

This must have constituted a record in energy for an oasis official, and seemed to exhaust his powers altogether. He refused to send a message round to the *'omdas* to have him detained if he appeared, and shortly after said something about supper and departed.

I was left to reflections that were not over-pleasant. There was no doubt that I had made a great mistake in asking to have Qway arrested, for, even if I could get him tried for the offence, I should have to find some motive for his actions, and I could not see how that could be done without raising the Senussi question in an oasis where, though their numbers were few, they possessed enormous influence. I decided it would be best to confine my accusation against him to that of stealing the rifle and telescope.

The possibility of my being able to secure him seemed extremely remote. The attitude towards me of the natives of the oasis left no doubt in my mind that they would all shield him. The Government officials were obviously of the same frame of mind, and though they might make some show of attempting to arrest him, I felt certain that they would be surreptitiously endeavouring to aid him in his escape. In the background I knew would be the Senussi, using all the great influence they possessed in the oasis, in order to shield their puppet, Qway, and to prevent his capture.

With only three Sudanese and an old Berberine cook at my back, it was difficult to see what I could do. Still, as I had foolishly insisted on his being brought to justice, I had to see it done. The task was not altogether hopeless, for in cases of this description one Sudani is worth a thousand *fellahin*. But for the time being the only thing to be done in the circumstances was to lie low and await developments.

They soon came. As is often the case when dealing with natives they were rather of the comic opera type. I first located Qway as staying in the Senussi *zawia* in Smint. But the clerk to the *qadi* in Mut, Sheykh Senussi, whom Qway had told me was "like a brother to him," finding that I was hot on his trail, and fearing that the Senussia might become involved, moved him on to Rashida, and then, like the mean sneak that he was, came round, and, to curry favour with me, told me where he was.

I went off at once and saw the *mamur*, told him I had heard that Qway was in Rashida, reminded him that this was "the day after to-morrow," on which he had promised to send "*a* man" to look for him, and called on him to carry out his promise.

The *mamur* endeavoured to avoid doing so; but after some trouble, I at length managed to get him to send a man at once.

I was in the *merkaz* the next day when he returned. He rode pattering up on a donkey, dismounted, shuffled into the room, saluted clumsily and made his report. According to instructions he had gone to Rashida and seen Qway, and given him the *mamur's* message that he was to come into Mut. But Qway had said that he did not want to come. The man had argued with him, and had done his best to persuade him to come; but Qway had stuck to it that he really did not want to, so he had climbed again on to his donkey and ridden back to Mut to report progress.

The *mamur* was greatly relieved. He had done everything I had asked him to do. He had sent a man on a Government donkey to fetch Qway; but Qway did not want to come. What more could he do? It was of no use asking Qway to come if he did not wish to. He was very sorry, but he had done the most he could.

I suggested that perhaps he might send a policeman—a real policeman in uniform with a rifle, not a *ghaffir*—and give him instructions that, if Qway again refused to come, he was to BRING him. But the *mamur* did not see his way to doing this. Why should he arrest Qway? What had he done? Stolen a rifle had he? Had he any cartridges? He still had twenty cartridges and a rifle had he? No, he could not possibly arrest him. Qway might be old, but the Arabs were very wild fellows, and he had no troops—only a few armed police.

A long discussion followed, and at last a solution of the difficulty occurred to the *mamur*. He said he could not arrest Qway, but he would send a policeman to bring back the rifle and cartridges. Did that satisfy me? It didn't. I said I must have Qway as well. After a long discussion he at last agreed to send to fetch him, if I would send a message by the policeman to tell Qway that he was not to shoot him!

The next day the *mamur* came round to see me, looking immensely relieved. He said that the policeman had gone to Rashida to fetch Qway, but found that he had left the village, so now there was nothing more to be done. He evidently felt that he was now clear of all responsibility in the matter.

I had thus lost track of Qway, and began to despair of ever being able to get hold of him. But the next day Abd er Rahman, who all along had been indefatigable in trying to pick up information of his whereabouts, told me that Qway had been seen near Tenida dressed up as a *fellah*[4]—a fact that caused the little Sudani the keenest amusement.

So I sent Abdulla to go off on his *hagin* to Tenida, under pretence of buying barley, and to try and find Qway, and, if he succeeded, to tell him from me to come at once to Mut.

The next day I went down to the *merkaz* to enquire whether there was any news. I saw the police officer, who told me that he had just had certain news that Qway had left the oasis and taken the road to the Nile Valley. So, as he was now out of his jurisdiction—which seemed to greatly relieve him—he was in a position to draw up the *proces verbal* about the telescope and gun that he had stolen, a piece of information that was distinctly depressing. I began to wonder what was the best thing to do next.

This problem, however, solved itself. I had just finished lunch when a timid knock came at the door, and in walked Qway!

The old brute had evidently had a terrible time of it. He had allowed himself to become the tool of the Senussi, but his plans having miscarried, he had got lost and nearly died of thirst in the desert, for, as I afterwards discovered, he had been nearly two days without any water—and two very hot days they had been—and it had only been the excellence of his camel that had pulled him through.

He looked ten years older. His eyes were bleary and bloodshot, his cheeks sunken, his lips parched and cracked, his beard untrimmed, and he had an unkempt, almost dirty, appearance.

He laid the rifle and telescope on my bed, fumbled in his voluminous clothing and produced a handful of cartridges, took some more out of his pocket, from which he also produced a rosary—the Senussi mostly carry their beads in this way and not round their neck as in the case of most Moslems. He then unknotted a corner of his handkerchief and took out two or three more cartridges and laid them all on the table.

"Count them, Your Excellency," he said. "They are all there." I found that the tale of them was complete.

He looked sadly down to the ground and sighed profoundly. "I have been working very badly," he said, "very badly indeed. I am a broken thing. I am the flesh and you are the knife." It certainly looked remarkably like it.

I asked him what excuse he had to make for his conduct. He looked at me for a moment to see what line he had better take, and the one that he took was not particularly complimentary to my intelligence.

"It was very hot, Your Excellency—very hot indeed. And I was alone and an *afrit* climbed up on to my camel."

At this point I thought it might be advisable to have a witness, so I sang out for Dahab.

"No, Effendim, not Dahab. Don't call Dahab," said Qway in a much perturbed voice. Presumably he thought Dahab would be less likely to be convinced by his story than I would. Dahab entered the room with surprising promptness—the doors in the oasis are not sound-proof.

I told Qway to get on with his story of the *afrit*, which promised to be a good one.

"There was an *afrit*, Your Excellency, that got up behind me on my camel and kept on telling me to go there and to do this, and I had to do it. It was not my fault the water was upset. It was the *afrit*. I had to do what he told me." Then, hearing a snort from Dahab, he added that there was not only one *afrit*, but many, and that that part of the desert was full of them.

I thought it time to stop him. I told him I had heard quite enough, and that he had to come round with me to the *merkaz*. This upset him terribly.

"No, not the *merkaz*, Your Excellency. Not the *merkaz*. In the name of Allah do not take me to the *merkaz*. Take everything I have got, but do not take me to the *merkaz*."

But to the *merkaz* he had to go. We called in at the camel yard to pick up the other men, as they might be wanted as witnesses, and then proceeded in a body to the Government office, Qway all the way attempting to bribe me to let him off by offering me his belongings, among which, with an obvious pang, he expressly offered me his camel.

We met the *mamur* at the door of the *merkaz*, and Qway immediately rushed forward to try and kiss his hand. The *mamur*, however, would have nothing to do with him. Like nearly all the *fellahin* he backed the winner, and I for the moment had come out on top.

"This man is a traitor, a regular traitor," said the judge, who had not yet tried him and who had previously told me he was a sportsman; but I had got the best of the deal, and, moreover, was shortly returning to Egypt and might report on him to one of the inspectors; so he determined to show me how an Egyptian official can do justice when he takes off his coat for the job. He bustled in to the office and began arranging the papers fussily on his table. The police officer also came in and prepared to take down the depositions.

Having got things to his satisfaction, the *mamur* ordered the prisoner to be brought in. He arrived between two wooden-looking policemen.

"Well, traitor, what have you got to say for yourself?" Then, as it occurred to him that he had overlooked one of the formalities, he asked Qway his name.

"Qway, Effendim."

"Qway what?" asked the *mamur* irritably.

"Qway Hassan Qway, Your Presence. My grandfather was a Bey."

"A Bey?" snorted the *mamur*.

"Yes, Your Excellency."

"Where did he live?"

"Near Assiut, Your Excellency. Perhaps he wasn't a Bey. I don't know. Perhaps he was a *mamur* or a police officer. I don't quite know what he was, but he worked for the Government."

"Bey!" repeated the *mamur* contemptuously. "Mr. Harden Keen says you upset some water. What do you say to it?"

"Yes, I upset the water. But I could not help it. It was a very hot day . . ."

"Liar!" said the *mamur*.

"*Na'am?*" said Qway, rather taken aback.

"I said liar," shouted the *mamur*, thumping the table. Qway, who was a high-spirited old fellow, found this more than he could stand, and began to get nettled. It was entirely characteristic of our position in Egypt at that time that at this juncture, Qway, the accused, should turn to me, the accuser, for protection from the judge.

"It *was* a hot day, Effendim, wasn't it?"

Badly as he had behaved, I was getting to be very sorry for him, and I had taken a strong dislike to that *mamur*. So I replied that it was one of the hottest days that I ever remembered.

The *mamur* could not contradict me, but looked distinctly uncomfortable and shifted uneasily in his chair. He told Qway to go on. Qway, who was beginning to recover his composure, proceeded to make the most of the victory he had gained over him.

"As I said, Effendim, it was a hot day—*very* hot, and I am an old man and perhaps it was the sun. I don't know what it was, but an *afrit*—"

"Allah!" said the *mamur*, spreading out his hands, "an *afrit*?" Qway began to get a bit flurried.

"Yes, Effendim, an *afrit*."

"Liar," repeated the *mamur*. "I *said* you were a liar."

Qway looked round again for help, but I was not going to bolster up that statement. The *mamur* began to examine him as to the exact nature of that *afrit*. Qway broke down, stammered and generally got into a terrible mess. At the last the *mamur*, having elicited from him in turn the fact that there was one *afrit*, that there were two, that there had been a crowd of them, and finally that there were none at all, went on to the next stage and asked what had happened afterwards.

Qway explained that after leaving the depot he had ridden for two days to the south-west, and then had turned back and circled round Jebel el Bayed and finally ridden off to the east.

"The east?" said the *mamur*. "I thought Dakhla lay to the north."

"The north-east, Effendim," corrected Qway. "Rather north of north-east."

"Then why did you go to the east? Were you lost?"

Qway stammered worse than ever. The *mamur* repeated his question. Two tears began to roll down Qway's cheeks and his great gnarled hand went up to hide his twitching lips.

"Yes," he said, with a great effort. "I was lost." Being an Arab he did not lie—at least not often.

"But you are a guide. And you got lost!"

"Yes," stammered Qway. To have to own to a mere *fellah* that he, the great desert guide, had lost his way, must have been most intensely humiliating; for the favourite gibe of the *bedawin* to the *fellahin* is that they are "like women," and get lost directly they go in the desert.

No Egyptian could have resisted such a chance. The *mamur* began to question Qway minutely as to where, how and when he had got lost, and to the exact degree of lostness at each stage of the proceedings; and Qway, to his credit be it said, answered quite truthfully.

When he could rub it in no further, the *mamur* began to question him as to the remainder of his journey. Qway described how he had had to go two days without water and had almost ridden his camel to death in order to get back to our tracks, and how he and his camel had eventually managed to get back to Dakhla more dead than alive.

"You were hiding when you got back. Where did you hide?"

Qway hesitated a moment, then asked him in a low voice if he need answer. The *mamur* did not press that question. It was a distinctly ill-advised one. Qway had been in the Senussi *zawia* at Smint. He put a few more questions to him, then told him again that he was a traitor and that his work had been "like pitch," and asked me what I wanted done next. I suggested that he might perhaps call a few witnesses, so Abdulla was brought in.

Abdulla had entirely recovered from the scare he had had in the desert, and, though Qway had tried to let him down, the *mamur's* treatment of him seemed to have softened his views towards him. There *is* a bond of union between those who "know the *nijem*" and Qway, too, was in difficulties, and Mohammedans are usually sympathetic towards each other in those circumstances, so Abdulla tried to get Qway off.

The *mamur* asked him what he knew about the case.

"Effendim," he said, "I think Qway went mad."

The *mamur* flung himself back in his chair and spread out his hands.

"Allah!" he exclaimed. "Are you a doctor?"

This little pantomime was completely thrown away on the stolid Abdulla. He looked at the *mamur* with the amused curiosity that he would have shown to a performing monkey.

"No," he said, in his slow stupid way. "I am not a doctor, of course—but I know a fool when I see one!"

The *mamur* concluded that he had heard enough of Abdulla's evidence. I began to wonder if the Sudani was quite so "feeble in the head" as he had been represented!

"I find that Qway is a traitor. His work has been like pitch. What do you want me to do with him?" asked the judge.

I suggested, as delicately as I could, that that was a question to be decided by the court, and not by the accuser. After a whispered conversation with the police officer across the table, the *mamur* announced that he intended to put him in prison and send him, when the camel-postman went, in about a week's time, to Assiut to be tried.

The attitude of the men towards Qway changed completely after his trial. There was no longer any need to be afraid of him. Their resentment at his conduct in the desert had had time to cool down. He had been bullied by a *fellah mamur*, been forced to confess in public that he had disgraced himself by getting lost in the desert, had been arrested by a Sudani and publicly paraded through the oasis dressed as a *fellah*. His humiliation was complete and could scarcely have been more thorough. The *bedawin* instinct for revenge had been amply satisfied. Hatred is generally largely composed of fear, or jealousy, and there was certainly no room for either where Qway was concerned. Moreover, the men had the usual feeling of compassion for those in adversity that forms one of the finest traits in the Mohammedan character.

So far as I was concerned, I was feeling rather sorry for my erring guide, to whom I had taken a strong liking from the start, for he had only been made a tool by the Senussi, who were the real culprits. So having once got him convicted, I told the *mamur* I did not want him to be severely punished, provided that "the quality of mercy was not strained."

Dahab told me Qway was confined in irons and being fed only on bread and water. So I sent him some tea and sugar, with a message to the police that they might take the irons off and that I would "see them" before I left the oasis. Dahab asked for money to buy a quite unnecessary number of eggs for my consumption. I never enquired what became of them all; but the same evening he asked for leave to go to the doctor's house, and started off with bulging pockets in the direction of the *merkaz*. He came back again with them empty shortly afterwards, saying that he had been told that Qway was resigned and very prayerful. The Sudanese, as I afterwards heard, sent him some cheese and lentils, to which Abdulla added a handful of onions, so altogether Qway must have rather enjoyed himself in prison.

CHAPTER XX

HAVING disposed of the question of Qway, I went off to Rashida for the fête of Shem en Nessim (the smelling of the breeze). The officials of the oasis were also there, and we celebrated the day in the usual manner. In the morning we put on clean clothes and took our breakfast out of doors to "smell the breeze." Then we went up among the palm plantations to a primitive swimming bath the *'omda* had made by damming up a stream from one of his wells. The natives stripped and disported themselves in the water, swimming about, splashing each other and enjoying themselves immensely.

After the bath they dressed again and we lay about under the palms till lunch was brought out to us. We lounged about on the ground, sleeping and talking till late in the afternoon, when a woman from the village appeared, who had been engaged by the *'omda* to dance. A carpet was spread for her to perform on, and we lay round and watched her. She looked quite a respectable woman, and it was certainly a quite respectable dance that would have been an addition to "Chu-Chin-Chow," but the *mamur* took occasion to be shocked at it. He sat with his back half turned to the woman, watching her out of the corner of his eye, however, and apparently enjoying the performance. Though I was unable to detect anything in the slightest degree wrong in the dance, the delicate susceptibilities of the *mamur* were so outraged that—as he was not on good terms with the *'omda* of Rashida—he felt it his duty to report him to the Inspector in Assiut for having an immoral performance in his private grounds. Government under the Egyptian *mamurs* is a wonderful institution!

The next day I returned to Mut to pack up. A number of callers came round to see me during the short remaining time I stayed in the town. For since I had come out on top, the whole oasis had become wonderfully friendly.

Among them was the Sheykh el Afrit from Smint. He was extremely oily in his manner and kept on addressing me as "Your Presence the Bey!" He gave me a lot of information about *afrits*. He spoke in the tone of a man who had had a lifelong experience in the matter. It was most important, he said, to use the right kind of incense when invoking them, as if the wrong sort were used the *afrit* always became very angry and killed the magician—it seemed to be a dangerous trade.

He told me a lot of information of the same nature and gave me a number of instances of encounters with *afrits* to illustrate his remarks. Among them he mentioned—quite casually—that it had been an *afrit* that had led Qway astray. The object of his visit had apparently been to put this opinion, as an experienced magician, before me, for he left almost immediately afterwards.

Among my other visitors was the *'omda* of Rashida, who said he had come into Mut as he had a case to bring before the *mamur* against his cousin Haggi Smain. He, too, stood up for Qway. He was the only native of the oasis who had the backbone to openly champion his cause.

Some time after he had gone, I had to go round to the *merkaz*. I could hear a tremendous row going on inside as I approached. Someone kept thumping a table and two or three men were shouting and bawling at each other and, judging from the sounds that proceeded from the court, all Bedlam might have been let loose there.

But I found that it was only the *mamur* "making the peace" among the Rashida people. The *'omda* of Rashida and two of his brothers were bringing an action against their cousin, Haggi Smain, who owned part of the same village. The row stopped for a while as I came in, and the proceedings were conducted for a few minutes in an orderly manner. Then they went at it again, hammer and tongs, bawling and shouting at each other, and at the *mamur*, who was endeavouring to effect a reconciliation, at the top of their voices. The *mamur* at first spoke in a quiet persuasive tone, but soon he lost his temper and was as bad as they were. He banged with his fist on the table and yelled to them to be silent and listen to what he had to say. The *'omda* shouted back that it was not he, but Haggi Smain that was interrupting the proceedings, while Haggi Smain himself foaming at the mouth and at times almost inarticulate with rage, screamed back that it was the *'omda* who was making all the noise.

The cause of all this hullabaloo was as follows: Haggi Smain had an orange tree growing on his property, one branch of which projected beyond his boundary and overhung some land belonging to the *'omda*. Three oranges had fallen off this branch on to the *'omda's* territory and the case had been brought to decide to whom these three oranges belonged. Their total value was a farthing at the outside.

I left next day for Egypt. As I got on my camel to start, the *mamur* and Co. announced that they intended to walk with me for part of the way. As this was calculated to increase my prestige with the other natives, I decided to keep them with me for some time.

I rode—and the *mamur* walked—which was quite as it should have been, for these little distinctions carry great weight among these simple natives. The *mamur*, I was glad to see, was wearing a pair of new brown boots fastened with a metal clasp over the instep, and having soles about as thin as dancing pumps. The road was rough and baked very hard by the sun in those places where it was not boggy. The *mamur*, I fancy, was not used to much pedestrian exercise and soon became very obviously footsore.

I saw him look longingly at an unloaded camel, so told Dahab to get up on it and ride. Several times he hinted that he had come far enough, but I merely had to look surprised and displeased to keep him trotting along beside me for another mile. He had not shown up well while I had been in the oasis, and he realised that in a very few days I should be seeing one of the Inspectors about Qway, so was desperately anxious not to do anything to displease me.

At last I decided to take a short cut. We left the road, such as it was, and went straight across country over a very rough stretch of desert. I called out to Abdulla to hurry up the camels, as they were going too slowly, with the result that the limping *mamur* and the fat old *qadi* began to fall behind. The farce was becoming so obvious that all my men were grinning at them and Abd er Rahman sarcastically whispered to me that he thought the *mamur* must be getting tired.

When I had got them well away from the road, and two or three miles from any habitation, I looked back and suddenly discovered the *mamur* was limping, and asked him why on earth he had not told me before that his feet were all covered with blisters. I insisted that he should go back at once to Mut.

On the way to Assiut, in the train, I saw old Sheykh Mawhub, the Senussi, going, as he said, to Cairo. But I was not in the least surprised to find that he broke his journey at Assiut, where he lay doggo in the native town, pulling strings in the *mudiria* to get his catspaw, Qway, out of his difficulties—unfortunately with considerable success.

I went round to the *mudiria* as soon as I got to the town, only to find that the English Inspector was away, so I asked to see the *mudir* (native governor of the province). The *mudir* did not think Qway had been tried, but would I go up into the town and ask at the *mamur's* office? There I was requested to wait while they made enquiries. They made them for about three-quarters of an hour, and then a man came in with an ill-concealed grin and announced that Qway had just that moment been tried and had been acquitted!

I went round to interview the *mudir* again—rather indignantly this time. He was bland and courteous—but firm. He had been acquitted, he said because I had said that I did not want him to be severely punished, and because I had given him a good character the year before. The course of true law never did run smooth in Egypt!

I tried to get this decision reversed by applying to a very exalted personage. He told me, however, that the Government did not want to raise the Senussi question and were anxious to avoid an incident on the frontier, and he was afraid that he could not take the matter up.

I had to get the best of Qway somehow and, as the regulation methods of dealing with him had failed me, I took the law into my own hands—which is quite the best place to keep it in Egypt—and fined him the balance of his pay, which amounted to about twenty pounds. I afterwards heard that the Senussi, in order to prevent Qway from having a grievance against them, had bakhshished him £42 worth of cotton; so I got at the real culprits in the end; but it was a roundabout way of doing it.

Thanks to Qway and the Senussi, the results of my second year did not come up to my expectations, for the main work I had planned for the season was, of course, the fifteen days' journey to the south-west of Dakhla, which I hoped would take me to Owanat. Instead of this we had not been able to get farther than the centre of the desert, so far as we could estimate where the middle lay.

CHAPTER XXI

DURING my first two seasons I had managed to get out to the middle of the desert and had succeeded in mapping a large area of it; but the main object to which these two years had been devoted—the crossing of the desert from north-east to south-west had not been attained—there seemed no prospect of my being able to accomplish it, for Owanat, the first stage on the journey, was evidently so far out that it could only be reached by adopting some elaborate system of depots or relays, that Qway's escapade had shown to be too dangerous. The Senussi had certainly won the first trick in the game; but I did not feel at all inclined to let them have things all their own way.

It was, however, pointed out to me that the omens to any further journeys were by no means propitious just then, as the natives were much excited over the Italian invasion of Tripoli, and, moreover, the Senussi were clearly prepared to take an active hand in the game and, even at that time, were evidently contemplating an invasion of Egypt, should a suitable opportunity occur.

The latter fact, however, seemed to me to cut both ways, for the Senussi were quite wide-awake enough to realise that, if an European got scuppered by them, some form of punitive expedition was extremely likely to follow, which might force them into hostilities at an inconvenient time—so I concluded that they would just as unwillingly start scrapping as I would myself—and that was saying a good deal.

As crossing the desert seemed an impracticable scheme just then, I abandoned that part of my programme, and as there were plenty of other large areas waiting to be explored, decided to try a different district, and set out to explore as much as possible of the unknown parts of the eastern and western sides of the huge depression in which lies the oasis of Farafra.

I intended, too, to visit the little oasis of Iddaila, that lies not far to the west of Farafra, and I hoped to score a trick off the Senussia by making a dash into the dunes to the south-west of Farafra and locating the oasis of Dendura, that was used sometimes by them as a half-way house when travelling from Egypt to Kufara.

Unfortunately—though I did not learn this till afterwards—before my start some rag of a native paper in Cairo announced that I had come out again to Egypt and intended to go in disguise to Kufara, and a copy of the paper had been sent out to that oasis itself. This was a piece of pure invention on the part of that journal that led to rather unpleasant consequences.

I was advised to take as my guide some man who was admittedly a member of the Senussia and camel drivers of the same persuasion. The advice did not commend itself very strongly to me; but in deference to the views of those whom I expected to know a good deal more of the country than I did, I so far accepted it as to decide on taking a Senussi guide and one or two of his camel men, while adding Abd er Rahman, Ibrahim and Dahab as well to the caravan—Abdulla unfortunately was not available.

I eventually engaged a man called Qwaytin, who was stated to be reliable. Haggi Qwaytin Mohammed Said—to give him his full name—though a native of Surk in Kufara Oasis, at that time was living in the Nile Valley, in the Manfalut district, near Assiut. For some time he had acted as a tax-collector among the Bedayat for 'Ali Dinar, the Sultan of Darfur, and when he was inclined to be communicative could impart a considerable amount of information about unknown parts of the desert. He seemed to have led a fairly wandering existence and to be at home in most parts of North and Central Africa; at any rate he had a Bedayat wife in Darfur, a Tawarek one somewhere near Timbuktu and one—if not two—others near Manfalut.

He was a queer fellow, and I did not altogether take a fancy to him. When I told him that I already had two camel drivers and did not want more, he was very much put out and declared that he could not trust his camels to strangers. Eventually we compromised the question by arranging that he should take three men and that I, in addition, should bring Abd er Rahman, Ibrahim and Dahab.

I asked to see the men he was going to bring with him. The three he produced—Mohanny, Mansur and 'Abd el Atif—were even less prepossessing than Qwaytin himself. They were typical specimens of the low-class *bedawin* camel drivers that the camel owners engage on nominal wages, to take charge of their beasts when they hire them out. They proved to be most indifferent drivers. But Qwaytin and his men were such an obviously feeble lot that, with my three men to back me up, I had no doubt of being able to deal with them, if they gave any trouble.

I intended to pump Qwaytin as dry as I could of the information he could give me of the unknown parts of the desert and, with the assistance of my own men, to compel him, by force if necessary, to take me within sight of Dendura, after we had left Farafra.

These preliminaries having been gone through, I sent for Abd er Rahman and Ibrahim to come up and join me in Assiut—Dahab was already with me. While waiting in the little Greek pub, where I stayed for the arrival of my men, I made the acquaintance of an educated Egyptian, who was engaged in some sort of literary work, the exact nature of which I was unable to discover. His English was excellent, and he was evidently anxious to practise it, for he stuck to me like a leech.

He was never tired of dilating on the beauties of Arabic as a literary language. In Arabic literature, he said, the great thing was to use as many metaphors as possible, and the best metaphors were those that were the most obscure or, as he expressed it, that made the reader "work his brain" the most. Certainly some of the examples he gave left nothing whatever to be desired in that direction.

He insisted in coming to see me off at the station, where he explained that he had lain awake for a considerable part of the night, in order to be able to think of a really good metaphor for me at parting.

It certainly was a poser. If, he said, he described a man as having a very cowardly dog, what should I think he meant? I suggested various possible solutions: that he was a brutal man who thrashed his dog unmercifully; that he was a very poor man who could not afford to buy a good one; or a very mean man who nearly starved the beast to death. As none of them was correct, I asked him to explain. But he preferred to keep me on tenterhooks and declined to do so, chuckling with delight at the way in which he was making me "work my brain."

SHEYKH SENUSSI.—Clerk to the Qadi in Mut and the village poet. (p. 44).

HAGGI QWAYTIN.—My guide during my last year in the desert. (p. 199)

SHEYKH IBN ED DRIS.—One of the Senussi Sheykhs in the *Zawia* in Farafra. (p. 228).

Left, HAGGI QWAYTIN. Right, HAGGI QWAY.—Qway was my guide during my first two years in the desert. (p. 26).

It was not until the train began to move, that he condescended to solve the problem. When he said that a man had a cowardly dog, he meant that he was so very hospitable that his dog got tired of barking at the innumerable guests who came to his house! As a literary language Arabic must be very hard to beat.

Near Nazali Genub, where I camped while buying my camels, I found an acquaintance whose job consisted in surveying and drawing the hieroglyphics on the tombs, where, to relapse into metaphor, in mere English:

"The long phantasmal line

Of Pharaohs crowned divine

Are dust among the dust that once obeyed them."

I shared a very comfortable tomb with him during the time I spent there.

After about a week, during which Qwaytin with Abd er Rahman visited the surrounding villages and markets in search of the camels that he required to complete the caravan, we moved over to Qwaytin's house, some seven miles away, and on the following morning, 24th March, started off for our journey into the desert; Ibrahim at the start, as usual, banging off his gun after the Arab custom to scare away evil spirits during our journey.

I decided first to make for an uninhabited oasis called Bu Gerara, which had not previously been reported, that Qwaytin said he knew of, and that lay some little distance off the Derb et Tawil, and not very far to the north-east of Dakhla. This oasis he said contained palms, wells and some old buildings, but had been deserted for many years.

The Derb ed Deri—the monastery road—that we followed starts from near an old *der*, or monastery, called the Der Muharug, from which it takes its name, and is a branch of the great Derb et Tawil—"the long road"—that, starting from the Nile Valley near Manfalut, runs right across the desert plateau to Dakhla Oasis.

On getting up on to the plateau, Qwaytin pointed out in the distance to the west a low hill, which he said was called the Jebel Jebaïl, where, he stated, there are many tombs.

The plateau was level and as featureless as that between the Nile Valley and Kharga Oasis, to which it bore a strong general resemblance. There were the same patches of sand and pebbles, interspaced with areas of limestone, showing all the same types of sand erosion—*kharashef, kharafish, battikh* and *rusuf*.

In many places the limestone appeared as marble, sometimes polished by the action of the sand blast. White, black, grey, yellow and beautiful rose pink, in various combinations, were seen in the stone. Much of it showed large cracks on the surface, but there were considerable areas of stone, especially of the grey marble with darker grey lines, that seemed to be quite solid. The rock in places was translucent and appeared to be alabaster, but of very inferior quality. Some of the pink marble looked to be of a fine colour and texture; but it is doubtful, in such an inaccessible position, if it would ever repay working.

Early on our second day in the desert we joined the main road—the Derb et Tawil, or "long road." Close to the east of the point, where the two roads met, was one of the low rocky hills with which the plateau was studded. From the foot of this ran a little used road leading to 'Ain Amur, via 'Ain Embares, an undiscovered well that I had tried to reach by way of the small depressions leading out of the 'Ain Amur wady. It was reported to be almost sanded up and to give very little water.

On the following day we passed the point where a road branches off to the west from the Derb et Tawil to go direct to Qasr Dakhl. This road, which does not appear to be much used, is known as the "Derb el Khashabi," or "wooded road," owing to the fact that about two days' journey from the point where it leaves the Derb et Tawil, there is a patch of dead trees about ten feet high. It is said to be an easy one to traverse.

The next day we reached the Abu Moharik dune belt that took us three hours and twenty minutes to cross, which at the rate of two and a half miles an hour, was equivalent to a distance of eight and a half miles. The dunes of which it was composed were all, so far as we saw, of the crescentic type, and were probably all considerably under fifteen feet in height. Where the road crossed the belt, was a sand-free gap, the dunes in that part being rather thinly distributed, though farther to the north they appeared to lie much closer together. The whole of the road, where it ran through the belt, was entirely free from drift sand. We camped that night in the middle of the dunes.

On leaving the dunes for Bu Gerara, I sent Qwaytin and Abd er Rahman off to look for another oasis that the former had heard of, that was said to lie some distance to the west of our road, which, however, he failed to find. In the evening before his departure, he came into my tent and announced that "his book said" that on the following day we should reach the Gara bu Gerara. There, he said, the road forked, and one branch, leaving the usual road followed by caravans going to Dakhla, and keeping more to the west, led to Bu Gerara—the oasis we were in search of.

This was the first mention he had made of any "book," so I enquired what the book was to which he referred. Qwaytin seemed rather surprised that I had not heard of it before, and said that it was his "book of treasure!"

Cautious questioning elicited the fact that he had never been to Bu Gerara before, but that he was relying entirely on the directions given in this precious volume to take me there, and evidently expected, when we reached the place that we should all fall to digging in search of the buried riches that the book said were to be found there, instead of getting on and mapping the desert.

He was clearly under the impression that he was conferring a great favour on me by taking me into the secret of the vast wealth that he expected to find. To have thrown any doubt on the reliability of his wonderful book would have mortally offended him, as natives are very sensitive on these subjects. But as following out his instructions did not seem likely to take me far from the part to which I wanted to go, and would lead me into new ground, I thought it best to humour him, trusting that, when he failed to find the place, he would be willing to come down to the more mundane occupation of mapping the desert. So, much against my inclination, I found myself at last fairly launched on a treasure-hunting expedition!

PINNACLE ROCK ON DESCENT TO BU GERARA VALLEY.

Soon after our start on the following morning one of the camels fell ill. What the particular disease was I was unable to discover; but the remedy that Mohanny applied was to bleed her from the tip of her tail—an operation that appeared to afford some relief. The *bedawin* veterinary methods are simple, but, on the whole, effective. They may be summed up in three words—"bleed, butter, or burn."

Eleven miles' march from our camp brought us to the Gara bu Gerara—a long, low, flat-topped hill with a small peak at its eastern extremity, where the road to Bu Gerara branched off from the Derb et Tawil, according to Qwaytin's book of treasure.

Qwaytin had given minute instructions to Mohanny as to finding the place, so, on reaching the hill, he came up to me and announced that it was now necessary to leave the Derb et Tawil, which turned off towards the east, and to follow a road that led straight on.

Our departure for Gara bu Gerara though had to be postponed for a short time owing to the camel developing another attack of whatever the complaint was that she was suffering from, necessitating that she should be again bled—this time from the nose. The operation having been successfully performed, we started off to look for our treasure.

Much to my surprise, we found a very well marked road branched off from the Derb et Tawil, though, judging from its appearance, it had not been used for a very long time. Away to the east of our route—by the side of the Derb et Tawil—was a small, but very conspicuous mound of bright yellow earth—probably ochreous—which I was told was the Garet ed Dahab (golden hillock).

Shortly after we passed through a tract of desert thickly studded with stones. Through this stony area ran a made road. The stones had all been cleared off its surface, which had then been smoothed over with a thoroughness that made it extremely unlikely that the work had ever been done by the *bedawin*, whose contempt for all forms of manual labour always induces them to put up with a bad part in a road, if they cannot circumvent it by a slight detour.

After traversing this stony part of the desert, we reached the top of a steep descent, where again it was evident that some more civilised race than the desert *bedawin* had been at work, for the road down on to the lower level had been notched out of the side of the scarp in a way that would not have done discredit to a modern engineer. After that I felt prepared for any developments.

After negotiating the Negeb Shushina, as the descent from the plateau to the level of the depression is called, we came on to a level sandy plain, where for a time Mohanny, who had been acting as guide by following the directions Qwaytin had given him from his wonderful book, succeeded in getting completely lost. After wandering about for a time, seeking the marble palaces and gilded domes of Bu Gerara, we at length caught sight of two figures in the distance, who, when examined through the glass, proved to be Qwaytin and Abd er Rahman.

CHAPTER XXII

WE found Abd er Rahman and Qwaytin diligently engaged in grubbing about in the ground. In reply to my question as to whether they had seen anything of Bu Gerara, I was told that we were standing on it. Qwaytin pointed out the foundations of several walls that could just be seen showing above the sandy surface of the ground and a lot of broken pottery lying about on the desert. He then led me a few yards away to where a circular patch of unusually sandy soil, a few feet in diameter, was to be seen, which he said was the mouth of a well, and produced as the first instalment of the "treasure" to be found, a piece of broken purple glass, that had apparently once formed part of a cup or bowl, and a copper coin of the Ptolemaic period, which he had dug up.

The sight of that coin was too much for my men. It was all I could do to get them to unload the camels and pitch my tent, before they were all off digging away into the ground for dear life, expecting every moment to find the untold wealth that the book had described. They continued until it was too dark for them to see. They then set to work to cook their evening meal.

Qwaytin's men were even more primitive in their culinary arrangements than Abd er Rahman and Ibrahim. Their food supply consisted of the usual leathern sack of flour, an earthenware jar, covered with raw hide, which contained clarified butter, that they slung on a camel, and several tin canisters containing a very anæmic-looking cheese. They mixed the flour, water, salt and butter together into a dough, which they rolled out into thick slabs with a stick about three-quarters of an inch in diameter on the top of one of my provision boxes. They then lighted a huge bonfire from the surrounding scrub, and when the sand was sufficiently heated and the wood was reduced to glowing embers, scraped the fire away, laid the slab of dough down on the heated sand and covered it over again with the cinders. After about a quarter of an hour's baking the bread was considered to be ready to eat. My men cooked their dough on a slightly dished iron plate called a *saj*.

Qwaytin came into my tent in the evening, highly elated at having found Bu Gerara. To my disgust I discovered that he was not thinking of going on into Farafra at all, but was fairly off on a treasure hunt, and seemed to imagine that he was going to drag me all over the desert with him searching for buried riches. His book, he explained, not only described the road as far as Bu Gerara, but said that close by there was a hill to the west, standing in the same wady—Qwaytin pointed out a hill standing by itself to the west as a conclusive proof that his book was correct—and that a road ran past the foot of the hill that, if followed, led to a big hill, on the top of which was a well in which the treasures of three Sultans were buried. He said he had seen the road at the foot of the hill in the morning. He had never followed it to see where it led to; but he had seen a hill some years before in the direction of which the road was going, and had noticed a lot of pigeons alight on the top of it, and thought that perhaps it was the one the book referred to, and that they had gone there to drink from the well.

His mind was fairly obsessed with the idea of treasure, and I could get him to talk of nothing else.

I tried to get some information from him about Farafra and Iddaila—but it was of no use; he got round again to treasure at once. The last time he was in Farafra, he said, he was on his way back from Tibesti, where he said he had found a seam of diamond that stood up two feet above the ground like a wall, and ran for a long distance. He had chopped some lumps of diamond off and they cut glass. But the Senussi sheykhs had apropriated them for the benefit of the Senussia. He was clearly very sore on the subject.

I tried to switch him off on to the Bedayat country—but it was almost equally useless. He said he knew of a number of places there where there were ruins that probably contained treasure and asked to see my map.

He studied it for some time, asking me to read out the names and then declared that it was all wrong, and asked for a pencil and piece of paper, saying that he would draw me a better one. He laid the paper on the ground, sucked the end of the pencil and began to draw the roads joining the places he was going to tell about, now and then consulting a cheap bar compass to make sure that he had got them running in the right direction. This framework, when completed, looked more like a broken spider's web than anything else.

He next proceeded to place on his "map" a number of enormous dots, to represent the positions of the places he wished to insert in it, and began to reel out a lot of names that are not found on any printed map. The conversation commenced to become interesting, and a good deal more in my line than fables relating to buried treasure.

But the names given to places by Arabs, Tibbus and Sudanese are not easily remembered, or even grasped, the first time they are heard. I allowed him to run on until he had completed his list, and then took the pencil from him and began to write opposite his dots the names of the places they stood for, and their distances and bearings from each other. Qwaytin at once became impatient, as I found he always did whenever I questioned him as to his statements, or he saw me writing them down, and I was not able to get more than two or three of the names before he took himself off in a huff.

He was a most exasperating man to get information from. If I questioned him about some part of the world that he had visited, he would very often give me no information at all. Sometimes a suggestion on my part that perhaps he did not know anything about it, would put him on his mettle and cause him to divulge some of his knowledge; but as often as not it only had the effect of making him reel out a lot of lying statements that probably appealed to his yokelish mind as being facetious, but which subsequent questioning showed to be incorrect—every statement that he made I had to check in order to guard against this peculiar sense of humour that he possessed.

I usually verified his information by getting him to repeat what he had said after an interval of a week or more, by which time I calculated that, if he had lied, he would have forgotten what he had said.

The first time I caught him misleading me, I pulled him up. But this proved to be quite the wrong line to take, and nearly had the effect of making him withhold his information altogether. He was greatly incensed, and for many days he would tell me nothing at all. Then late one night, while I was sitting up, waiting for a star to come on to the meridian in order to get a latitude, just when it had almost got there and I was going to take the observation, Qwaytin came quietly up and said that he would tell me about the country of the Bedayat. I had to give up the observation and go and sit down in the tent, where under a coat thrown over my knees, under pretence of feeling cold, so that he should not see me doing so, I took down all he said in writing.

The information that he volunteered in this way I found to be nearly always reliable—but he generally chose some time when I was going to bed, or in the middle of some other work, to come and impart his knowledge, and broke off at once if he saw me writing it down. During the day's march, too, I would sometimes get him in a communicative mood, and he would describe to me the route that joined two places. The difficulty of writing all he said down before I forgot it was easily solved in this case, by stopping to take a compass bearing, as he had often seen me do before, and then by writing in my route book the information he had volunteered under pretence of keeping up the survey.

Collecting data from natives on which to base a map is not quite so simple as it sounds. The habit that so many *bedawin* have of deliberately misleading one, makes it necessary to check the routes described most carefully. But even bona-fide information collected in this way will make a most inaccurate map unless some means for adjusting it can be found.

The plan I adopted was to get the data whenever possible, in the form of through routes, joining two places whose positions had been previously fixed. Roads so described can then be plotted on the map, their accuracy tested and the route as a whole adjusted, so as to fit the positions of the places that are already known. In this way the errors can be minimised as far as possible.

But collecting this information from Qwaytin was anything but easy. Like nearly all the *bedawin* he was entirely illiterate, and so could not give me the spelling of the names of the places that he gave me in the Libyan Desert, the Sudan, Tibesti and Endi, and these could not be found on any map. Many of them were almost unpronounceable, and in some cases introduced sounds that could not be reproduced by even the Arabic alphabet. They were presumably those of the Tibbu or Bedayat languages—the latter being a tongue that Qway had described to me as sounding like "the chattering of monkeys."

It will easily be imagined that to take down a long string of new names such as these, when rapidly reeled off, was a matter of some difficulty.

But it seemed worth taking some trouble to get them. I had been asked to get any information I could about the unknown parts of the desert, for the Senussi question was in the air—the Government were by no means so fast asleep as people were led to suppose—and at that time, moreover, a rod was being laid in pickle for 'Ali Dinar, the Sultan of Darfur, whose goings on did not always meet with the approval of the authorities; so information on these unknown parts was likely to be of some practical use, beyond spoiling the virginal whiteness of this part of the map of Africa.

Qwaytin's knowledge of the least known parts of North and Central Africa was profound, and he had the great virtue, from my point of view, of being so densely stupid that he was unable to realise the value of all that he let out. Before I had done with him, he gave me enough data to form a fairly complete map of the unknown portions of the Libyan Desert, with a great deal of the Bedayat country and Endi. In addition I learnt from him much information of the orography of the desert and the distribution of the sand dunes. The map when completed contained the names of some seventy places that, I believe, had not previously been recorded; many of them have been found since, approximately in the position in which they were shown. Maps of this kind do not, of course, err on the side of accuracy, but they have their uses—principally in giving future travellers that definite objective to look for, that I had so greatly needed when starting work in this desert. If I had been able to collect during my first year the information I eventually obtained, mainly from Qwaytin, in my last, I should certainly have tackled the job in an entirely different way.

The morning after our arrival at Bu Gerara, the men fell seriously to work to dig about in the site, with the result that by midday a few pieces of broken pottery and glass and two or three more small copper coins had been unearthed. As I wished to ascertain whether any water was to be found in the well, in the afternoon, much to their disgust, I set the men to clear it out.

Qwaytin's men, after they had been working for a short time, downed tools, declaring that that sort of work was a job that was only fit for the *fellahin*, and beneath the dignity of the Arabs. It was not until I pointed out that the well was the most likely place in which to look for treasure, and reminded them that the three Sultans were said to have buried theirs in the well on the top of the hill described in Qwaytin's book, that they could be induced to resume their work. Then they fell to with a will and soon had the well cleared out to the bottom.

It was about nine feet in diameter, and eight feet deep. On the side towards the site of Bu Gerara, a ramp, cut in its side, led down to the bottom. The part of the desert in which it had been sunk was covered with a thin layer of rock, below which lay a bed of clay, extending down to another layer of rock, which formed the bottom of the well. Before we commenced to dig, the well was completely filled with sand that had drifted into it. About half-way down our expectations were raised by the sand becoming damp; but though the well was cleared out to the very bottom, and the sand got considerably damper as we descended, no water was to be seen. This was a considerable disappointment, as a well at this point on the long Derb et Tawil would have been of the greatest value to the travellers using the road.

The nut of a dom palm that I dug up, and the trunks of some palm trees that had been built into the walls, showed that, at one time, there must have been a plentiful supply of water in the neighbourhood. The place was probably a small fortified station built, or at all events occupied, during Ptolemaic times, to protect the well, which from its position on "the long road" must once have been of considerable importance.

The existence of fossilised tree-trunks and old river-beds in the Libyan Desert shows conclusively that, in the remote past, this portion of the world must have been a well-watered country. But whether this desiccation reached its limit before historical times, or whether it is still going on is one of the most disputed points in connection with this district. The failure of the well at Bu Gerara may, of course, have been due to some purely local cause, which was not apparent. But in the absence of some explanation as to its nature, this little abandoned settlement affords a very strong argument in favour of the view that the water supply—apart from that derived from the artesian wells—has failed appreciably in comparatively recent times, owing probably to a decrease in the rainfall. From this point of view, our discovery was of some importance, though the place itself was of no consequence at all.

But it was found by following instructions in Qwaytin's book of treasure. Works of this description, to put it mildly, are regarded in Egypt with a considerable amount of incredulity. This scepticism, I own, I fully shared—until my discovery of Bu Gerara.

Since then, however, I have taken a different view of the case, and believe that the almost universal suspicion with which these books are regarded, may not, after all, be entirely justified, and that part of it at least is due to the strong prejudice that so often exists towards any native beliefs or customs that do not admit of a ready explanation, or that savour in any way of the occult, or of buried riches.

These books of treasure, it is true, are mostly written by natives of the astrologer class, who clearly expect their readers to rely largely upon charms and various occult means to discover the hidden riches to which they profess to give the key. Many of them lived in the Middle Ages, but the race has not died out. There are hundreds of the same class of men still to be found practising their arts on the credulous natives of Egypt, and one of the principal subjects upon which they are even now consulted is the recovery of buried treasure. There is a *sheykh el afrit* (ruler of spirits) in almost every village, to whom the inhabitants resort to induce him by means of the pool of ink, or some similar method, to foretell the future or to guide them to where treasure has been buried. Some of them perhaps believe in their own powers, but the majority are probably little more than impostors. So far, so bad.

But there appears to be a very fair amount of grain among all the chaff contained in these books, for in many cases they not only refer to places, such as Esna, which are perfectly well known, but they describe the roads that lead to them, when these roads are still in use.

For this reason I think they are worth careful—or perhaps it would be better to say cautious—consideration. It is true that in many cases they mention places and describe roads which perhaps were perfectly well known at the time when the books were written, but that cannot now be identified; but this proves nothing. There are many old sanded-up wells, little deserted oases and small outpost stations of the Roman and other periods, such, for instance, as Bu Gerara, scattered about in the desert, and the vestiges of many old roads are still to be seen, whose ultimate destination is now unknown, but which, I believe, lead to these abandoned oases, which very probably, in the fifteenth century, when the book of Johnson Pasha's that has already been referred to was written, were populous villages and oases; but which, owing to failure of the water supply, the encroachment of the sand, or to some other cause, have long since become deserted.

On these grounds I believe these books contain—among a great deal that is useless except as a curiosity—some valuable information as to old places in the desert that have long since been lost to sight, and whose very names may now be forgotten, information that is of a geographical character.

Why not? Is it the age of the book, or the fact that the descriptions in it are associated with magic and hidden treasure, that presents the difficulty? If it be the former, ask any archæologist whether he would hesitate to look for the site of some ancient city, because the only references to it were to be found in some old papyrus or temple hieroglyphics; besides, did not the Royal Geographical Society have a paper read before them on the identity of the Garden of Eden with Mesopotamia? The description that led to the identification being taken from the Book of Genesis, which was written long before any of these books were thought about.

If it be the treasure that presents the difficulty, has there not been endless discussion among geographers as to the identity of the Wakwak Islands and other places, mentioned in the "Arabian Nights," a large proportion of the stories in which have no pretensions to be anything more than fairy-tales—and certainly there is enough buried treasure mentioned in them to satisfy the most ardent fortune hunter in Egypt.

Are not educated Europeans, even now, continually setting out to look for the fabulous riches hidden, a hundred or two years ago, by some old pirate or buccaneer, usually on an island—say, in the West Indies? Of the identity of the island there is generally no doubt at all—but the treasure does not seem to be often found!

We stayed for a day or two more at Bu Gerara, during which time the men found a small earthenware pot, some broken fragments of glass and pottery and one or two more copper coins—and that was all! Then as we had drawn a blank, so far as treasure was concerned at Bu Gerara, the men all wanted to be taken off to the hill where the riches of the three Sultans was buried with the least possible delay. Qwaytin was the most insistent of them all, evidently assuming that I had given up my plan of going to Farafra and had committed myself to a whole season's treasure hunting instead.

The hill where the mystical Sultans had buried their riches was not far off, though it did not lie in the direction in which I had intended to go; but it was in a part of the desert that had never been mapped, so I thought it best to humour him once more and let him take me there.

We got off early the next morning. Qwaytin led us straight towards the hill in the wady, near the foot of which we found the promised road.

As we increased our distance from the cliff lying to the north of Bu Gerara, the surroundings of the place could be better seen. The view to the north was, of course, cut off by the cliff, which as soon as we had got some distance from it, could be seen stretching away for many miles to the east, forming the continuation of the escarpment that bounded the Kharga depression on its northern side.

To the south-east was a considerable expanse of elevated ground, evidently the plateau in which lay some small depressions I had found to the north of 'Ain Amur. So far as I could see, there was no cliff on the northern side of this tableland, the ground only sloping up to it from the lower level. A well— 'Ain Embares—that I had tried to reach by way of the chain of small depressions, with little doubt was situated between the foot of the scarp of the main plateau and this high ground that lay to its south.

On the west, the scarp of the plateau was visible for a long way. Qwaytin's old road led us in a southerly direction, roughly parallel to the cliff of a detached plateau. It was chiefly noticeable for the large number of small patches of bushes, known as *roadhs*, that were scattered along it. These seemed to be a favourite feeding ground for gazelle, to judge from the number of tracks we saw, most of which, however, were fairly old ones. In one place, instead of the usual small bushes, a couple of small acacia (*sunt*) trees were seen.

We sighted the hill we were in search of in the afternoon, and, an hour before camping, reached the top of a steep descent on to lower ground, about two hundred and fifty feet below us, that Qwaytin said was called in his book the "Negeb er Rumi" (descent of the European). The road down to the valley below was obviously to some extent an artificial one, and, though extremely steep, was negotiated without difficulty. We pitched our camp below.

This lower ground was so covered with sand and pebbles that I was unable to see whether we were still on the limestone. But the ground level rose again considerably as we neared the hill, and for the last part of the way the limestone was showing again on the surface. Possibly a fault exists in the neighbourhood.

We reached the hill itself at noon, and camped on its southern side. It was a small limestone-capped hill, chiefly remarkable for the extent to which the limestone was honeycombed by the wind-driven sand. At the foot of the hill, near the camp, was a boulder that had evidently rolled down from the top. It was almost four feet in diameter, and literally riddled with holes like a sponge.

As soon as the camp was pitched, the men rushed up the hill and began minutely searching every nook and cranny for the reported well, while Qwaytin wandered disconsolately along its base, vainly searching for the broken glass that his book had foretold would be found there. He thought that perhaps he had mistaken the hill, and said, if we could not find the well or any glass, that we had better follow the road farther, to see if there was not another hill upon it that might be the one referred to in his book; but to waste any more time in looking for that hill was the last thing I intended to do.

By sunset the well had not been found, though every inch of that hill must have been most carefully examined several times.

This was a serious blow to Qwaytin's hopes, and a distinct wet blanket to the whole caravan with the exception of Ibrahim, who, as he explained to me, would not have minded a little *bakhshish*, but would not in the least know what to do with sacks of gold, or diamonds, even if he found them.

In the evening Qwaytin, Abd er Rahman, Dahab and I held a serious consultation. The position of the hill tallied so well with the description of it in Qwaytin's book that he felt sure that it was the right one; but he was terribly worried over the failure to find the well.

Dahab said that he thought that probably it was there all right, but that it was hidden by enchantment, and that it would be necessary for us to burn some incense before it would become visible.

Qwaytin cheered up rather at this idea; but said that we had no incense with us, and added it was awkward stuff to play with, as it was most important that we should have the right kind, and should be quite sure that we knew how to use it.

Abd er Rahman agreed with this, and was very emphatic in saying that we ought to be quite sure that we had enough of it, as he had heard a story of a Maghrabi Arab, who had joined with two *fellahin* in a search for treasure that was buried in some tombs in the side of a hill that had a spell over them, and so could not be opened without proper formalities. They found the place where the tombs were hidden, and then had gone through the necessary incantations and burnt some incense and the tombs immediately opened. The two *fellahin* had then gone in to collect the treasure while the Maghrabi had remained outside to look after their camels and to keep the incense burning. Unfortunately the incense ran short, and, as soon as the last of it had been burnt, the tombs closed again with a bang, burying the two unfortunate *fellahin* alive. The Maghrabi had then gone home with their camels, and Abd er Rahman was clearly of opinion that that Arab had done something that was quite exceptionally clever.

He suggested that, to be on the safe side, we had better go and fetch Sheykh Ibrahim, the *Sheykh el Afrit* from Dakhla, to come out and do the necessary incantations. But this did not meet with Qwaytin's approval at all. Sheykh Ibrahim, he said, was a member of the Senussia and he knew all about him. He had the right books and the proper incense and was very clever at his work. But he was such a bad man that sometimes the spirits would not obey him; and he pointed out that if an *afrit* went on strike in the middle of the performance, we might find ourselves rather badly in the soup.

After much serious discussion, we came to the conclusion that, in the circumstances, it was no use for us to waste any more time in examining the hill, but that at the end of the trip we would go and get a really first-class highly certificated magician from Cairo, or some big town, and get him to come out and do the job. In the meantime, as Qwaytin had told me that there were some mounds in the Kairowin *hattia*, that we should go there through the eastern part of the Farafra depression and see if they did not contain treasure. Qwaytin had heard that they contained buildings, and so thought that it would be a likely place for buried riches, though, as he said lugubriously, he did not expect that we should find anything like what we might have done if we had discovered the treasure of those three Sultans. The following morning a rather crestfallen caravan set out for the eastern side of Farafra.

CHAPTER XXIII

ON leaving the hill we took a road that led us towards the north. We first rounded the western end of the scarp of the detached plateau parallel to which we had marched on coming from Bu Gerara, and, about two hours after our start, ascended a steepish bank on to the top of the plateau, which here was only about fifty feet high.

From the summit of a small hill close by, a huge cliff stretching to the north and south, as far as it was possible to see, was visible, far off in the east; this was evidently the eastern boundary of the Farafra depression, and, as I afterwards discovered, the continuation of the cliff to the north of Bu Gerara.

The scarp was too far for me to be able to see any details of its surface, with the light behind it, and as the top of it showed as only a straight line, there were no points on it to which I could take a bearing.

In these circumstances it was impossible either to fix its position or to estimate the direction in which it ran. I several times met with this difficulty, but found that, when a cliff faced towards the south, it was only necessary for me to wait till the sun came round far enough to begin to light up its surface, and then a rough estimate of the direction in which it ran could be obtained by taking a bearing on to the sun itself. This dodge was especially useful when it was necessary to map the continuation of a cliff, part of which had already been surveyed and the remainder of it could only be seen from one point, such as the top of a high hill.

The part of the Farafra depression in which we found ourselves was an absolutely featureless plain, of hard level sand, that sloped slightly towards the foot of the scarp on our east. Here and there we came across patches of greenish clay, with white lines running through it, showing above the surface of the sand.

The Persian King, Cambyses, during his occupation of Egypt, sent a great army across the desert to destroy the oracle of Jupiter Ammon in Siwa Oasis. The army never reached Siwa; but was lost in the desert. Its last resting-place is unknown, but, according to native reports, the whole host perished of thirst in this huge depression in which the oasis of Farafra lies.

I happened to mention to Qwaytin the subject of singing sands, and asked him if he had ever heard any. He told me that somewhere in the north of the Farafra depression there was a rock that was supposed to be the "church" of the spirits of the lost Persian army. It was called the "infidel rock," because it "sang on Sunday." It appeared to be some form of musical sands.

It was not until the third day after our start from the treasure hill that we sighted in the west the field of dunes that occupies the centre of the Farafra wady. They appeared to be almost white in colour, and lay a long way off.

Qwaytin told me that we should reach the Kairowin *hattia* on our third day after leaving his hill. It will give some idea of his utter incompetence as a guide when I say that we did not actually get there until two days later.

He came into my tent on the first evening and began yarning in an aimless sort of way, as he generally did as a preliminary to serious business, and I endeavoured to extract some information from him as to the topography of the Bedayat country, with which he was well acquainted.

But he at once got impatient and changed the subject to that of his confounded hill. He ended by asking—almost demanding—that we should go back there to have another look at it, and to make certain that there was not another hill in the neighbourhood which might be the one indicated in his book. On my refusing to do so, he flounced out of the tent—he was certainly a queer customer to deal with.

Whenever I spoke to him the next day he began gassing about his wretched hill, and saying that he wanted to go back to it; but towards evening he rather recovered himself, and when he came to my tent I again threw out feelers about the country of the Bedayat, though he declined to tell me anything about the district, he started giving me a lot of information about the Bedayat themselves, which, as they are an almost unknown race, proved extremely interesting.

They claim to be descended from an *afrit*, whom, for some crime, either David or Solomon shut up in a box, till he grew to such an enormous size that he burst it open. There still exists apparently a mongrel Bedayat—Tibbu tribe, known as the M'Khiat er Rih, that possess the miraculous power of being able to walk over sand without leaving any tracks behind them—a most useful accomplishment in the desert for a race of born freebooters. This peculiarity they owe to the fact that wherever they go they are followed by a wind that immediately obliterates their footprints!

On our fourth day after leaving the treasure hill, our road converged towards the dunes lying on our west, and, as Qwaytin seemed to be hopelessly lost, I climbed one of the biggest of them with him to try and make out our position.

From the top, the east and west scarp, with a break in it leading up to Baharia Oasis, that lies on the north of Farafra, could be seen in the far distance, but no sign of the *hattia* Kairowin was visible. In front of us, however, was a high three-headed *sif*, or longitudinal sand dune, that Qwaytin declared to be the landmark for the *hattia* from the south.

As we were getting very short of water, the news that the *hattia* was not in sight caused something like consternation among my men. They all started grumbling at Qwaytin's ignorance of the road, and Ibrahim went so far as to ask him point-blank why he called himself a guide, if he knew so little about the desert.

This coming from a young Sudani, hardly out of his 'teens, to an elderly Arab guide, who, moreover, was a sheykh of his tribe, was a great *ayb*, and Qwaytin was intensely put out. Qway, under the circumstances, would have retaliated with some stinging remarks on the inferiority of "slaves" and the respect that was due from a boy to his elders and superiors in rank; but Qwaytin lacked his ready powers of vituperation. He was a slow-witted old curmudgeon, and failed entirely to put Ibrahim in his place. His own men stood up for him in a feeble sort of way. But they were no match for Ibrahim, and eventually gave up any attempt to defend their sheykh, probably feeling themselves that there was not much to be said in his defence. As I rather wanted to encourage a certain amount of friction between my men and Qwaytin's, I left them to settle their differences as best they could, with the result that Qwaytin and his men got much the worst of the wrangle.

Kairowin *hattia* measures some eighteen miles from north to south, by seven from east to west. It consists of a level scrub-covered area, in which, here and there, are to be seen a few neglected-looking palms. A number of wells have been sunk here at various times; one on the extreme eastern edge of the *hattia*, where the road coming from Assiut first enters the scrub, is known as Bir Murr. This well, which I did not visit, is said to be sanded up. Another well somewhere to the north, I believe, is known as Bir Abd el Qadr. There are also several others, all of which seem to be impartially named Bir Kairowin. Probably water can be found under all the lower lying parts of the *hattia* by digging for a few feet into the ground, which throughout this district consists of chalk.

The wells in every case apparently give water so thick with chalk particles that when first drawn from them it is almost as milky as whitewash. Attempts to clear the water by passing it through a Berkefeld filter failed, as the chalk clogged the filter after a few strokes. But when it had been allowed to stand for a few hours, most of the chalk settled down to the bottom, and the water that was poured off passed quite easily through the filter, after which it proved to be of quite good quality.

I, unfortunately, forgot to wind my watches the first night in the *hattia*, and so allowed the half chronometer I had been using in taking my observations to run down. As I was depending on it for my longitudes, this necessitated a stay of two or three days in the camp in order to ascertain its new rate after it had been rewound.

These watches are for some reason only made so as to run for one day. As oversights of this kind must be of common occurrence with travellers, it would seem to be preferable that they should be made so as to run for two days, and be furnished with an up and down indicator to show how long an interval has elapsed since they were last wound.

I spent a considerable part of the time while in the *hattia* in trying, without success, to get a shot at gazelle. There appeared to be very few in the district, though a considerable number of old tracks were to be seen where they had been feeding on the scrub.

This scarcity of game may perhaps have been due to the fact that a few *bedawin* were at that time living there in charge of some camels belonging to the Senussi *zawia* at Qasr Farafra. These men kept away from the camp, but I saw them and their camels several times wandering about in the scrub, and twice found small hovels constructed of brushwood, in which they had been living—they had, so far as I could see, no tents.

My men spent most of their time in grubbing about in some large mounds. On the top of one of these, about thirty feet high, Ibrahim found some burnt bricks. The whole mound was covered by a thick growth of *terfa* bushes, among which the sand had collected, completely hiding any building there might have been beneath it.

It must have been originally a building of some size and of considerable height, and was perhaps a tower. The men unearthed part of a small room at the base of the mound. It had been well built, of the same burnt bricks, and the interior was covered with plaster. A few pieces of broken pottery were found, one of them covered with a green glaze. There were four or five other mounds of a similar nature in the neighbourhood; but we had neither time nor implements thoroughly to examine them.

As the total result of their treasure hunt in Kairowin the men only unearthed one corpse and a few bits of broken pottery, without finding even a single copper coin to gratify their cupidity. They were consequently considerably disillusioned with their occupation, and I experienced no difficulty in getting them to start for Qasr Farafra.

I made first for the main well, that is known as the Bir Kairowin, in order to close my traverse. The water lay about eight feet below the surface; access being gained to it by the usual sloping path, cut out of one of its sides. By the top of the well was a mud-built trough for watering camels, with an empty paraffin tin lying beside it for use as a bucket.

Immediately on leaving the *hattia* we got into the dunes, which cover a large area in the centre of the Farafra depression. The first two or three dunes gave a little difficulty, but we found the rest of them quite easy to cross. They were all, so far as I could see, of a very elongated whalebacked type, which ran roughly from north to south, in the direction of the prevailing wind.

Qasr Farafra lay almost due west from our camp. Soon after we got into the sand it became clear that Qwaytin was again hopelessly lost, as I found we were marching almost due south. I was obliged to put it to my guide, as inoffensively as I could, that if he would change the direction in which he was leading us by a mere right angle, we might perhaps reach our destination, instead of going on to Dakhla Oasis as we seemed to be doing. Qwaytin was so hopelessly lost that he accepted my suggestion without the slightest argument.

Soon after this we got out of the sand on to level desert, where a large number of black nodules of iron pyrites were to be seen lying on the surface. Further on some fine specimens of sand erosion were met with in the shape of chalk "mushrooms" and table rocks. Otherwise this part of the desert was quite featureless. The road lay entirely over white chalk, which caused a rather trying glare in the blazing sunlight.

We sighted Qasr Farafra on the evening of the second day after leaving Kairowin *hattia*; but as night fell before we could reach it, we camped a few miles away from the village. Two hours' march on the following morning brought us into the oasis. On the outskirts we passed a patch of ground on which the sand was encroaching, some palms lying on the north of it being almost entirely submerged.

We camped on the northern side of the village. A large crowd of natives came out and stood watching us while the tent was being pitched. Among them was a sulky-looking fellow whom I was told was the *'omda*; so, as soon as the tent was pitched, I invited him and some of the other men standing by to come in.

We had foolishly camped too close to the village, with the result that throughout the greater part of the day the camp was surrounded by a crowd of men and children watching all our actions, peering into the tent, thronging round the theodolite, when I began to take observations, and generally showing an ill-mannerly curiosity that was in great contrast to the conduct of the natives of the other oases in which we stayed. Farafra being the least known of the Egyptian oases, the advent of a European was an event of such rare occurrence that the natives had evidently decided to make the most of it.

The natives of Farafra Oasis, who are known as the Farfaroni, or sometimes as the Farafaroni, are a far more vigorous lot than those of Kharga and Dakhla. They were a surly unpleasant-looking crowd.

The day after our arrival, I went out with the *'omda* and Qwaytin to see the village and plantations. With the exception of an *ezba* at 'Ain Sheykh Murzuk, where there are a few houses, a Senussi *zawia* and a family or two continuously resident to tend the cultivation near the well, Qasr Farafra is the only permanently inhabited spot in the whole Farafra depression. It is a poor little place with a total population of about five hundred and fifty inhabitants. The houses are of the usual mud-built type, and in most cases little better than huts; almost the only exception being that of a square tower, showing in places the remains of battlements, attributed, perhaps rightly, by the natives to the Romans, who are said to have erected it as a keep to protect the village.

This proved to be rather an interesting place. It is not inhabited, but the door is kept locked with a watchman perpetually on guard over it. The building is used solely as a storehouse, each family in the village having the right to the use of one of the rooms that it contains—there were said to be no less than one hundred and twenty-five chambers in the building.

The *'omda* showed us over the tower. The entrance lay through a strong wooden door, at the top of a flight of steps, in a passage entered in the middle of one of the outer walls, the walls on either side of which were pierced with apertures, apparently intended for use as loop-holes. The passage extended the whole height of the building and was unroofed, in order that stones might be dropped from above on to any assailant attempting to attack the door.

BOY WITH CROSS-BOW, FARAFRA.

The interior of the tower was a perfect labyrinth of breakneck stairways and little rooms opening out of narrow dark passages. After scrambling up several sets of steps and repeatedly banging my head in the dark against the low roof, we at length emerged into a sort of courtyard at the top, surrounded by two tiers of small chambers, each provided with its own locked door. Some further scrambling landed us on the roof that covered the rooms and formed a kind of platform surrounding the courtyard. From here a wide view could be obtained over the oasis and depression.

There was not much of consequence to be seen. Below lay the village, looking, when viewed from above, even more squalid than from below. Scattered round it, within a radius of a few miles, lay a number of small patches of cultivation, showing the positions of the various wells and springs. Seven or eight miles away to the west was a cliff of considerable height, forming the scarpment of the Guss Abu Said—an isolated plateau beyond which, though invisible from the tower, lay a well, "Bir Labayat," and the little oases of Iddaila and Nesla, in another large depression, the dimensions of which were unknown. Here and there on the floor of the depression a few isolated hills stood up to break the level monotony, the most conspicuous amongst them being Jebel Gunna el Bahari, about fifteen miles to the northeast. Otherwise the view over the depression was singularly monotonous. The only other noticeable features being the cliffs in the far distance to the north and east that marked the limits of the higher plateau.

On descending from the tower the *'omda* took me round the village. Except for its poverty-stricken appearance, it differed little from those in Dakhla and Kharga Oases. There seemed to be few houses with a second storey, and the palm leaf hedges, that usually topped the wall surrounding the flat roofs in the other oases, were seldom visible.

Having completed our survey of the village, the *'omda* took us to his house. It was a very poor residence for a man of his position in the village, and was overrun with fowls, goats and filthy little children, mostly suffering from ringworm. He gave us some dates and very bad tea, but no cigarettes were produced, probably because, like most of the inhabitants of the place, he "followed the Sheykh."

In the afternoon I went with Abd er Rahman and the *'omda* to see the winch of a boring machine that had been given to the *zawia* by a wealthy Egyptian in Cairo, in order that they could sink a new well. They wanted my opinion on it, as two of the cog wheels had been broken and the work of sinking the well had had to stop in consequence. It was obvious that there was nothing to be done, except to replace the wheels. I took measurements of the broken parts and promised to have duplicates of them made in Cairo, when I got back, and to have them sent to the oasis.

I was engaged in noting down their dimensions, when Abd er Rahman informed me that the Senussi sheykhs from the *zawia* were coming, and I caught sight of two men, with Qwaytin in their train, stalking along in my direction.

The *zawia* was run by three sheykhs who were brothers, the eldest was, however, at that time away in Cairo. The other two were not a prepossessing-looking couple. Sheykh Ibn ed Dris, the elder, was a fine-looking Arab, and would have been even handsome if his face had not been marred by its dour, truculent expression. His youngest brother, Sheykh Mohammed, was apparently hardly out of his 'teens, and seemed to be somewhat of a cipher, being completely swamped by the aggressive personality of the elder sheykh. The only impression he made was one of extreme sulkiness. Qwaytin told me that they had come to take me for a walk round the plantations that surrounded the village, adding that as I was a stranger in the oasis they felt that they ought to entertain me.

They did not seem to relish the job very much. Sheykh Ibn ed Dris was extremely taciturn, and his brother never opened his mouth during the whole of our tour of inspection.

Compared with the other Egyptian oases, the plantations in Farafra contained comparatively few palms and a much larger proportion of other fruit trees—olives, vines, apricots, white mulberries, figs, pomegranates, limes, sweet lemons, a few orange trees and a small apple, which, being regarded as a rarity, was very highly prized. Formerly there used to be a considerable export of olive oil to the Nile Valley, but for some reason, perhaps because the trees were getting too old, the crop was said to have diminished considerably, and barely to suffice for the wants of the oasis.

The fields surrounding the plantations were planted so far as I saw only with wheat, barley and onions, but durra and rice are also said to be grown in the oasis. The areas under cultivation seemed small, but the plants all looked healthy, and even luxuriant. I saw no patches of salty ground, such as were often to be seen in Dakhla.

A Bride and her Pottery.

A bride from the poorer classes can only contribute a small amount of earthenware towards furnishing her new home. In her wedding procession she carries this on a chair on her head. Note the sequins on the front of her dress. (p. 253).

Farafra is such a small place that administratively it is under Baharia, the nearest oasis, lying about three days' journey away to the north-east. In the whole oasis of Farafra there are only about twenty wells, the two most important ones were said to be 'Ain Ebsay, lying four to five miles to the south of the village, which I did not visit, and 'Ain el Belad (the town well), both of which were said to be of Roman origin and to resemble those of Dakhla Oasis.

Some of the wells are said to be connected with long underground infiltration channels cut horizontally, at some depth below the surface, similar to those at 'Ain Um Debadib, but I had no opportunity of examining any of these. The 'Ain el Belad, that supplies the village, flowed into a large pool covered with green weed and to some extent surrounded by palm groves, that in the glow of the setting sun made a most lovely picture.

We ended our promenade at the door of Sheykh Ibn ed Dris' house in the *zawia*. It was a gloomy mud-built building, without a trace of the European furniture that characterised the *zawia* and houses of the Mawhub family in Dakhla. Here I took leave of my unpleasant companions, much, I fancy, to our mutual relief. As the sheykhs had to a slight extent thawed during our walk, I asked Ibn ed Dris to let me photograph him, to which, rather to my surprise, he grudgingly consented. He did not make a pretty picture. He was wearing his normal expression, a scowl that "never came off," and nothing that I said would induce him to look pleasant.

Supplies of all kinds were very scarce in the oasis. No fruit or vegetables were procurable, and the only eatables to be bought were fowls, eggs and onions. Owing to nearly the whole of the inhabitants being members of the Senussia, tobacco was also very difficult to obtain, as the members of the sect are forbidden to smoke. The men had all run out of cigarettes, and were much upset at not being able to renew their supplies.

The morning after my walk with the sheykhs, Ibrahim, who was always keen on any kind of sport, told me that quail were beginning to arrive in the oasis, so I went out with him to try and shoot some. I only, however, saw two—one of which I succeeded in missing twice.

The natives of Qasr Farafra were so unfriendly that I was unable to see as much of the place as I should have wished, and I was only able to take a very few photos.

The next morning we packed up and set out to Bu Mungar. After an uneventful journey of about eight hours to the south-west, over a featureless level desert, we reached the little oasis of 'Ain Sheykh Murzuk—the only permanently inhabited spot, besides Qasr Farafra, in the whole depression.

Three or four men came to meet us as we approached the plantation, and greeted Qwaytin with enthusiasm. The oasis was a very small one, extending to only a few acres. The cultivation consisted of only a few palms and fruit trees and a field or two of grain. Among the palms were hidden two or three houses, which I, however, inspected only from a distance. One of them, I was told, was a Senussi *zawia*.

CHAPTER XXIV

WE started the next morning at dawn. Soon after leaving 'Ain Sheykh Murzuk, Qwaytin showed me a pass ascending the scarp of a small plateau, the Guss abu Said, on our right, over which, he said, passed a road to Iddaila. From Iddaila, he said, a road ran direct through Nesla and Bu Mungar to Dakhla Oasis.

Two hours after our start we reached a very small oasis, only an acre or two in extent, known as 'Ain el Agwa. It contained a few palms and evidently a well, though the place was so covered with drifted sand that the palms in some cases were buried nearly to their crowns, and the well was completely invisible.

About an hour farther on we reached a similar oasis, called 'Ain Khalif. There were no traces of inhabitants at either of these places; the dead leaves left hanging on the palms showed that they were entirely uncultivated, and at 'Ain el Agwa the trees themselves seemed to be dying.

These little places do not seem to have been previously reported, though Rohlfs' route must have passed fairly close to where they were situated. From the size of the palms they seemed to be only about twenty years old, so possibly the wells were sunk since the time of his visit.

Though the sand had to some extent encroached on the oasis at 'Ain el Agwa, it had not done so to anything like the same extent as at 'Ain Khalif, and the feeble well, discharging into a tiny pool a few yards across, was still quite clear of sand.

As the water proved to be good, we stopped here for half an hour, while we refilled the *gurba* and examined the oasis.

Shortly before sunset we reached a place where the road forked. A line of small stones had been laid across the right-hand track—a common sign among the Arabs that the road was not to be followed. Qwaytin took the left-hand branch and soon afterwards we came to the top of the descent into Bu Mungar. The path at this point was a narrow cleft, a few yards long and not more than a foot or two wide, that proved as difficult to negotiate as the very similar one leading from the 'Ain Amur plateau down towards Dakhla. Below it lay a sandy slope that extended to the bottom of the cliff and presented little difficulty.

On reaching the bottom of the slope we set out for Bu Mungar, which lay a short distance ahead of us. But on reaching the *hattia*, Qwaytin, as usual, got lost, and it was some time before we could find the well.

It had been a stiflingly hot day and we had marched for over thirteen hours, with only a short halt at 'Ain Khalif. I had done the whole distance on foot, so I was dog tired, and extremely thirsty. So, as the evening of our arrival was cloudy, and as to get in a set of observations would probably have meant that I should have had to sit up for several hours for the clouds to clear off, I put off the work until the following day, meaning to leave the place in the afternoon.

My tent was pitched on the extreme eastern end of the *hattia*. The cliff of the plateau formed a huge semicircular bay on our east, the southern point of which could be seen about twenty-five miles away to the south-east of the camp. In the middle of this bay lay a second large detached scrub-covered area.

Bu Mungar contains at least two wells, as in addition to the one near which we were camped, the men found a second one, about a quarter of a mile away to the south-west, the position of which was marked by a group of trees—acacias and palms, so far as I can remember.

The other well, that lay about two hundred yards to the north-west of the camp, seemed to be an artesian one, similar to those in the Egyptian oases. A little stream ran from it for a short distance till it lost itself in the sandy soil. So far as I was able to see the trees were larger and the vegetation more luxuriant than in the Kairowin *hattia*.

To the south, a huge area covered as far as the horizon with sand dunes was visible. A large dune overhung the camp on its eastern side, and drift sand seemed to be encroaching in many places on the vegetation. In the neighbourhood of the camp was a praying place, or "desert mosque," made according to Qwaytin after one of the Senussi models. This consisted of a line of stones laid out on the ground much in the shape of a button-hook, the straight portion of which pointed in the direction of Mecca, to indicate the direction in which worshippers should face when performing their devotions. It was the only praying place of the shape that I ever saw.

SENUSSI PRAYING PLACE, BU MUNGAR.

The wells of the *hattia* perhaps dated from Roman times, as at a short distance to the south of the camp was a small mud building (*der*) which the natives attributed to that period. The remains of the vaulted roofs and the arched tops of the openings in the walls tended to confirm this view.

I managed the next day to get the necessary astronomical observations to fix the position of the place, but was not able to make a thorough examination of it, as complications with the Senussia that, from numerous indications I had seen since leaving Assiut, I had been expecting for some time suddenly came to a rather unpleasant head.

It was not until I got to Bu Mungar that I discovered that all the men in my caravan belonged to the Senussia. Qwaytin and his three men, I knew, had always been of that persuasion, and, while in Farafra, Abd er Rahman, Ibrahim and Dahab had all been so worked upon by Sheykh Ibn ed Dris that, just before we left that oasis, they too had joined the order, and showed all the fanaticism to be expected from new converts.

A party of thirty Tibbus, sent from Kufara for my entertainment, by Sheykh Ahmed Esh Sherif, at that time head of the Senussia, were hanging round somewhere in the neighbourhood of Bu Mungar, close enough for Qwaytin to start signalling to them by firing shots at imaginary pigeons and lighting an enormous and quite unnecessary bonfire at dusk—a well-known Arab signal.

Twenty more men had been sent from Kufara to reinforce the Mawhubs at their *ezba*, in the north-west corner of Dakhla, which I should have to pass in order to enter the oasis on my way to Egypt; while the inhabitants of Farafra—the only other oasis I could fall back upon with my small caravan—were members of the order almost to a man, and were on the look out for me if I returned that way. It was explained to me that they had allowed me to go to Bu Mungar instead of to Iddaila—my original intention—in order that I should leave Egypt, and then, as I had altered my plans, no one would know "where it happened!"

It was a neat little trap that I had foolishly walked into; but it had its weak points. It was nearly dusk when Qwaytin fired his signal shots that led to my enquiries, and, better still, a howling sandstorm was blowing. If once we got out into the desert in these circumstances, I felt confident of getting away without difficulty. But the prospect of having the camp rushed before we could get off gave me such a bad attack of cold feet that I decided to start running as soon as possible in order to get them warm.

Qwaytin and his men, however, when told to do so, flatly refused to leave the *hattia*. But he and his crowd were such a feeble lot that I had little difficulty in reducing them to order. We lost so little time that I got the tanks filled and the caravan off just after sunset.

Before starting it occurred to me that I might borrow a trick from Abd er Rahman. So finding a sand-free space near the well, I scratched the Senussi *wasm* with a stick deeply into the ground, and then, to mislead the Senussi when they came as to the direction in which we had gone, drew a line from it pointing towards the west—the direction in which I knew they feared that I should go—and then set out towards the south-east to Dakhla.

Almost immediately after leaving the camp we got on to the sand hills. I then left the road, and, to Qwaytin's intense disgust, struck out into the dunes to the south, where the tearing gale that was blowing very quickly obliterated our tracks.

After marching for two and a half hours, the dunes became considerably larger, and, as the moon had set, travelling was attended with such great difficulty that we halted till daylight.

But after leaving Bu Mungar our journey to Mut began to get too much in the nature of "adventures" to be described in detail. It took me all that I had learnt, during seven seasons spent in the desert, to get my caravan into Dakhla, without creating that incident that I had been warned to avoid, and which might easily have resulted in something in the nature of a native rising.

No one in the caravan but Qwaytin had been over the road before, and he, of course, got hopelessly lost, and in any case was not reliable, so I had to take over his job and do the best I could as guide.

After leaving Bu Mungar our road for the first day lay all over the dunes. Late in the afternoon we came across three *sifs*—dunes with an A-shaped section running up and down wind—which, since they stretched across our path, gave us some difficulty. They were all under twenty feet in height, but their sides were at such a steep angle that the camels were quite unable to climb them, and the men had to scoop paths diagonally up the face of the dunes and down again on the farther side, over which the camels one by one with difficulty were forced. Small as these *sifs* were they caused a considerable delay. But these three ridges proved to be the last of the dune belt, and the remainder of our road, till we reached the dunes near Dakhla, we found to be easy going.

A long cliff runs from Bu Mungar to Dakhla Oasis, the road between the two lying at its foot.

The sand dunes that form a long north and south belt to the south of the great hill—Jebel Edmondstone—that lies some fifteen miles to the west of Qasr Dakhl, gave us considerable trouble, not only on account of their height, but because of their extreme softness. The camels sank into them in places literally up to their hocks.

In the softest parts the caravan absolutely came to a standstill, being quite unable to make any progress without assistance. I had to put one man on either side of each camel, and make them take the weight of the loads on their backs, and lift them up with every step that the camels gave, in order to get them along at all. Then having got a beast through the soft places, I had to fetch the others across, one by one, in the same manner. Our rate of progress consequently fell to something like half a mile an hour.

On the evening of the fifth day after leaving Bu Mungar we arrived in Mut, having lost some of the baggage, two men and two out of our seven camels, and with the rest of the caravan pretty well foundered from over-driving.

During the journey down from Bu Mungar, my own men, as I expected, finding that, as members of the Senussia, they had to give up smoking, gradually came round and recovered from their attack of Senussism. So, before reaching Mut, we halted out of sight of the town, and I put Abd er Rahman up on a camel and sent him in to find out how the land lay in the oasis.

He returned extremely pleased with himself. He had left his camel tied up among the dunes and had then gone into Mut "like a thief," as he expressed it, so that no one should see him and had gone to the house of a friend of his, who told him that some Tibbus had been several times into Mut, but had not been seen there recently. They had gone back to the *zawia* at Qasr Dakhl. Here, as I afterwards heard, they were seen and photographed by a native who happened to have come into the oasis from the Nile Valley. His friend thought it would be quite safe for us to come into the oasis, as when once we had been seen there, the Senussi would not dare to molest us. So we packed up our traps again and started.

On reaching Mut, I again put up in the old store. Having seen my baggage safely deposited there, I went round to the post office to get my mail.

I found Sheykh Senussi—the poetical clerk of the *qadi*—had managed to get his son appointed as postmaster in the oasis, a position that must have been of considerable use to the Senussi, on account of the thinness of the envelopes used by the natives.

Though office hours, so far as they can be said to exist in Dakhla, were long over, the door of the office itself was open, and I entered without being heard. I found the intelligence department of the Senussi in the oasis, consisting of Sheykh Senussi and his son, hard at work examining the mails. They held each letter up in turn to the light, and, if the contents were of interest, read them through the envelope. A letter lying on the top of a basin of hot water had presumably been undecipherable in this way, and so the flap of the envelope had to be steamed open. A stick of wax and a bottle of gum, lying on the counter, seemed to indicate that sometimes they experienced some difficulty in reclosing the correspondence after it had been read.

I walked quietly away from the door, and then returned clearing my throat loudly and making as much noise as I could and asked for my mail. Sheykh Senussi welcomed me most cordially. The basin of water, the gum and the sealing wax had all disappeared. The postmaster was busily engaged in sorting the letters. But I fancy that I had just seen one of the many ways in which information gets known in Egypt!

Affairs in Mut I found to be in a very queer state. A new *mamur* had arrived on the scene, who, according to reports, both drank and took *hashish* to such an extent that he had gone practically mad. He had quarrelled so violently with the police officer, his understudy, that one day he had fired three revolver shots at him, from a window in his house, as he crossed the square by the mosque. I was shown the places where the bullets had ploughed up the ground, so something of the sort had probably happened.

The *mamur*, after this exhibition, shut himself up in his house and never went out even to the *merkaz*, and declined to see anyone. The policeman was doing his feeble best to keep things going; but as he was afraid to go to the *merkaz*, which lay close to the *mamur's* house, for fear that he should be shot at again, he was somewhat handicapped in his work.

I passed once through the mosque square and caught a glimpse of the *mamur* peeping at me through the crack by the hinge of his half-opened door, but this was the only view I had of him.

He sent me, however, a roundabout message to the effect that he had seen me pass his house and he considered it an *ayb* that I had not called on him as he was the head of the Government in the oasis, and a much more important person than I was myself. He added that he expected me to do so at once. As my views as to our relative importance differed from his, I continued to *ayb* him in the same way till I left the oasis.

The day after our arrival, Qwaytin asked permission to go for the day to the village of Hindau. There was, I knew, a small Senussi *zawia* there, but it would have been useless for me to refuse him permission, so long as he was at liberty, and with the existing state of affairs in the oasis it was quite out of the question to try and get him arrested. So I thought it best to pretend I did not see what he was driving at and allowed him to go.

Later in the day I was in my room in the upper floor of the store when, rather to my surprise, I heard Qwaytin's voice in the court below talking to Dahab and Abd er Rahman. As I had not expected him back so soon, I suspected that he was up to some mischief, so had no hesitation at all in listening to the conversation, especially as I wished to know more exactly the terms on which he stood with my men.

They were immediately below my window; but Qwaytin was speaking in such a low voice that I could only catch a word here and there of what he was saying. But I caught enough of the conversation to become greatly interested.

He was apparently giving them instructions from a certain Sheykh Ahmed, whose identity I was unable to ascertain. Repeatedly I heard him mention a certain *kafir* (infidel) and once a "dog," of whose identity I entertained no doubt at all—listeners proverbially hear no good of themselves. Several times I heard him state "Sheykh Ahmed says—" something that was quite inaudible, followed by expostulations from Dahab and Abd er Rahman, and then again they were told that "Sheykh Ahmed says—" something else that the *kafir* would have given a good deal to have heard.

Eventually, I heard Qwaytin take himself off, and, shortly afterwards, Dahab, looking terribly scared, came into the room, announcing that Dakhla was a very bad place indeed, and that we must get out of it as quickly as possible.

Abd er Rahman next burst unceremoniously in and asked abruptly when I intended to start. I told him I meant to get off as soon as I possibly could. He looked immensely relieved, and said that the sooner we started the better.

I tried to find out from them exactly what was in the wind, but native-like I could not get them to be in the least explicit.

I went out and interviewed Qwaytin and told him I intended to start the next day. He grinned and refused absolutely to let me have the camels. I felt inclined to take them, but a large trading caravan with several *bedawin* had come in during the day, and these men all hung round listening to our conversation in what seemed to be anything but a friendly frame of mind, and I thought it best not to make the attempt. I sounded one or two of the traders with a view to hiring their camels, but met with a surly refusal. I might, of course, have tried to get the Government authorities in the oasis to force Qwaytin to fulfil his arrangement with me; but it does not do, in a case of this sort, for a white man to appeal to a native official for assistance, so I had to look round for some other means of continuing our journey.

After some difficulty, I succeeded in hiring three other camels that were in the oasis. Then, having arranged to leave part of my baggage, for which I had no immediate use, in safe keeping in Mut till I could send for it, I prepared to start on the following morning.

I told Abd er Rahman to send his friend out into the village to gather information as to the Senussia. During our visits to Mut, this man on several occasions made himself considerably useful to us; but fearing to appear openly as being favourable to us, he always conducted his operations in a clandestine manner.

Abd er Rahman, who was always in his element in anything in the nature of an intrigue, introduced him secretly into the store in the middle of the night, and brought him up to my room. His information was entirely satisfactory. I was unable to get out of him exactly what scheme the Senussi had devised for our benefit, but he declared that our intention to make an early departure had entirely checkmated them, and that they were furiously angry in consequence.

But the Mawhubs, he said, were extremely cunning, and as we had now got the better of them, their one desire was that the whole episode should be forgotten and that they should now appear as our best friends. He said that, if we got away quickly, we had nothing to fear from them; but he emphasised the importance of not wasting any time. I sent him off with a thumping *bakhshish*.

CHAPTER XXV

THE police officer and the Government doctor—a Moslem this time—insisted on accompanying me across the oasis. They told me they had sent a messenger to Tenida to say that we intended to stay the night there, so as to give the *'omda* time to prepare for us.

My little caravan of three camels and three men seemed extremely small after the one we had been accustomed to; but the men were in good spirits at the prospect of soon returning to their homes, and the camels were good ones and stepped out well.

As we left Smint, Sheykh Senussi, the poet from Mut, in a most excited state, rushed past us, waving his arms wildly in the air and called out to the policeman something that I could not catch.

On reaching Tenida we went to the *'omda's* house, lying a mile or two to the north of the town, where we drank the usual tea. Afterwards our host invited us to come and sit in his garden.

It was a large place covering several acres, enclosed by a wall and planted with a variety of palms and fruit trees, all looking extremely healthy. Judging from the size of the trees, they could not have been planted more than twenty years. There was a plentiful supply of water, as a small stream coming from a well, the Bir Mansura 'Abdulla, ran through the plantation with a babbling sound that was very grateful after our hot ride across the oasis. Altogether the garden was a delightfully shady place.

The *'omda* led the way, directing my attention to the different kinds of trees we passed. Behind came a crowd of officials and the leading men of the district, laughing and chaffing each other in the usual noisy manner of Egyptians. Finding a smooth level place under a palm, with the stream running close beside it, I suggested that we might sit down there; but the *'omda* declared that the best place was a little farther on, just beyond a thicket in front of us, and made way for me on the path to go in front.

The other natives suddenly all stopped talking and followed us in a most unnatural silence. I led the way, turned round the thicket—and found myself face to face with old Sheykh Mawhub!

He was sitting on a rug in the shade of a small fig tree, apparently engaged in pious meditation. It was an idyllic scene, to which a pergola covered with vines and roses that stood behind him made an effective background.

He was apparently prepared for a journey, his baggage consisting of a small sack containing only a few clothes showed that his wants were easily satisfied. A jug of water and a handful of dates, left over from his meal, showed that he had been demonstrating to the luxurious *fellahin* of the oasis, the simple life that the Senussia lived in their *zawia*—with the help of a Turkish cook.

The situation was perfectly clear. The little ramp of the Senussia having missed fire, they were desperately anxious that it should be overlooked. So the natives of the oasis, with their usual kindly instincts, had arranged this meeting in order to "make the peace." I was quite willing to fall in with their views—there was no use in raising the Senussi question.

Old Mawhub greeted me with a benevolent smile, that was almost fatherly in its friendliness. He patted the rug beside him, as an invitation to sit down, and we entered into conversation.

He expressed himself delighted to see me; but I noticed that he omitted the formality usually made to one returning from a journey, and did not praise Allah for my safety. He made no reference at all to my having been in the desert, beyond saying that his son, Sheykh Ahmed, was very angry, very angry indeed, that I had passed so close to his *ezba* without partaking of his hospitality. I felt quite sure of his anger, but I rather doubted the cause of it.

Mawhub explained that he was on his way to Cairo to "sell some horses" he had with him. The fact that one of his rare visits to the Nile Valley happened once more to coincide with my return to civilisation after a bother in the Senussi country, was not one that I overlooked. I concluded that he would break his journey to Cairo at Assiut, so as to see Qwaytin through any complications that might arise in the *mudiria*—he did.

After ten minutes' conversation, during which we both carefully avoided dangerous topics, his youngest son, 'Abd el Wahad, who was travelling with him, acting as a most attentive and devoted servant, intimated to me, in a whisper, that his father was tired, and as he was an old man and had a long journey before him on the morrow, wanted to sleep. So I took leave of him and we returned to the *'omda's* house, where a meal was served, after which I rode back to the camp for the night.

Shortly after dawn the next day, Mawhub's caravan—a most wretched-looking collection, consisting of a couple of camels and a miserable horse, passed our camp in charge of two dejected-looking blacks. A few minutes afterwards old Mawhub himself rode up with his son, mounted on two sorry looking screws, that were apparently the horses he was taking into Cairo for sale.

They dismounted on reaching the camp, and the old sheykh suggested, as we were both of us travelling to Kharga, that we should join forces and make the journey together. He was an interesting old fellow, and I felt rather tempted to do so. But though I was ready to let bygones be bygones to a certain extent, I was not prepared to go to this length, so finding that he was intending to travel by the lower or Gubary road, I decided to take the route across the plateau via 'Ain Amur. Mawhub, apparently much disappointed, jumped up again in his saddle with a nimbleness surprising in a man of his age, and rode off wishing me most cordially *tarik es salaama* (safe road, i.e. journey).

We kept a careful look-out at night and took no risks during our remaining time in the desert, but our precautions were probably quite unnecessary. Our journey to Kharga was entirely uneventful.

Here we found great changes. The English company that had been endeavouring to make the desert blossom like a rose, had only succeeded in gathering the thorns. A shortage in the water supply, leading to interference between the wells, the saline character of the ground, the drifting sand and tearing sandstorms had proved to be too much for them. The company was practically in liquidation. The European staff had mostly gone and taken up work elsewhere. Only one member of it remained, and he was busy in the final preparations necessary before leaving the place in the charge of a native. Finding himself thrown out of a job, he was looking round for a new one, and was hoping to have the old office of Inspector of the Oases revived in his favour—I found myself regarded, in consequence, with a somewhat jaundiced eye as being a possible rival.

He need, however, have had no anxiety on that account. One can put in a fairly interesting time in mapping the unknown parts of the desert, collecting weeds that no one wants, studying the natives' habits and peculiarities, listening to their stories of buried treasure, and enchanted cities, and in chasing will-o'-the-wisp oases round and round the desert; but to settle down in these wretched oases for the term of my natural life, to seeing that the native officials did not extort more than a reasonable amount of *bakhshish* from the wretched *fellahin* under their charge, and to settling disputes as to oranges that fall on the wrong side of a wall, was not one that greatly appealed to me.

The night's rest that I got in Kharga was most welcome; there had not been a night since leaving Qasr Farafra, a fortnight before, when I had been able to get more than a very limited amount of sleep.

A sleeping man is so utterly defenceless that I had been put to great shifts to get any rest at all on the five days' journey from Bu Mungar to Dakhla. It was not till we got to Mut that I felt I could trust my men enough to risk being caught by them asleep. Even while inhabiting the old store, Dahab and I took it in turns to keep watch during the night.

I awoke the next morning feeling more alive than I had done for some time, and in the train I continued my night's rest at intervals during the journey.

On reaching Qara, the base of the railway on the edge of the Nile Valley, the train stayed for some minutes and I got out and walked along the platform. I found that I had been a fellow-passenger on the train with old Sheykh Mawhub. The train was packed with natives, but the compartment which he and his son occupied had been left entirely to them.

They were an unobtrusive looking couple. The old man sat huddled up in the far corner of the third-class carriage, on an old rusty looking sheepskin with a *gula* (water bottle) and a handful of dates beside him on the wooden seat. Both he and his son were almost shabbily dressed as ordinary *bedawin*—his "glad rags" being probably contained in the patched and dilapidated *hurj* he carried with him. No one unacquainted with his identity would have troubled to look at him a second time. But for all that he was a man who probably had as much influence among the Mohammedans in Egypt as any other native.

He was still travelling in his character of a horse dealer, and sold one of his screws to the engineer in charge of the line for £5—it looked a stiff price.

Shortly afterwards, Abdulla Kahal, an old thief of a carpet merchant, living up in the native quarter of Cairo, who acted as head sheykh of the Senussia in Egypt, was removed by them from his office and Sheykh Mawhub was appointed in his place. If there were any emoluments attached to the job, I have sometimes wondered if I could not have made out a claim to some sort of commission on them.

I stopped a few nights with a hospitable friend, on the way to Assiut, to allow Qwaytin time to get through from Dakhla. As I slept most of the time, I must have been a remarkably dull guest. I then went on to Assiut to have it out with my guide.

Having arranged that matter fairly satisfactorily, I took the train for Cairo, left the "romantic desert" to look after itself, and exchanged the heated atmosphere of the "Arabian Nights" for the saner one of Europe.

. . . .

The following are the main results of my visits to the Libyan Desert:

1. A map of practically the whole desert was compiled from information collected from natives. This contained the names of about seventy new places, not shown on any previous maps. It also showed the distribution of the sand dunes and many unknown hill features.[5]

2. The farthest point that was reached to the south-west of Dakhla was practically the centre of the desert. This journey showed that the pre-existing ideas of this district were entirely wrong, and that the hundreds of thousands of square miles, shown in this part on the old maps as being covered with

gigantic dunes, were in reality practically free from drift sand, and that the large dune-field lying to the west of the Egyptian frontier, that Rohlfs had found such an impassable obstruction, came to an end about a day's march to the south of his route, the sand being all banked up by the high sandstone plateau that we found occupying the centre of the desert.[6]

3. The position of Bu Mungar *hattia* was astronomically fixed, and the cliff running from there to Dakhla was mapped for the first time.[7]

4. The cliff forming the eastern boundary of the Farafra depression was mapped, thus showing that the escarpment of the east and north of Kharga is a continuation of the cliff that runs west from Iddaila Oasis, the whole escarpment—except for a narrow break to the north of Farafra—is consequently continuous and runs for some 450 miles. It forms the southern limit of the limestone plateau, and is the main hill feature of this part of the desert.[7]

5. Two small new oases—'Ain el Agwa and 'Ain Khalif—were found in the western portion of the Farafra depression. The site of Bu Gerara was also discovered, and most of the isolated little plateau that lies on its south-west was mapped.[8]

6. A survey of the desert to the north of 'Ain Amur showed that the plateau there was riddled with a curious network of little depressions.[9]

7. Several months were spent in studying the sand dunes and their method of formation.[10]

8. A considerable amount of material was collected on the manners, customs, legends, measurements and superstitions of the natives.[11]

9. Notes were also made upon their methods of well sinking, and dividing the flow from the wells.[12]

10. Over 240 characters and inscriptions of the "Libyan" type were found and copied.

11. A number of plants growing in the desert and oases were collected and their geographical distribution worked out.[13]

12. A zoological collection, mainly of insects, was also made.

CHAPTER XXVI

CUSTOMS, SUPERSTITIONS AND MAGIC

THE natives of the oases in Egypt are known as the Wahatys, and are a feeble lot as compared with the inhabitants of the Nile Valley, with whom they seem racially to be intimately connected. This deterioration in the race is probably due to their poverty, insufficient food, poorer housing accommodation and to the prevalence of the serious form of malaria known as oasis fever.

In their customs the inhabitants of the oases closely resemble the natives of the Nile Valley; but in some respects they are peculiar. Until the railway into Kharga was constructed, the oases were very much more cut off from the outside world than at present. Consequently the inhabitants are in many ways much more primitive than the *fellahin* of the Nile Valley, and still follow customs which in some cases may have been followed there, but which have long since become obsolete. Many of their peculiarities in this respect are probably confined to the oases, and may never have existed elsewhere.

As an example of the primitive conditions of life in Kharga, it may be noted that the old method of producing fire by rubbing two pieces of wood together is still used by some of the older inhabitants, though the introduction of matches is causing it to die out. Fire is produced in this way by two methods. In one, a stick is held vertically upon a block of wood and rapidly twirled between the palms of the hands; in the other it is rubbed backwards and forwards in a groove on the block with the action of a carpenter sharpening a chisel on a hone. In both cases a pinch of fine sand is sometimes placed between the two pieces of wood in order to increase the friction.

Marriage Procession in Dakhla Oasis.

Note the clown and band in front, the bride's friends firing guns and carrying flags, her tea things and her wedding dress on a cross above the procession behind. She herself wears old clothes. (p. 252)

Vegetation in Hattia Kairowin.

This shows the neglected palms and scrub to be seen in a *Hattia*, or uninhabited oasis. (p. 222).

Auguries as to the future of a child are drawn by his parents from events that happen about the time of his birth; thus, if his father, or any member of his family should meet with an accident, or fall ill at that period, it is considered that he will be unlucky. If, however, some stroke of luck should fall to his father, such, for instance, as his being able to conclude a good bargain, it is thought to be a good omen for the child's future.

It is said to be unlucky to be born on a Wednesday, for this day of the week throughout the year is considered to be an ill-omened one in the oases—the last Wednesday of the month of Safar being considered to be the most unlucky of all.

As soon as a son has been born, in either Dakhla or Kharga Oases, a little ceremony takes place, which cannot be described here, but which is intended to cause the child when he grows up to become a very fast runner. In both these oases, a very curious ceremony takes place on the seventh day after his birth, which is known as "sieving the baby." A pinch of salt and a small quantity of each of the grains—wheat, barley and rice—grown in the oases, is placed in a round sieve. In this sieve, too, is placed the baby. It is then shaken, as though it were being used in the ordinary way, while a woman close by beats as loudly as possible with a pestle on a mortar, as though she were pounding rice.

The grain and salt that pass through the sieve are then carefully collected and taken by the father of the child and thrown into the air to the north, south, east and west in various places throughout his village. The ceremony is completed by the father taking the sieve and bowling it like a hoop along the village streets.

The effect of this quaint proceeding is said to be as follows: the grain and salt put into the sieve with the child are supposed to protect him against want and cause him to have plenty to eat throughout his life. The pestle and mortar are beaten close to him to ensure that he will not be frightened by any noise when he grows up. The seed is thrown to the four points of the compass in his village to act as a charm to enable him to travel in security in any direction should he leave it. The bowling of the sieve about the streets is another charm intended to make him a fast runner.

These elaborate precautions, taken to ensure that the child shall be able to travel safely, and that he shall turn out a fast runner, seem quite out of character with such an eminently unathletic and sedentary race as the dwellers in the oases. They seem to be more in accordance with the character of the

Arabs, from whom it is possible that these ceremonies may be derived, or perhaps they may owe their origin to some tribe in the Sudan. This sieving ceremony is said to be also occasionally performed in the Nile Valley.

The first cutting of a child's hair and finger-nails is attended with some ceremony, and takes place when it is a year old. In the case of a boy, a tuft of hair is left long on his forehead, to remind his parents that they should be grateful to Allah for giving them a son—a male child being always considered of much greater value than a girl.

As it is for some reason considered to be unlucky to open a pair of scissors before a child's face—perhaps for fear of accidents—its nails are always first cut with its hand behind its back; more usually, however, they are bitten off short by its parents. The ends of the fingers are then dipped into newly ground flour to "prevent them from growing again."

If a child is regarded as being unusually handsome or well conditioned, so that the mother fears it may incur the evil eye of other matrons less favoured in their progeny, a black cross as a protection is smeared on its forehead, if it is its face that is likely to be envied; or on the back of its hand if it should be its plumpness that it is feared will cause heart burnings. This custom is most probably derived from the Copts.

The fear of the evil eye is widely distributed, especially in the East, and in the oases many precautions are taken to guard against it. To ensure a good crop on a palm, for instance, an animal's bone—frequently a skull—or a piece of manure, wrapped up in a cloth, is hung in its branches, and sometimes small doll-like figures are used in the same way. Charms, in the form of texts, or cabalistic signs, written either by a religious sheykh, or by certain men who are supposed to have a special gift in this direction, are sometimes done up in a little packet, made generally of leather, and hung round the neck of a child or valuable beast as a protection from the evil eye; but they are not very much in request.

They have also a charm that they recite before lying down to sleep, or sitting down in a place they suspect to be infested with scorpions or other poisonous creatures. Having recited it they spit to the north, south, east and west, and then consider themselves to be safe from attack. I attempted to get a copy of the spell that was given to me translated, but was unable to find anyone who could do so. It appears to be merely gibberish.

Boys in the oases are usually circumcised between the ages of three to five years—the parents, if poor, wait till they have saved enough to make the necessary feast; they also, if possible, endeavour to make the circumcision coincide with a marriage in their village, in order that expense may be saved to both parties by combining the marriage and circumcision processions. The richer families for the circumcision feast will kill a sheep, or even a cow, but with the poorer classes a very much simpler meal suffices.

Girls are married at an extremely early age—sometimes when only eight years old. But in these cases the wife probably merely acts at first as an attendant upon her husband. When between twelve or fourteen years old, however, they begin to have children, ceasing to do so between forty and forty-five.

Divorce is extremely common. I was shown a young girl in Dakhla, whose age I was told was only twelve—she did not look to be more—who had already been divorced three times. The state of morality in these oases is very low indeed, and this, combined with the very early marriages, probably has a good deal to say to the feeble character of the inhabitants.

Marriages are celebrated with great pomp—especially in the case of the richer inhabitants—and their ceremonies differ in some noticeable points from those in the Nile Valley.

Mahr, or dowry, is paid by the man to the bride's family in all but the case of the very poor. This preliminary having been settled, the ceremony of the *katb el kitab*, or "writing of the writ," is gone through, though, as in the case of the Nile Valley, it is seldom that any written contract of marriage is drawn up. The bridegroom, accompanied by a friend or two, goes to the house of his intended bride, where he meets her representative, to whom he pays over the portion of the dowry agreed upon. Everyone recites the *fatha*, or first chapter of the Koran—from which proceeding the ceremony is often alluded to as the "saying of the *fatha*"—and then the bridegroom and the representative of the bride squat facing each other on the ground, and, prompted usually by a religious sheykh, take hold of each other's hand and swear the marriage contract.

About a week later, the *Zeffet el Arusa*, the procession of the bride to the bridegroom's house, takes place shortly after noon. A procession of this kind that I saw in Dakhla Oasis, was headed by a *sutary*, or jester, who had tied the end of the long leaf of a palm to his waist in front and then passed the other end through his legs and up his back, so that it had very much the appearance of a bushy tail. He carried a staff in each hand, and hopped about on these in a most grotesque manner.

Behind him followed a man beating a drum of the kind known in Egypt as the *tabl beladi*, beside him walked a blind man clashing cymbals (*kas*). Then followed a crowd of the friends and relations of the bride.

The bride herself, unlike those of the Nile Valley, does not wear her wedding dress. This is borne behind her, held above the heads of the procession so that all can see it, by being supported on a couple of sticks lashed together to form a cross. She herself wears an ordinary robe, and a shawl, usually red or of a bright colour, on her head.

The gala dress worn by the women of these oases differs somewhat from that usually worn by the women of Egypt. It is generally either black or of a very dark blue, and is worked on the front in coloured wools—usually red and yellow—in a sort of "herring-bone" pattern. The richer women usually cover a great part of the front of their dress, down to rather below the waist, with silvered sequins sewn closely together on to the material of which the dress is composed, producing an effect much resembling old scale mail.

Their hair usually hangs down their backs in three or four long plaits, which are frequently decorated at the end with strings of beads.

Another peculiarity of the wedding ceremonies in the oases, is that the bride's *gahaz*, that is to say the articles contributed by her to the joint household, are not, as in the case of the Egyptians, sent to her future home in a separate procession, but are borne in the *Zeffet el Arusa*. In the case of a rich bride these may consist of tea and coffee cups, a huge kind of brass urn, not unlike the Russian samovar, for heating water when making tea, and a brass tray. These will be carried by one of her male friends on the tray in the procession.

But in the majority of cases, amongst these poverty-stricken people, the bride's *gahaz* only consists of a few bowls and water bottles, made of the local terra-cotta, and in that case they are carried on a stool, which the bride herself places on the top of her head when she walks in the procession, to her future husband's house. This stool perhaps corresponds to the canopy under which the bride walks in the Egyptian villages, or possibly it may be the representation of the chair for the bridegroom to place his turban on, that Lane mentions as usually forming one of the articles of the bride's *gahaz*.

Two large flags, generally green in colour and covered with suitable texts, are usually carried in the procession, which also includes some male relations of the bride armed with guns, which they blaze off at frequent intervals as it advances. At the rear of the *zaffeh* is frequently a man beating a *tar*, or tambourine, and a boy dressed all in white and riding on a horse, who has been introduced into the *zaffeh* to save the expense of a separate circumcision procession for him alone.

The *zaffeh* is followed by a feast at the bridegroom's house, after which the guests all offer presents, usually in the form of money, to the bride. During this entertainment there is the usual native band playing and sometimes a dancing girl performs—but this is only in the case of the richer natives. Among the poorer ones, that is to say a large majority of cases, there is no music or dancing, and sometimes even no feast or presents.

The funeral procession to the grave presents some features not to be seen, so far as I am aware, in the Nile Valley. While I was staying in the Dakhla Oasis, quite a sensation was caused by the death of the guardian of a sheykh's tomb in the district, and I subsequently saw his funeral procession, which much resembled that of a bride going to her future home. The *buffoon* at the head of it was of course absent, but instead of the usual group of chanting men to be seen in Egypt, there were the same men as in the case of a wedding, beating drums and cymbals. These were followed by male friends of the deceased, and the same flags that figured in the bride's procession. Behind them came the bier, covered with a shawl, after which followed the usual crowd of wailing women, the rear being brought up by a woman carrying a tray covered by a cloth, containing bread and dates for distribution to the poor after the ceremony.

After the funeral, the female portion of the procession, accompanied by the drum and cymbals, formed up again and returned to the house of the deceased guardian in a sort of slow dance, occasionally emitting short, shrill shrieks of the usual type.

In the evening the funeral feast and what is known as a *khatma* is held at the deceased's house, when one or more *fikis*—holy men of a humble kind, frequently the village schoolmasters—chant from the Koran the sixty-seventh chapter known as the *Surat el Mulk* (the chapter of the kingdom) which deals largely with the punishments that await unbelievers when they get to hell. Food is usually provided for all present. That carried in the procession is distributed at the grave.

The night following the funeral is usually called by Mohammedans the *Leylet el Wahsha*, or night of desolation, though it is also sometimes known as the *Leylet el Wahada*, or "night of solitude," because Moslems believe that the soul remains with the body during this first night after burial.

The female relations of the deceased go to visit the grave daily in the oasis for fifteen days, and longer if he was much beloved.

The grave, I have heard—I have not looked into one—is of the usual Moslem pattern, with the *lahd*, or recess at the side of the bottom, in which the body is laid. They are so oriented that the corpse, when lying on its side, faces towards Mecca. The recess is walled up before the grave is filled in.

Mohammedans believe that as soon as the mourners have left the cemetery, the grave is visited by two coal-black angels with china blue eyes, called *Munkar* (the "Unknown") and *Nakir* (the "Repudiating") whose business it is to question the dead man as to his belief in Mohammed and Allah, and if necessary to inflict upon him the "punishment of the grave." One of them seizes him by the tuft of hair that most Moslems have on the top of the head, and raises him into a sitting position, while the other puts the questions. Should his answers prove satisfactory the grave is greatly enlarged and filled with light, and the defunct is thrown into a deep sleep that lasts until the Resurrection. But if the corpse proves to be that of an infidel, he is beaten to a jelly with an iron club.

In view of the visit of these two angels, it is usual, before the burial party leaves the grave, for a *fiki* (holy man) to seat himself before it, and proceed to instruct the corpse as to the answers he is to give when they come.

The funeral processions I saw in the oases seemed to have little of the solemnity associated with a European interment. That of the guardian of the tomb already referred to—although the corpse was that of a man who might have been supposed from his occupation to have been somewhat of a saintly character—on seeing me standing by with a camera, hesitating to take a photograph for fear of intruding on such a solemn occasion, of their own accord came in my direction, and one of them volunteered the information that I could photograph them if I wished to do so. Unfortunately the light was too bad to enable me to avail myself of the invitation.

It is curious to note that in Dakhla Oasis—though this is not so apparently in Kharga—both funeral and circumcision feasts are sometimes held at the tombs of the local religious sheykhs.

The methods of celebrating some of the religious festivals differ slightly in the oases from the usages of the Nile Valley. The tenth day of Moharrem, the first month of the Moslem's year, is the anniversary of several important events in their religion, and is kept as a fête throughout Egypt; it is known as *Yum Ashura* "the tenth day."

It is said to be the anniversary of the day on which Noah first issued from the ark after the flood; and Adam and Eve—who, according to the Moslems, somehow lost sight of each other on their expulsion from the Garden of Eden—are said to have met again for the first time afterwards on this day. Some say that this is the day upon which Allah created them, and also that heaven, hell, life and death, the pen with which Allah wrote down the predestined actions of all mankind, and the exact number of all things that were to be ever created and the tablet upon which they were all recorded, were all created on this day. But more especially it is the anniversary of the day upon which El Hussein, the son of 'Ali, and the prophet's grandson, was killed in the Battle of Karbala.

On this last account it is held of much greater sanctity by the Shia branch of Mohammedans, to be found in Persia and India, than by the Sunni branch, to which nearly all Egyptian Moslems belong.

In both Dakhla and Kharga Oases it is customary on this day for everyone to receive a present as on our Christmas Day. A boy is given a chicken, a girl a pigeon, a man a cock turkey, duck or other large bird, while a woman receives a hen bird of the same species. All the eggs in the village are saved up for this feast, and for a week or so before it is almost impossible to buy any. These eggs are hard-boiled and dyed, and are used by the people to pelt each other with—this, I believe, is also done in some parts of the Nile Valley, but not on the occasion of this feast, but on that of *Shem en Nessim*. A sort of game is also played by the men in the oases, who knock their eggs together, the one that breaks first being taken by the owner of the egg that broke it.

"Pace" eggs are used in Cumberland at Easter in a game exactly similar to that described. "Pace" being supposed to be a corruption of the French "Pasque."

In these oases they believe, as the inhabitants of the Nile Valley also do, that on the night following this festival a benevolent *jinni* (female spirit, or fairy) wanders sometimes round the villages, in the form of a mule, known as the Baghallat el Ashar, or "mule of the tenth," bearing a pair of saddle-bags filled with treasure to be bestowed upon some deserving Moslem. In order that the mule may have every opportunity of selecting its inmates as the recipients of its bounty, the door of every house in the village is left open during the night.

In the Nile Valley they believe that the mule has a string of bells round her neck, and the head of a dead man on her back between the saddle-bags, and that on arriving at the house of the fortunate individual whom she intends to enrich, she shakes her head, so ringing the bells, at the door, and remains there until the owner comes out and empties the saddle-bags and fills them up with straw. This, however, he will be unable to do, unless he can muster up sufficient courage to remove the dead man's head from her back, a proceeding made somewhat formidable by the fact that the head rolls its eyes and scowls at him in what, I was told, was a most terrifying manner. I could not, however, hear that this belief holds good in the oases.

At the beginning of summer comes the *Khamasin*—the "fifty days," during which the hot *simum* wind may be expected to blow. The first day of this is known as *Shem en Nessim*—"smelling the breeze." It is the day after the Easter Sunday of the Coptic Church, and is kept as a festival throughout Egypt.

On this day in the oases, barley from the new crop is hung over the outer doors of the houses to bring plenty in the following year. Onions too—which overnight have been placed under the pillows of the inhabitants of the house—"to make them energetic"—are hung with the barley in order that they may "bring refreshment" to the family till next season. The onions grown in the oases appear to be unusually pungent, and I have several times seen a native "refresh" himself by stuffing a small one up one of his nostrils. Perhaps inhaling air through one of these odoriferous bulbs in this manner produces a cooling sensation on the air passages similar to that caused by peppermint.

In some cases branches of the *oshar*[14] tree are placed with the barley and onions over the door in order to keep off scorpions, reptiles and venomous insects, and to prevent the family from being lazy. This use of *oshar* I believe to be peculiar to Dakhla and Kharga Oases.

It is also usual on this day for the natives to bathe before dawn in order that they may be "refreshed," till the following year—when presumably they take their next bath. This custom I have heard also obtains in the Nile Valley.

The *oshar* tree, when cut, exudes sap freely, and this sap is occasionally inserted by men, who wish to avoid enlistment, into their eyes. It is said to set up violent inflammation for a few days, resulting in more or less total loss of sight. Fibre from the dried fruit of this tree is also used to stuff pillows with; but I was unable to ascertain whether it was supposed to have any peculiar properties.

The most interesting festival to be seen in Kharga, which is not, I believe, held in Dakhla, is the *Aid el Mahmal*, or fête of the *Mahmal*, which takes place on the 15th day of the Arab month, *Sha'aban*. This day is a religious anniversary in the Nile Valley, the night being known as "the night of the middle of *Sha'aban*."

It is believed that there is a lote tree in Paradise known as the "Tree of Extremity," which bears as many leaves as there are human beings living in the world, and that each leaf has the name of the being it represents written upon it. On the night of the middle of *Sha'aban* this tree is shaken and the leaves inscribed with the names of those who are going to die during the year fall off. Many pious Moslems accordingly spend a great part of the night reciting a special form of prayer in the Mosque. But, so far as I know, no other ceremonial takes place in the Nile Valley on this day, so although the date is identical with that of the *Aid el Mahmal* of Kharga Oasis, there does not appear to be any connection between them.

Nor does this Kharga festival appear to be in any way connected with the *Mahmal*, whose annual departure from Cairo for the pilgrimage to Mecca is such a well-known sight for the tourists in Egypt. The Kharga *Mahmal* in appearance much resembles the Cairo one, but its red and green covering is not so gorgeous. It is carried in procession round the village of Kharga, accompanied by the usual crowd bearing flags, beating drums, banging off guns and carrying on the *fantasia* usual to ceremonial processions.

Instead of being merely an empty litter, as in the case of the Cairo *Mahmal*, a man sits in it, who collects *bakhshish* from the inhabitants of the village. Each gives him a handful or two of dates, grain or the produce of some other crop of the neighbourhood. This *bakhshish* he keeps as a perquisite.

I was unable to find out the origin of the custom. The Kharga natives claim that their *Mahmal* is a much older institution than the Cairo one, which they say was copied from theirs. They say it dates back to the time of the Fatimide dynasty, who ruled over Egypt from A.D. 908 to A.D. 1171, while the Cairo *Mahmal* is only supposed to date from about A.D. 1265. The privilege of riding in the Kharga *Mahmal* is hereditary; the family enjoying the right to do so being described to me as a family of *fikis*.

When I was in Kharga, the representative of the family was the village schoolmaster—Khalifa Zenata by name—and may possibly be the descendant of some petty sultan who ruled over the oasis, or perhaps of some holy sheykh.

In the latter case possibly the *Aid el Mahmal* is a form of *mulid*, or anniversary birthday fête; but I could hear of no other *mulids* for any of the local sheykhs in either Kharga or Dakhla. *Mahmals*, however, are used at a few places in the Nile Valley for carrying a carpet to the tomb of a deceased sheykh on his *mulid*.

The *Mahmal* that is taken on a camel from Egypt on the pilgrimage to Mecca, consists of a square box-like structure, about five feet square, surmounted by a pyramidal top, and is covered all over with richly embroidered black brocade. It is quite empty, being merely an emblem of royalty.

It has an interesting history. The Sultan, Es Saleh Nejm ed Din, owned a lovely female Turkish slave—Shagher ed Durr—who eventually became his favourite wife. When his last son died, the dynasty of the house of Aiyub, of which he was the last representative, came to an end. Shagher ed Durr then managed somehow to get herself acknowledged as Queen of Egypt; and in that capacity performed the pilgrimage to Mecca, borne on a camel back in a gorgeous covered litter. During the remainder of her reign, she sent this litter empty on the pilgrimage, as an emblem of her sovereignty. This custom of sending an empty litter with the pilgrims to Mecca has been kept up by the rulers of Egypt ever since.

A native doctor in Mut kindly supplied me with the following particulars. During the three years he was in the oasis, 1906-1908, there were 110 male children born in Mut and 106 female, the males consequently being in the proportion of 100 to 96.36 females. In the same period there were 76 male deaths to 70 female, the male deaths being in the proportion of 100 to 92.1 females.

The women appear to be very careless mothers, leaving the children very much to look after themselves. It is noticeable that swing cradles, such as are to be seen in some other parts of North Africa, are quite unheard of in Dakhla Oasis.

Crime, in its more serious forms, is very rare indeed. The chief misdemeanours are petty thefts of food, the result probably of extreme poverty. Squabbles about the irrigation water sometimes lead to assaults, but weapons are scarcely ever used. Illegitimate children are very numerous and are occasionally destroyed. A very large percentage of the women are immoral, but this, as a rule, is taken as a matter of course, and little jealousy results in consequence.

Albinos, epilepsy and deafness were said by one doctor to be unknown; but the man who followed him in office knew of one case of epilepsy at Qasr Dakhl.

There were one or two cases of insanity known in the oasis, and one instance of St. Vitus' dance, in the case of a partial idiot.

There were said to be four or five cases of dumbness among the population of Mut.

There was only one case of phthisis—a man who had been for some time in the Nile Valley, but who had fallen ill on his return to Dakhla.

The commonest complaints were malaria, chronic bronchitis and emphysema, the last two being largely due, according to the native doctor, to weakness of the lungs caused by smoking *hashish* and in some cases opium. Bronchitis and bronchial pneumonia were also among the commonest complaints among children. Venereal cases, considering the character of the population, were extremely rare, the natives apparently being almost immune from them. Digestive troubles were extremely common, and were largely due to the extremely strong tea they consume at every opportunity.

As might be expected with such a primitive race as the natives of these oases, the remedies used in case of disease are sometimes rather curious. If a man, for instance, has an attack of fever, one of his friends will sometimes invite him to come for a walk, during the course of which he will lure him unsuspectingly to a pool of water and suddenly push him in. It is said that the nervous shock, combined with the sudden immersion in cold water, not infrequently effects a cure—but it sounds a drastic remedy.

Ophthalmia—a rather common complaint in these "islands of the blest"—due probably to dirt and the irritation to the eyes caused by the dust during the frequent sand storms, is treated by poultices formed of onions and salt, or of raw tomatoes; occasionally, too, a vegetable called *borselain*, that I was unable to identify, is used pounded in the same way.

A plant called khobbayza[15] is sometimes pounded and applied as a poultice to a sting of a scorpion in Dakhla, and is said to give considerable relief. It is interesting to note that in the oases they say that the sting of a "thirsty" scorpion, i.e. one that lives far from water, is much more likely to prove fatal than the sting of one living near a well. It is possible that this may point to the existence of two different varieties.

The families in the oases are usually large, seven to eight children being, I was told, about the average. A childless woman, as is usual throughout the East, is much looked down on by her more fortunate sisters, and many expedients and charms are in use in order to remove the disgrace. It is only possible to mention one of them. Near Mut in Dakhla Oasis is a well, known as 'Ain el Masim, which runs into a small pool. A childless woman will repair there on Friday afternoon, taking with her a *gula*—earthenware bottle used for cooling drinking water—filled with water taken from seven different wells. She throws small pieces of bread, grain, etc., into the pool and then bathes in it. On her emerging from her bath, a second woman, who accompanies her, smashes the *gula* over her head. This is said to be a sovereign remedy.

Women also sometimes go to a disused cemetery to pray for children, or to a tomb of one of the local sheykhs and vow *bakhshish* to the sheykh in the event of their prayers taking effect.

During five visits to the western oasis, I never remember to have seen a single case of baldness. Perhaps this is due to the frequent shaving of the head having a strengthening effect upon the hair. But cases of premature greyness due perhaps to dirt and the excessive dryness and heat of the climate, seemed to be unusually common. It is possible that these may be racial characteristics.

There are some curious superstitions about the sand dunes in the oases. In both Kharga and Dakhla they say that there were no sand belts in the oases in Roman times, but that they have come down since from the north. In this they are probably correct, for remains—apparently of Roman origin—are to be seen in several places underneath the dune belt to the west of Kharga. A native, too, told me that he had once ridden for a long half-day on a *hagin* (riding camel) to the west from Dakhla Oasis, when, after passing extensive ruins among the dunes at several places on the way, he found some rock-cut tombs. I have heard reports of ruins in this direction from several people, and, though the size of them may have been exaggerated, have little doubt that they exist.

On the plateau to the north of Qasr Dakhl, there is said to be a place where the sand gives out a loud "bur-r-r-r-"ing sound when stroked, which can be heard for a long distance to the south. I have also heard that it gives out a musical sound when struck, so apparently it is a case of the ordinary "musical sands" that have been found in many parts of the world.

It is said that there used to be a Roman *tulsim* (talisman) here that stopped the dunes from entering the Dakhla depression. The talisman in question may very possibly have been a wall, intended to stop the drifting of the sand, as remains of one, built of unmortared stone, are said to be still visible here.

In Kharga Oasis they say that the Romans had another talisman in the shape of a brass cow on the top of the scarp to the north of the depression that—until it was removed—swallowed up all the sand that was blowing into the oasis and kept the Kharga depression free from dunes.

In the neighbourhood of the village of Rashida in Dakhla Oasis, there is a large dead tree—a *sunt*, or acacia, apparently—which is known as the "tree of Sheykh Adam," and is supposed to possess a soul. The wood is reported to be uninflammable.

There is another *sunt* tree in Dakhla that has curious attributes attached to it, and possibly the superstitious views of the natives with regard to these trees may be a relic of some very old form of tree worship, such as exists at the present day, I believe, among the Bedayat of the south of the Libyan Desert.

This second tree is at Belat, and is known as the "Sunt 'Abd en Nebi." When a man in the oasis hears that an enemy of his has died, he exclaims "*Kabrit wa Sunt el Belat*"—"a match and the acacia of Belat"—meaning that he wishes he had a match and the *sunt* tree of Belat to burn him with. Sometimes he will also say "*Wa Jerid el Wa*"—"and the palm leaves of the oasis"—meaning that he would like to add them to the fuel as well.

The agricultural appliances used in the oasis are naturally of a very primitive character. The whole of the cultivation, so far as I saw, was done with the ordinary *fas*, or hoe, to be met with in the Nile Valley. In reaping and pruning a curious toothed sickle is used. The actual blade is pointed and almost at right angles to the iron shaft, the end of which is inserted into a wooden handle. Ploughs are, so far as I saw, never used.

FLOUR MILL, RASHIDA.

At Rashida I was shown a flour mill belonging to the *'omda* which was of a rather interesting type. The two stones between which the grain was ground were of unequal size—the upper one being considerably smaller than the lower. The bottom stone was hollowed out, and the upper one, rotated by an ox walking round and round in a circle, revolved in the recess in the lower stone, which was fixed in the ground. Suspended over the millstones, by a four-legged wooden frame, was a box in which the grain to be ground was poured, a tube from the bottom of the box delivering the grain to the junction between the upper and lower millstones. The flour was drawn off through a hole in the lower stone into a basket placed in a cutting in the ground in which this stone was embedded.

A large part of the grain consumed in the oases is not ground in a mill, but prepared by the women in a much more primitive manner—this is especially the case with rice, which is largely consumed by the poorest inhabitants. Basin-shaped hollows, about a foot in diameter, are roughly scooped in the rock, frequently by the roadside, the grain is placed in these and pounded to powder by means of a large stone wielded with both hands.

Rashida is one of the few villages in the oasis which grows any number of olives. These are cultivated in sufficient quantities to warrant the erection of appliances for extracting the oil.

The olives are first crushed in a mill, a somewhat primitive arrangement consisting of an enormous stone wheel, about five feet in diameter, by eighteen inches thick, which is made to travel on its edge round and round a circular trough about six feet in diameter, by a man pushing against a beam, revolving the vertical pivot to which it is attached.

The mass of crushed olives when taken out of the trough is placed in a bag and squeezed under a screw press, also worked by a man pushing a bar on the principle of a capstan, the oil as it oozes out being collected in earthenware pans, or rather basins, placed below the press.

Butter is made by shaking the cream in a skin bag. A stick about ten feet long with a fork at the top is leant against a wall, and a goat-skin full of cream suspended by a rope from the fork. This is swung to and fro with a jerky motion until the butter has formed.

Unlike the natives of Dakhla and Kharga, who have no pretensions to a sporting character, those of Farafra Oasis are keen hunters. While in that oasis I saw several most ingenious appliances for catching game.

The most interesting of these was a trap for catching gazelle. It consisted of a basketwork funnel, open at top and bottom. This was 7 inches long, 5½ in diameter at the top, tapering down to 2½ inches at the bottom. The trap is set at the foot of a bush where the gazelle are accustomed to feed. A hole is first excavated in the ground, and the funnel buried in this with the large end flush with the surface of the soil.

OLIVE MILL, RASHIDA.

Into its open end is fitted an arrangement like a hubless wheel, the rim of which is formed of plaited palm leaf, through which about thirty strong thorns from a date palm, representing the spokes, are passed; the points of these meet together in the centre. Resting on this wheel is placed a noose, at the end of a cord, the other end of which is tied to a small log of wood.

The trap is concealed by covering it with asses' manure; the rope is covered with sand.

On putting its foot on the wheel, the gazelle goes through it where the hub should be, its foot is then held by the thorns till the noose has had time to tighten round it. The wheel then generally falls off, but the log attached to the rope so hampers the gazelle's movements that it can be easily run down and caught.

OLIVE PRESS, RASHIDA.

There were several traps for catching birds; these seemed to be chiefly set for quail. One consisted of a hole in the ground with a slab of rock or a large clod, supported in position to form a sort of lid by an arrangement of sticks, like the familiar trap made of four bricks used in England. A few grains of wheat seemed to be the usual bait.

There was also a very ingenious net trap. This consisted of two semicircular nets, about eight inches in diameter, A and B, which, when the trap was set, were at right angles to each other. The curved portion of the frames of these nets were of *jerid* (mid ribs of the palm leaf), while the straight side of the semicircle was made of palm fibre rope. The framework thus formed was filled in with net, made of narrow strips from a palm leaf.

A long stick, C, held the two frames together, by passing underneath the frame, A, through the meshes of the net and through the rope of the frame, B, in such a way that, when B was raised at right angles to A, the rope became twisted sufficiently to cause B to fly back on to A when released, and so catch the bird between the two nets. B was held perpendicular by a stick, D, the lower end of which was pointed and fitted into a ring, E. The bait, F—a large yellow grub in the trap I saw—was tied to the ring. The upper end of D was tied back by a string, G, on to the end of C. A pull at the bait dragged down the ring, E, thus releasing D, and leaving B free to fly down on to A.

I saw many small boys in the oasis using a very primitive crossbow. The "stock" of this was simply a stout *jerid*, near one end of which a large slot had been cut. The bow, another *jerid*, fitted loosely into this slot and was not secured to the "stock" in any way. When bent the string of the bow caught in a notch on the upper side of the "stock," on the top of which the arrow was kept by being held between the finger and thumb of the left hand. The string was released from its notch by being pressed upwards by the first finger of the right hand.

When loading the camels the men nearly always struck up a chanty. I managed to get the words of a few of them. In some cases it is doubtful if they had any meaning, but, where they seemed to admit of a translation, I have inserted one as a suggestion. The men, for some reason, disliked being questioned about them, and I am not sure that I have always got the words quite correctly.

In loading, one man stood on each side of the kneeling camel, and they usually placed a portion of the baggage on his back in turns, singing a line of the chanty as they did so. The commonest chant was "*Elli hoa li al li*" (this is higher than that?). This they would go on singing over and over again till the loading was completed.

Another was in three lines, which they sang alternately *ad infinitum*. It ran as follows:

Ya tekno ni

Ya lobal li

Ya tawal li

A more complicated chanty had five lines, which when finished was repeated. The first two lines were sung over twice by each of the two men, then the third line was repeated in the same way once, the fourth line was sung twice by each man. They then began with the first two lines again and repeated the whole process. The last line was only chanted once, by the man who added the last package to the load. The whole song ran as follows:

Ana wahdi (I am alone).
Repeated twice by each man.

Wa Nawar hade (and I will teach you something).
Repeated twice by each man.

Shufi jebbi di (Look! I bring you this).
Once only by each man.

Ya ho debbi di (Oh! Ho! I pack this with it).
Twice by each man.

Ma saffi an (Do not arrange any more for me).
Once only as the last pack is put in place.

During the march the men often burst out singing, but on these occasions it was in a shrill falsetto and quite different from the loading chanties, which were in their normal tone of voice. I was never able to catch the words of any songs to the camels on the march, and the tunes, being in a different scale from that used in Europe, were still more baffling. Once or twice, however, during a long night march, I heard Abdulla, who was said by the men to have come from somewhere Abyssinia way, start crooning to himself a song, in what sounded like the European scale. It was a low, plaintive ditty that bore a faint resemblance to the old British song, "The Bailiff's Daughter of Islington." I tried to pick up the tune, but being distinctly "slow in the uptake," where anything musical is concerned, I foolishly asked him to sing it over, so that I could get hold of it. But Abdulla was evidently very sensitive on the subject, and never sang again. Even to my European ears it was a distinctly pretty song, very different from the discordant squalling one usually hears from the Arabs.

The camel drivers' singing is supposed to help their charges on their way, and does seem to have some effect in this direction—presumably because the beasts know from experience that, if the singing fails to take effect, it will be followed up by a whack from the *kurbaj*.

The Egyptians are a superstitious race, and the inhabitants of the oases are probably the most credulous of all Egyptians. I was able to learn a good deal about the native beliefs and occult practices from the Coptic doctor in Dakhla, Wissa—previously mentioned.

One day he got on to the subject of the Coptic priests, and, being a Copt himself, probably knew what he was talking about. He said that they were all very good astrologers, but were very cunning and would never own to knowing anything about the subject.

They work by means of the signs of the Zodiac, used in conjunction with tables. He himself had one of the tables, but was unable to use it, as he had not got the key. There are a number of these tables, each compiled by one of the great philosophers—Solomon, Socrates and so on, after whom it is called.

The tables and key are generally written in Coptic. By means of the key an answer to a question can be got from the table in rhyme, which he said is generally correct. His family owned an answer drawn up for his grandfather in which Arabi's rebellion and the British occupation of Egypt were foretold—presumably in very vague terms.

Magic and clairvoyance were subjects in which he was deeply interested. At Qasr Dakhl he said there was a boy, about twenty-three years of age, who was much consulted by the natives of the oasis when they had lost anything, wanted information about treasure or wished to have the future foretold.

The boy had a familiar—a female *afrit* (spirit)—who sometimes appeared to him during the night. He always knew when she was coming, as he felt drowsy and stupid for a day or two beforehand. After her visit he remained in a clairvoyant state for some hours. He would let it be known beforehand that he was expecting a visit from his *afrita*, and those who wanted information would then apply to him. When she arrived he would question her. Sometimes she replied verbally, but usually he saw or heard the answer to the question while in the clairvoyant condition following her visit. The doctor, who had seen the medium, said he judged him to be epileptic.

He told me the following extraordinary story, which I am sure he believed himself. He was once called in to see the wife of a famous *Sheykh el Afrit* (magician) living near Cairo—at Zeitun. She complained to him that her husband neglected her in favour of his familiar spirit, a male *afrit*, to whom he was always speaking. The doctor, when he saw the husband—an old Maghrabi Arab, called 'Abd ul Atif—began chaffing him about this, and asked him to foretell something that he wanted to know. 'Abd ul Atif promised to do so, if he would come round some day and bring a young boy with him. The doctor selected a boy that he knew, and took him round to the magician's house. The *Sheykh el Afrit* sat him down on a divan, and placed the boy on another facing him at some distance away. He then seated himself at the other end of the room, where he began banging the end of his staff in a rhythmic manner on the floor.

The boy almost at once began to get drowsy, and after about two minutes shrieked and fell to the ground. The doctor rushed across to examine him; found that he showed every sign of asphyxiation and thought that he was dying. But the magician assured him that he was in no danger, and told him to question the boy in any language that he liked. The doctor began to interrogate him in English—that he knew for certain that the boy was unable to speak. The boy replied in the same language, and the answers to the questions that he gave came true, except for some minor particulars. After this séance the boy was ill for a month, during which time he attended him!

Through the agency of the doctor, I was able to see a performance of the *mandal*, or clairvoyance by means of a pool of ink, performed by the magician from Smint previously mentioned.[16] I suggested that we might get hold of him and make him do the *mandal*, so he undertook to interview him and arrange it.

Soon after the magician and doctor came round to my house together. The *Sheykh el Afrit* carried a staff in one hand and a rosary in the other. He came up the stairs on to the housetop muttering what I presumed were incantations. He was a burly looking individual, with a large flabby face and small cunning eyes. He condescended to partake of some tea, and then we got down to business and I asked whether he would perform the *mandal*.

He expressed his willingness to do so, and promised that he would go through the performance provided that there was a bright sun and no wind—conditions that he said were indispensable for a successful séance. He suggested that we should have a young boy brought round to meet him, to play the part of the *tahdir*, i.e. the one who gazes into the magic mirror.

The magician was at great pains to explain that he did not deal at all in black magic, though he said that he knew all about it.

We were anxious for him to start doing his magic art at once; but that he declared to be impossible, as he had not got the right kind of incense with him to use in the *dawa* (invocation). He told us that it was of the first importance that the correct sort should be used, as otherwise the Genii would get angry and might kill him, or even destroy the whole house. He explained that there were many kinds of perfume employed in magic, according to the nature of the *dawa* (invocation) for which they were intended.

First Sight of the "Valley of the Mist."

The Oases of the Libyan desert lie in depressions several hundred feet deep in the main plateau. This huge depression had not previously been reported. (p. 95).

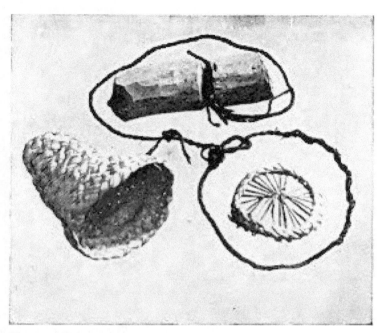

Gazelle Trap. (266)

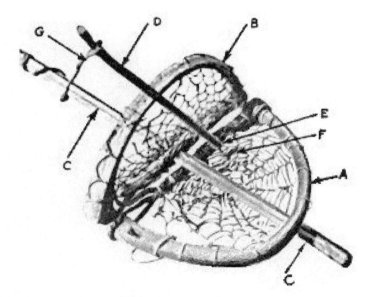

Trap for Quail and Small Birds. (268)

These two ingenious traps are used by the people of Farafra Oasis, many of whom are great hunters.

After some discussion, during which he displayed much learning in his occult science, it was at length arranged that he should go through the performance on the following day.

The next morning he arrived with his staff and rosary and came up the stairs muttering prayers, or incantations, as before.

After he had drunk the usual tea, and approved of the boy that had been provided, he declared himself ready to start work. He asked for a charcoal fire in a brazier, some paper and ink. He then retired to the room that had been cleared for him, and, having closed the door and shutters, so as to produce an imposing dim religious light, seated himself in the darkest corner on a black sheep-skin, with the brazier beside him, and requested to be left alone while he went through the preliminary ceremonies. The doctor and I accordingly retired to another room, taking the boy with us.

Soon a faint smell of incense that reached us from next door, the sound of much muttering and an occasional shout, as the magician invoked the spirits, told us that he had got to work.

After his *dawa* had been going on for some ten minutes the magician called out to us that he was ready, and that we could bring in the boy. He made him sit down on the sheep-skin cross-legged in front of him, patted him and told him there was nothing to be afraid of, if he only did as he was told, and at length soothed him sufficiently to enable the performance to be continued.

The magician first drew in ink the *khatim* (seal) on the palm of the boy's right hand. He then put a written slip of paper on his forehead, licking it to make it stick to his skin, and finally, as that did not make it adhere, slipping the top edge of it under the rim of his cap. He then proceeded to complete the *khatim* by putting a large blot of ink in the centre of the square he had drawn—the whole when completed having the following appearance:

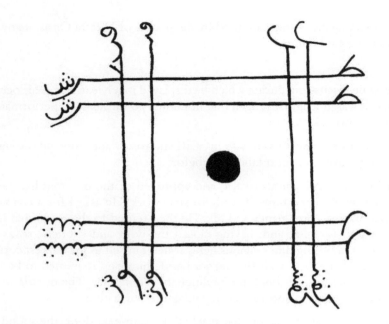

The magician told the boy to gaze in the pool of ink in his hand and to fear nothing, and started again with the spells.

He soon got seriously to work, repeating his incantations over and over again at an extraordinarily rapid rate, swaying himself to and fro, sometimes dropping his voice to a whisper that was almost inaudible, then suddenly raising it to a shout as he called upon Maimun, or some other *afrit*. At length he worked himself up to such a pitch that the perspiration fairly streamed from his face. Now and then he dropped pieces of incense into the earthenware dish that he used as brazier; once he pulled out a leather pouch and produced a knife and pieces of stick, from which he cut off shavings to drop into the fire. Soon the whole room was filled with the sweet sickly smoke of burning perfumes.

Occasionally he peered through the smoke at the boy to judge how far he had been affected by his magic. After a time he apparently concluded that the end of the incantations was close at hand. He redoubled his efforts, jabbering at such a pace that it was impossible to catch a single word and working himself up to an extraordinary pitch of excitement. Then he suddenly dropped his voice till it became almost inaudible, and followed this up by shouting out something as loud as he could bawl. He stopped abruptly; leant back panting against the wall, mopped his streaming face and told the boy to say "*Ataro.*"

The boy repeated the word after him. The magician, evidently considering that his labours were over, then asked the boy to tell us what he saw in the ink.

The experiment, however, proved a distinct failure. The boy was unable to see anything, and, though the magician tried again to reduce him to the clairvoyant state, he was equally unsuccessful on the second attempt.

On a subsequent occasion, when I met this magician, I induced him to write out the necessary incantations, etc., required for the performance of the *mandal*. The translation of what he wrote on the paper that he placed on the *tahdir's* forehead was as follows:

"We have set forth your propositions, and according to the Koran we beg our Prophet Mohammed to answer our prayer."

He commenced the incantations by calling on the spirits he was invoking thus:

"*Toorsh, toorsh, Fiboos, fiboos, Sheshel, sheshel, Koftel, koftel, Kofelsha.*"

The first four names, which are each repeated twice, are those which are written so as to form the frame of the *khatim*, the first being that at the top, the second the one on the left, the third the bottom one and the fourth that on the right-hand side. The last word, "*Kofelsha*," does not appear in the *khatim*, and may be some word used in magic.

The *dawa*, or invocation proper, ran as follows:

"Descend this day, Oh! Celestial Spirits, so that he here may see you with his own eyes and talk to you with his own mouth and set before you that which he desires. Descend quickly, and without delay, this very minute. I call on you in the name of Solomon, in the name of Allah the clement and gracious, to obey and to submit yourselves to my orders for the love of Allah. *Zaagra zagiran zaafiran hafayan nakeb, Zaagra Zagiran Zaafiran hafayan nakeb, zaagra zagiran zaafiran hafayan nakeb.*"

This *dawa* was repeated over and over again, punctuated occasionally with a loud shout of "*Maimun*," which was presumably the name of his own familiar spirit.

The last part of the *dawa*, which it will be seen is a series of words three times repeated, is untranslatable. It is either the names of some fresh spirits or, more probably, some magical gibberish designed to impress the *tahdir* and spectator.

He told me that if the séance had not been a failure, and he had been able to get the spirits under his control when summoned, that it would have been necessary for him to have liberated them afterwards by means of a second incantation which he called a *saraf* (change?), the form of which was as follows:

"In the name of Allah who has sent you, subdued to my orders, I pray you, Oh! spirits, to go back whence you came. I pray Allah to preserve you for ever to do good and to fulfil all that is asked of you."

Later on, while staying at Luxor, I made another attempt to witness the *mandal*. This time I was rather more successful.

The *dawa*, so far as I could see, was practically the same as the invocation of the magician in Dakhla; but the *Sheykh el Afrit* made no attempt to be impressive, and went through the performance in the most perfunctory manner. The boy appeared to be merely bored, and anxious only to earn his *bakhshish*, and to get away again and play.

When he had finished the incantations, the magician asked the boy what he saw in the ink. He replied that he saw a broom sweeping the ground. The magician told him that, when the sweeping was finished, he was to tell "them" (presumably the spirits) to pitch a tent.

After a short interval, during which the boy attentively watched the ink, he said that the tent was pitched. He was then told to command them to place seven chairs in it. When the boy declared that this had been done, he was told that they were to summon the seven kings. Shortly after, the boy declared that the kings had arrived and were seated on the chairs.

The *Sheykh el Afrit* then asked me what it was I wanted to know. I told him I wished the boy to tell me of what I was thinking, and I pictured to myself a young man of the Tawarek race I had once met in the desert.

The boy peered into the ink for some time before answering. Then, in a rather hesitating voice, said that he saw a woman.

I asked if she were veiled. The boy replied that she was. I told him to describe the veil. He said it was black, and in two parts, one covering the lower part of her face and the other the upper portion.

This was correct. The man I had seen was wearing the usual *litham*, or mask, carried by his race, consisting of a long strip of black cotton, wrapped twice round his head, the lower strip covering his face up to the level of his eyes and the upper one concealing his forehead, a narrow opening being left between the two through which he could see.

I next asked the boy if he could see the woman's hair. It was a long time before he replied to this question. Then, in a very doubtful tone, as though he felt he were not describing it properly, he said he could see it sticking up from the top of her head.

This was also correct, as the *litham* the man had been wearing did not cover the crown of his head, and consequently his hair was exposed. It was remarkable, owing to the fact that Moslem women are even more particular to conceal the top of their heads than to cover their faces. The crown of their head must not be seen by their own father, or some say even by the moon.

I then told the boy that his description was perfectly accurate, except that, as the figure he saw was veiled, he had very naturally concluded it to be that of a woman instead of a man. I asked him whether the man carried any weapons, and pictured to myself a curious dagger he had been wearing, which lay along the under side of his left forearm, secured to it by a band round his wrist, with the hilt lying in the palm of his hand.

The boy replied that he carried a sword. This was true, though I was not thinking of it at the time. I asked him to tell me what he was doing with it. He said he could see a drawn sword, and the man was holding it in his left hand. He again seemed doubtful in making this statement.

The left hand is considered as unclean among Moslems, and consequently left-handed natives are very rare, so, although his statement as to his holding a drawn sword in his hand was wrong, the connection with the left hand, on which the man had been carrying the sheathed dagger I had had in my mind, was rather curious, unless he were seeing his image reversed, as he would have done if he had seen him in a mirror. I asked him whether he was sure that it was a sword that he saw, and not a dagger, but he was quite positive on the point, and added that it was an unusually long one. This would have tallied well with the sword, which was a long and straight one, much like the ordinary Dervish type from the Sudan. But I had been thinking of the dagger and not of the sword, so on this point he was wrong.

At this point in the proceedings the wretched dragoman from the hotel, who had led me to the magician, shoved in his oar, asked the boy some stupid question, causing him to look up from the ink to reply, and the magician declared it would be useless to ask him any further questions, as the spell had been broken.

This method of clairvoyance, if such it be, has been seen by several reliable Europeans—Lane, for instance, gives an account of it in his book on "The Manners and Customs of the Modern Egyptians"—and there can be no doubt at all that, in some unexplained manner, correct answers have often been given to the questions asked of the boy when the possibility of collusion was out of the question.

The phenomena of thought transference have been considerably investigated of late years, and many serious scientists believe in the possibility of communicating ideas in this way, without the medium of either speech or hearing. Assuming this to be feasible, thought transference affords a ready means of explaining the phenomena of the *Derb el Mandal* in a case like that I have just described.

But the *mandal* is said to be used with success for other purposes besides the mere reading of another person's thoughts. The finding of hidden treasure, or articles that have been lost, is a very frequent reason for it being employed, and I have been assured, by natives, that the results are often satisfactory; but reliable evidence on this point is certainly desirable.

One of the railway guards in the Nile Valley used to have a great reputation for doing the *mandal*. He was once called in to diagnose the case of the young daughter of a man I knew, and to prescribe treatment. This, I was told, he did successfully, and the girl completely recovered. There is nothing, however, remarkable in this, as most complaints will cure themselves if doctors and other magicians will only leave them alone. The influence, too, of faith-healing and suggestion in this case would also have to be considered.

The railway man used a small mirror instead of a pool of ink. The boy, who was looking into it, stated subsequently that, after gazing at it for some time, it appeared to become greatly enlarged, and a room seemed to be reflected in it. This he was told to order to be swept and then sprinkled. I have seen a glass of water used instead of a pool of ink, and believe that a basin of oil is also sometimes employed. The whole question is an extremely curious one, and might possibly repay investigations on the ground that it is *not* magic.

CHAPTER XXVII

NATURAL HISTORY

THE intense heat and dryness, with the resulting great evaporation, combined with the almost total absence of rain, and the cutting action of the sand, when driven by the furious desert gales, makes the existence of vegetation in the desert almost an impossibility.

Still here and there a few blades of grass, or even a green bush or two, are to be met with, though one may travel for several days' journey in any direction from them before any other growing plants are to be seen.

The plants that grow in the desert are all especially adapted by nature to withstand the heat and drought. The stems of the bushes have a dense outer covering to prevent evaporation. Their leaves are small and leathery for the same reason. But their chief peculiarity is perhaps the extraordinary development of their roots, which stretch for enormous distances in search of water.

Some of the wild plants I collected in Dakhla Oasis were found growing on very saline ground—in a few cases the soil around them being white, with the salt lying on the surface. The date palm seems to have been specially designed by nature to flourish under desert conditions. A palm will grow in soils containing as much as four per cent of salt, providing its roots can reach a stratum containing less than one per cent, and, if it can find a layer with a half per cent of salt only, it is capable of yielding an abundant crop.

The animals in the oasis are no less interesting than the plants.

The nights in Dakhla—especially at Rashida and Mut—are made hideous by the dismal howling of the jackals. The dog tribe in the oasis are probably unusually interesting. I collected a number of skins, but, when I went off into the desert, was unable to take them with me, and had to leave them behind in a half-cured state in Mut. Insects swarm in the hot weather, with the result that, by the time I returned from my various desert trips, I invariably found that they had got at my skins to such an extent as to render them worthless to any museum.

One jackal skin that I managed to bring in in a fair state, and gave to the Natural History Museum in Kensington, was most kindly identified for me by Mr. Martin A. C. Hinton as being identical with the large Egyptian jackal, or "wolf," *canis lupaster*. All the jackals of Dakhla are of an unusually large size, and are locally called wolves. I was told that they breed freely with the village dogs. In addition to the jackals, foxes are extremely numerous, some being apparently identical with the common greyish fox of the Nile Valley.

There are probably some species of the dog tribe in the oasis which are new. One evening near Mut I happened to be returning to the town about sunset, and noticed a fox that struck me as being of an unusual appearance. Shortly after I first saw him, he went to the far side of a low mound of earth; I was consequently able to approach him unseen, and managed to get within about ten yards of him before attracting his attention. He then bolted; but not before I had had a good view of him.

He was a fairly large fox of a greyish brown colour, and carried a very fine brush. But his most striking peculiarity was that he was covered with large black spots, which appeared to be about an inch and a half in diameter. On questioning the inhabitants, I found that a spotted fox was occasionally seen in the oasis, but was not apparently very common. Markings of this nature are, I believe, quite unknown in any fox, so that this one probably was of unusual interest. Unfortunately, I was unable to secure a specimen.

In addition to the jackals and foxes, an occasional hyena is said to appear in the oasis, but none, so far as I heard, were seen while I was there.

A curious fact in relation to the jackals in Dakhla is that they appear to be to a great extent vegetarians, living largely upon the fallen fruit in the plantations—a fact which recalls the story of the fox and the grapes.

Gazelles used to be fairly numerous in the scrub-covered areas in and around the oases, but I invariably found them extremely shy and difficult to approach. Once, in the distance, I caught sight of a pair that looked interesting. One of them had an extremely pale coat, and was perhaps a *rim* (Loder's gazelle); but the other was of a deep reddish—almost chestnut—colour that, from a distance, looked unlike any known variety. The usual gazelle found in these parts is the common Dorcas; but these two looked entirely different. The natives do not seem to distinguish between the various varieties, all of which bear a strong resemblance to each other, classing them altogether as "gazelle."

Scorpions swarm in the older buildings of the town, and the natives get frequently stung, sometimes, I was told, with fatal effect. The leaves of a round-leaved plant known as *khobbayza*[17] are pounded and made into a poultice to apply to their stings—it is said with considerable effect. A native quack doctor from the Nile Valley used to do a considerable trade in little blackish wafers of a composition that he kept secret, which were also said to be very beneficial not only against the stings of scorpions but also in the case of snake bites. One of the native doctors I met in Mut tried them on some of his patients with, he told me, great success. Very large, hairy, yellow spiders, tarantulas perhaps, I saw once or twice, and found the natives very much afraid of them.

In the Nile Valley, curious mud-built tables supported on a single thick leg are used on which to place young children to secure them from the attacks of scorpions and tarantulas that, owing to the overhang of the table, are unable to climb to the top. The table-top itself is surrounded by a low wall to prevent the children from falling off, the crest of the wall itself being often fantastically decorated.

I never came across any snakes at Dakhla, but more than once saw the skin they had shed. There is said to be a long black snake, generally found in or near the water channels, whose bite is considered to be extremely dangerous. The ordinary horned cerastes viper, though often met with in the desert, seems to be rare in the oasis—and the same may be said of the unhorned viper that so much resembles it at first sight. Insects swarm during the hot weather in the oases. Butterflies are scarce, but moths are fairly numerous. In Kharga I caught the cotton moth, but I did not see it in Dakhla. Locusts are almost, I believe, unknown, but the grasshopper tribe are in some parts— Tenida for instance—extremely numerous.

SCORPION-PROOF PLATFORM.

Bristle tails (silver fish) were unpleasantly destructive, and boring bees do much damage by perforating the palm-trunk joists and rafters of the houses and rendering them unsafe. House flies were quite common enough to be a nuisance, though not to the extent usually found in the Nile Valley.

Mosquitoes were present in only small numbers in Mut, owing probably to the scarcity of water in the neighbourhood.

Dragon flies were conspicuously numerous—a dark red, a greenish variety and a beautiful steely blue kind being, so far as I saw, the most common.

In the spring there is a large immigration of birds into the oasis, coming up from the south-west. Sand grouse—both a pintailed and a spotted variety—are to be met with on the outskirts of the oasis and in the parts of it remote from the villages. Quail, duck, snipe and various water birds abound in the oasis at certain seasons. Kites I never saw or heard, but eagles were several times seen. Also a bird of the hawk species. Ravens exist in small numbers.

Pigeons are fairly well represented, a large wild pigeon—the blue rock apparently, which lives largely in the cliffs surrounding the oasis—being common. These at times give very good sport; in the open they are far too wary to be approached within gun-shot. But in the evening they come down to the wells to drink, usually choosing one that is removed some distance from the villages.

But these pigeons proved to be very poor eating, their flesh being hard and dry, and not to be compared with sand grouse for the pot.

The sand grouse, too, were singularly hard to bag. The only place where I ever succeeded in shooting any was on the Gubary road between Dakhla and Kharga Oases. I found them fairly numerous there, being generally to be seen in the early morning at the places where the *bedawin* camped for the night. As the day grew older they left the road altogether and flew off into the desert.

The birds that interested me most in the oases were the *kimri*, or palm doves. There are at least two kinds in Dakhla, the *kimri beladi*, or local palm dove, and the *kimri sifi*, or summer dove. The former seems to be resident in Dakhla all the year round; but the latter are migrants, coming into the oasis in March and returning in the autumn after the date harvest. They take somewhat the place in Dakhla that the cuckoo does in England, their advent being regarded as a sign that the winter is past and the summer close at hand. The palm groves of the oasis, when the hot weather comes on, swarm with these pretty little birds, whose soft cooing as they sit swaying in the palm tops is a most melodious sound—extremely pleasant and soothing after a long hot desert journey.

The whole question of the animal and vegetable life in these desolate regions is one of great interest. In spite of the intensely arid nature of these deserts, they support in some marvellous way a considerable amount of life.

Small lizards were often to be seen in the desert scuttling about the ground. They run with extraordinary speed, and are very difficult to catch. The usual way, I believe, is to throw a handkerchief on the ground and to drive the lizard towards it, when it will frequently run under the handkerchief to shelter, and can then be easily picked up. I found that, though they could run very fast for a short distance, they very soon tired, and, if steadily followed up for a hundred yards, without allowing them time to rest, they became so exhausted that they could be easily secured.

I never saw a specimen of the *waran*, or large lizard, in the desert, but on one occasion saw what looked like its track. It resembled the trail of a large-bodied lizard crawling slowly over the sand. My men, however, declared it to be the track of an *issulla*, which they described as a creature between a snake and a lizard in shape, which, when approached, will fly at an intruder, rising into the air after a rapid run on membraneous wings stretched between its legs—acting apparently somewhat like an aeroplane. They said its bite was poisonous, and generally fatal, but that, if it failed to strike home during its flight, it fell on the ground and burst! The existence of such a reptile—if we exclude the bursting part of the story—is perhaps not absolutely impossible. One has to take native statements of this kind with more than the usual amount of salt; but it does not do to ignore them entirely.

Its track corresponded well with the description of the reptile given me by my men, for, outside the marks where its feet had been placed, something had clearly been dragged along the sand, leaving a trace that showed upon its surface as a scratch. What that "something" was it is difficult to say—unless, as my men declared, it was part of the membrane upon which the *issulla* is said to sail through the air. It could not have been caused by its tail, as it appeared in places upon both sides of the track at once.

With regard to the capacity it is said to have of being able to rise into the air from the ground, that, I think, presents but little difficulty. I gathered from my men's account that it would have been nearly three feet long. The small fast-running lizards previously mentioned are mostly under six inches in length, and must be able to travel at nearly ten miles an hour, as it takes a man on foot all his time to catch them up. As the *issulla* must be five times the length of these little lizards, it is not unreasonable to assume that it can run quite twice as fast, or say at twenty miles an hour, which, if it were running against a stiffish breeze, would be equivalent to say fifty miles an hour through the air—a speed that would probably easily cause it to rise from the ground—but it is a tall story.

Snakes are very common in the desert—the *lefa'a*, or horned viper, and a very similar viper without horns being in places rather unpleasantly numerous. In addition we killed a very thin sandy-coloured snake, about four feet in length, which, so far as I could judge from its head, did not appear to be poisonous.

The *naja*, or Egyptian cobra, sometimes seen in the Nile Valley, is, I believe, quite unknown in the desert and oases.

I several times heard rumours of a feathered snake. At first I put this down as being a myth, but I afterwards found that this creature had been seen by at least one European, who had been long resident in the country. The specimen he saw was one killed in the Nile Valley. He described it as being a short, stout, sandy-coloured snake, having along its back, for some distance behind its head, a sort of crest of elongated scales considerably frayed out at their ends.

The existence of this creature is by no means an impossibility, for reptiles and birds are closely related.

Insects in the desert are comparatively few in number. I once found a few small ants, pink and silver in colour. Large grotesque-looking mantids were often seen running about on the sandy portions of the desert. Some of them were of considerable size, many of them being quite three inches long. They were curious creatures, and apparently very pugnacious, as, when approached, they would often turn round and face me, raising themselves slightly on their squat fat bodies and pawing the air with their big front legs.

If I pushed my foot towards them they frequently attacked it, grappling my toe with their legs and trying to bite. I picked up one of the larger ones and gave him the end of my thumb to bite—a rather foolish proceeding, it struck me afterwards, as, for all I knew to the contrary, his bite might have been poisonous. He bit furiously at the end of my thumb with his rather formidable jaws, foaming at the mouth and doing his feeble best to damage me. He managed to get hold of a small pinch of skin between his jaws, which closed in a horizontal direction, and gave me a nip I could distinctly feel.

Once, in the desert west of Dakhla, I found a mosquito, which considerably raised my hopes that I might be getting near water. But it proved to be only a wind-born specimen, coming probably from Nesla or Bu Mungar. Lace-winged flies frequently came into our camp, even when far out into the desert, and on most nights a few moths flew into my tent and came to my candle; occasionally they were in considerable numbers.

The common house flies, though a nuisance in the oasis, are fortunately unknown in the desert, though frequently a swarm of them, if there is no wind, will follow a caravan when starting from an oasis; but they disappear in a day or two.

Once while riding in a desert with my caravan, when, having left an oasis the day before, we were considerably bothered with these pests, a swarm of which kept buzzing round our heads, I was relieved of them in a rather unexpected manner. A swallow—evidently migrating—came up to the caravan from the south, and being presumably very hungry, kept flying round and round our heads, snapping up a fly at every circle. Owing probably to its hunger, the little creature was extraordinarily tame—its wing tips several times almost touched my face. Having remained with the caravan for a few minutes, it circled round us half a dozen times to make sure that there were no flies that it had overlooked, and then flew off and pursued its way to the north.

A list of some of the insects I collected will be found in Appendix II.

The road that we followed to the south-west from Dakhla lay in the direction from which the birds were migrating, so I not only noted every specimen that we saw, but put down in my route book every feather that I picked up, and even the marks on the sand where these migrants had alighted, as this was all valuable evidence that we were still travelling in the right direction.

In addition to palm doves and the smaller migrants, we several times saw storks and cranes, or their tracks; but this, of course, only occurred during the season of their migration. There was a large white bird, which appeared to be an eagle, that we frequently saw at all seasons, but I was never able to get very close to it, as, unlike most desert creatures, it was extremely wild.

The only place where I ever saw any sand grouse, outside the oases, was on the road between Kharga and Dakhla. They seemed to be entirely absent from the desert to the south and south-west of Dakhla, and also from the desert surrounding Farafra Oasis—the reason of their absence presumably being the lack of food.

Not only were insects, reptiles and birds fairly well represented in the desert, but even mammals were not unknown. In addition to the desert rats, about eighty miles to the south of Dakhla I came across the remains of a gazelle, but possibly the poor little beast had only wandered out into the desert to die. Small foxes, though they existed in the oasis, I never saw in the desert— the rats would not have been so numerous if I had. The tracks of a larger fox were seen several times, often several days' journey away from an oasis. The tracks of jackals, or wolves, I could not be sure which, were still oftener encountered.

The dog tribe, of course, could live on the rats and lizards, but, unless they obtained sufficient moisture from the blood of their victims, they must have returned occasionally to the oases to drink. One wonders why these animals, who can live also in the oases, should prefer to exist in the desert, where the conditions under which they are forced to live must make life almost impossible.

The problem of how the desert rats exist has caused much discussion, and cannot yet be said to be solved. I have found them certainly a good hundred and fifty miles from any oasis, in a part quite barren, yet they were obviously perfectly healthy, plump and lively.

I was once camped for several weeks in the dune belt that runs through Kharga Oasis. One evening I had just sat down to dinner, when I noticed one of these little kangaroo rats hopping about in the candle-light just outside the door of my tent. A sudden movement that I made scared him. He jumped about four feet and was gone in a flash.

But in a minute or two, prompted probably by curiosity, he was back again in his old place, hovering about just outside the tent. Hoping to get a better look at him, I flipped a small piece of bread so that it fell just in front of him. After some hesitation, he pounced on to it, and carrying it a few yards away, proceeded to eat it.

He then came back again, stationing himself a little nearer in, and seized another piece of bread I threw him that dropped about half-way between us. Soon I had him taking pieces actually out of my hand—he was extraordinarily tame.

I was just finishing my meal, and had forgotten all about him, and was reading a book propped up on the table as I ate, when I suddenly felt a tap on the top of my thigh, and on looking down to see what it was, found that he had not only returned, but had actually jumped up on to my leg as I sat at table. In a moment more, he had hopped up on to the table itself and was eating the crumbs.

He was so absolutely fearless that he even allowed me to stroke his back with my finger; but directly I attempted to close my hand over him he jumped off the table in alarm on to the ground, where, however, he remained restlessly hopping about with his extraordinarily springy movement, till I threw him another piece of bread.

Apparently, however, he had had as much as he wanted for the moment, for, instead of eating it as he had done before, he picked it up, hopped out of the tent, and disappeared for several minutes. Presently, however, he came back again. I threw him another piece that he again made off with, and after an interval returned for more. He must have carried off about ten pieces in this way that evening, each piece about the size of a filbert. I kept on feeding him so long as he continued to return; but at last, being perhaps tired after carrying so often what must have been a heavy load for him, he ceased to appear.

He returned again on the following night, and for eight consecutive ones. Each night I gave him as much bread as he would eat and carry away. He seemed to be a very small eater; but he must have taken off with him enough bread to make two or three loaves. In addition, he levied toll on the grain for the camels, which he obtained by gnawing holes in the sacks.

This last, however, proved to be his undoing, for one of my men happened to catch him in the act, and promptly, much to my disgust, killed him. It was unquestionably the same rat that had come nightly to my tent that had also carried off the grain, for there was no possibility of mistaking him, owing to the fact that he had lost an eye.

I felt quite sorry to lose the little beast, which had become quite a pet, and latterly became so tame that he would allow me to pick him up and stroke him. When my man, however, grabbed hold of him in his hand, he promptly bit him in the thumb.

These little kangaroo rats are wonderfully pretty little creatures, just the colour of the sand itself, with large black eyes and a very long tail. Their most striking peculiarity is the enormous muscular development of their hind legs, which seem quite disproportionately massive in comparison with their small bodies.

It is this great muscular development of their long hind legs that gives them such wonderful powers of locomotion. Once, while travelling with my caravan over a large area of level sand, I came across the track of one of these rats, quite clearly visible on the smooth surface, and as it happened to be travelling in practically the same direction as I was going myself, I followed it for a long distance.

The track consisted of a series of double dots where the hind feet had landed on the sand, occurring at regular intervals of three to four feet apart. I followed those tracks for over nine miles in practically a straight line, till a change in the direction of my route from that of the rat compelled me to leave them.

During the whole of the time during which I followed them, I only found three or four places where the rat had abandoned his regular pace and stopped for a moment or two to turn round and round apparently to play with his tail.

The speed at which these little beasts can travel is little short of marvellous. The fastest runner would not have the remotest chance of catching them; when frightened, they will go off at a pace that the natives say even a horse cannot equal. The steady rate which the one whose tracks I had followed had kept up for so many miles, shows that they can travel long distances without tiring, and that they not only can, but do.

It is in this marvellous capacity for getting over the ground, and their habit of hoarding up provisions, that the explanation of their ability to live in these districts can, I believe, be found.

Absolutely barren as this district seems to be, there are here and there patches of grass, quite dead to all appearances, but which have probably shed their seed on the surrounding ground. Even in these arid districts rain is not unknown—there were stories in Dakhla of a regular downpour that was said to have occurred not many years before, when rain fell in such quantities that many of the mud-built houses of the oasis melted before it and fell down. Rainfall such as this, or even a heavy shower, might cause the seed to sprout. The grass is usually found growing on the stiffest clay, which would hold the moisture from the rain for a considerable time, and, aided by the great heat of the warmer months, cause the grass to grow with extreme rapidity. Upon this grass and its seeds these rats could easily live, and from it they could store up in their underground burrows provisions to last them for a very long time. Rats are known to be able to subsist on hard grain alone, that does not contain more than ten or fifteen per cent of moisture.[18] They are probably acquainted with a number of places where these grasses grow, and, as it is known that they never drink, by making a store near each, and travelling from one to another as their depots become exhausted, they can maintain themselves for several years of drought. The tracks that we saw running continuously for nine miles at a stretch, with hardly a break, may have been those of a rat travelling from one of his storehouses to another. A journey such as this could hardly have been undertaken without some definite object in view. A fifty mile run would be nothing to one of these little creatures, so they would be able to draw their supplies from thousands of square miles of country, within which, even in this arid desert, they would be able to find plenty to live upon. In one place, too, we found green *terfa* bushes, from which they may perhaps have obtained some nourishment, and possibly sufficient moisture from the green portions of the plants to enable them to exist without drinking—though an occasional journey of a hundred miles or so, into an oasis to procure water, would be quite within the locomotive powers of these extraordinary little creatures.

APPENDIX I

THE GEOGRAPHY AND WINDS OF THE LIBYAN DESERT

THE views on the geography of the Libyan Desert, current at the time of my visit to the country, are summarised by Mr. F. R. Cana in the valuable paper and map that he contributed to the "Geographical Journal."[19] Writing of this desert he says: "Some knowledge of its character has been obtained where it borders the Nile, and to the north along the edge of the Cyrenaican plateau . . . the general character of the desert is that of rocky wastes in the north and east, and a vast sea of sand in the centre."

The rocky wastes begin on the north, immediately to the south of the cultivable belt along the North Egyptian coast; the desert here rising to form a plateau. This tableland is succeeded by a vast depression, portions of which lie below sea-level. This hollow runs from Siwa Oasis in an easterly direction towards the Nile. Reference will be made to this huge valley later on.

The southern side of this depression has never, I believe, been mapped, but, beyond it, the level of the desert rises again to a limestone-capped plateau, that in places is over a thousand feet above sea-level. The western limit of this has not, I believe, been ascertained in its northern part, but towards the east it is bounded by the Valley of the Nile, where it forms the towering cliff on its western side that is familiar to all visitors to Egypt. About the latitude of Qena the plateau narrows down to a width of about a hundred miles, its western limit being the great escarpment that bounds the oasis of Kharga on its eastern side.

The geography of this limestone tableland, and of the desert beyond it up to the Egyptian-Tripolitan frontier, was tolerably well known at the time of my arrival in Egypt; but, with the exception of Kufara and the other oases in the same group, practically the whole desert beyond it was a *terra incognita*, the domain of the Senussi, and, as stated in Mr. F. R. Cana's paper, considered to consist of an impassable sea of enormous sand dunes.

I made altogether eight journeys into the desert to the south-west of Dakhla, only some of which have been described. In addition to these, and to the others into Farafra and elsewhere already referred to, I made some to the north of 'Ain Amur, where I found a perfect network of small depressions.

These little hollows, which were only about a hundred and fifty feet in depth, mostly opened out of each other, and fairly honeycombed the limestone plateau. Entrance to them was gained by a gap in the cliff on the northern side of 'Ain Amur Valley, from which a small belt of sand dunes issued. They were mostly only a mile or two in width, though some of them were of considerable length, one in fact stretched for some thirty-four miles from north-east to south-west. There was one extraordinary little hollow that formed as it were an isolated pot-hole, nearly circular in shape, in the limestone plateau, about a hundred and fifty feet in depth with almost vertical sides. It was difficult to see how it could have been formed. Judging from the jagged skyline, shown by some of the cliffs surrounding these hollows, there were probably several other depressions that time did not allow me to explore.

A curious fact in connection with these little hollows was that, although many of them were floored with clay, they contained practically no vegetation. On the limestone plateau that surrounded them, however, bushes and even small patches of scrub were not infrequently seen.

The origin of the depressions in this limestone plateau has been the subject of some dispute. The action of water, sand erosion and folding of the strata have all been put forward to account for them by various writers. It may be interesting in this connection to mention that the southernmost of these little hollows to the north of 'Ain Amur contained the bed of a perfectly distinct watercourse, containing well-rounded shingle, running towards the entrance into the 'Ain Amur Valley.

In addition to these journeys I made one for three days to the south of Belat, in Dakhla Oasis. On the edge of the oasis we got into some very rough salt-encrusted ground, containing some patches of rock salt.

Beyond this lay a large scrub-covered area known as Dhayat en Neml, or sometimes as El Girgof, which was fairly thickly overgrown with bushes.

On leaving this we got into the open desert, whose level here rose fairly rapidly towards the south. Here we found traces of an old road, which, however, we lost on the third day after leaving Belat. It was probably only a branch of the Derb et Terfawi.

Early that afternoon our road led us to the top of a cliff about two hundred feet in height. A few hours' journey farther on and a second cliff, two hundred and forty feet in height, was reached, beyond which lay an expanse of level sandy desert, dotted here and there with a few rocky hills. This second scarp was apparently the eastern continuation of the cliff that forms the southern limit of the sandstone plateau to the south-west of the oasis of Dakhla, which, however, breaks down into a gradual slope to the south of the town of Mut, on the western side of Dakhla, where the road from Mut runs to Selima Oasis.

I endeavoured to make the most of the few opportunities that presented themselves of gathering such information as I could of the unknown areas beyond the Egyptian frontier. But opportunities of this kind unfortunately were few. These parts were regarded by the Senussi as being their particular reserve, and they did their best to keep them closed to outsiders. It was consequently only members of this sect and their friends who had any knowledge of the district, and the Senussi were so extraordinary secretive about their country that it was with the greatest difficulty that I was able to extract any information concerning it. Enquiries, too, had to be conducted with caution, for collecting data of this kind was apt to prove an unhealthy occupation.

Part of the map I was able to compile from the data given to me has since been verified from other sources; as much of it has thus been found to be correct, the remainder of it is presumably equally reliable. The absolute positions, so far as latitude and longitude are concerned, are, of course, considerably in error in most cases, but the relative bearings and distances of each place to those surrounding it are, in most instances, represented with reasonable accuracy.

A map based on native information can, of course, never hope to compete in precision with one constructed by the methods of a modern survey; but it need not be very far behind those produced by the rough-and-ready methods of the geographers of a hundred, or even fifty, years ago. Its object is to give a general idea of the district it covers, and, more especially, to give future travellers an objective, and sufficiently accurate information as to its position, to enable them to find it.

No definite system of spelling was adopted in my map. Many of the names are clearly not Arabic, but either those of the Tibbus or Bedayat, whose alphabets—if they have any—have not, so far as I know, been reduced to any system of transliteration. It was impossible to get the spelling of even the Arabic names, as all my informants were illiterate *bedawin*, so I have spelt them as nearly as I could phonetically. Probably the pronunciation that I heard differs from that in vogue in Sudan, so the comparison may be of use.

The information was collected as far as possible in the form of through routes, joining places that had already been more or less accurately fixed by previous travellers. The remainder of the data was then fitted into these routes, or plotted from more or less reliably fixed points on other maps.

The three main routes on which the map was based were as follows:[20]

Route I. From Tollab, in Kufara Oasis, to Bidau.

Three days south to the well of Bushara.

Four days south to Asara, or Sarra (a well only).

Six days from Asara, S.S.W., to Tikeru.

Half a day west from Tikeru to Erwully, a well.

Three days west to Guru.

Three days south-west from Guru to Ungoury.

One day S.S.W. to the village of Ertha.

One day west to Bidau.

Route II. From Tikeru to Abesher.

Three days south to Wanjunga Kebir. Another Wanjunga, known as Wanjunga Sgheir—little Wanjunga—lies one day's journey to the east. Both are inhabited. This district is sometimes called Wanjungat.

Three days south to Bedadi, a well belonging to the Bedayat.

Three days south to a well called Funfun, belonging to the Bedayat tribe.

One and a half (or two) days south to Wayta Sgheir.

A short day south to Wayta Kebir.

Five days south—I was also told four—to Mushaluba (Um Shaloba), which has recently been fixed by the French. The route then continued via Lughad and Aratha to Abesher.

Route III. From Wayta Kebir to El Fasher.

One day east to Um el Atham, a Bedayat well.

One day south to Baky.

One day south to the well of El Guttara.

Two days east to 'Ain el Baytha, a Bedayat well.

Two days east to Baou, a Bedayat well, or pool, in a fertile valley inhabited by Bedayat.

One long day, or a day and a half, south to Kuffara, a valley with plenty of water.

One day east to Medjoures, a valley containing many wells.

Three days and two "hours" east to Wady Howar. The road crosses the Howar Wady, and, after leading for a two days' journey further east-south-east, it enters one of its tributaries—the Wady Faruwiah. After crossing the wady, the road leads for two days south-east to Musbut.

Musbut and Faruwiah are both said to be large wadies containing many wells. Musbut is said to be on the Derb el Arbain, the old "forty days" caravan road from the Sudan by which slaves used to be taken to Egypt.

Two "hours" south from Musbut to Buhuruz, two days south-east from Buhuruz, the road reaches Formah, a Zaghawa well.

Two days farther east, and it arrives at Kafut, a village in a wady of the same name, which, half a day to the south, receives a tributary known as the Wady Kobay. Wady Kafut itself, some seventy miles farther north, unites with the Wady Kuttum to form the Wady Meleeat, itself a tributary of the great Wady Howar.

Mr. Boyce's survey shows a short section of the Wady Kuttum running east and west. Mr. Sarsfield-Hall shows Kuttum on his map as a village, situated upon an unnamed wady—presumably the Wady Kuttum—of which only a short section, running north-east to south-west is shown. But farther north he shows a large unnamed wady, discharging to the north, that corresponds well with the description I was given of the Kuttum-Meleeat Wady.

Three days farther east the road ends at El Fasher.

These routes were all taken as starting from Tollab, and when plotted on the basis of a day's journey of twenty miles in a straight line, closed with the following errors, from the positions of their termini as shown on the maps: Bidau, 95 miles 34° from the true position, on a route from Tollab of about 430 miles as plotted—in other words, with an error of about 22 per cent of the total route. Abesher, 95 miles 98° from the true position, on a route of about 680 miles, i.e. about 14 per cent of the total distance; El Fasher, 160 miles 59° from the map position, on a fifty days' journey of 1,000 miles, or 16 per cent of this distance. Considering the nature of the material upon which the routes were mapped, this compares not unfavourably—except in the case of Bidau—with a probable error in a prismatic compass traverse of about 10 per cent.

But this data may perhaps be misleading, for Colonel Tilho—a very accurate observer and equipped with a wireless installation for getting longitude by means of the signals from the Eiffel Tower—found that Nachtigal's positions for some of the places in Tibesti were as much as fifty miles in error; so presumably his position for Bidau is not to be greatly relied upon. Rohlfs' positions for Tollab, and other parts of Kufara Oasis, also remain to be checked by modern and more accurate methods than were available at the time of his journey.[21]

In constructing the maps, the routes were treated first as being three separate roads, joining Tollab to Bidau, Abesher and El Fasher respectively, and were adjusted separately by the ordinary graphic method, to their respective termini. This gave three separate positions for Bushara, Asara and Tikeru. These three positions in each case were meaned and accepted as correct, and from the position of Tikeru thus found the route to Bidau was plotted afresh and adjusted to Nachtigal's position.

The routes south to Abesher and El Fasher were again plotted from the new position thus found for Tikeru, and were again adjusted to the map positions of Abesher and El Fasher, as two separate routes running to those places from Tikeru. This gave two separate positions for Wanjunga Kebir, Bedadi, Funfun, Wayta Sogheir and Wayta Kebir.

The mean of these two positions was taken as correct, and from this mean position for Wayta Kebir, the roads to Abesher and El Fasher were plotted and finally adjusted to their termini. Many of the places on these routes were consequently adjusted five times.

Route IV. Dongola to the Howash Valley.

From Dongola a road runs five days south-west to Bu Senata—a well belonging to the Kebabish tribe.

Four days farther west-south-west, and Jebel Maydob is reached. From there, five days due west, and the road comes to Bu Zibad, and, three days farther west, reaches the Howash Valley.

It was not until long after I had been given this route that I heard of the existence of old Dongola, which lies some sixty-five miles about south-south-east of the better-known new Dongola.

When plotted on a twenty-mile-a-day basis from either of these places, the road is considerably in error, if the position of Maydob can be relied upon. The route starting from old Dongola closing, however, much better on to Maydob than the one from new Dongola. The positions on the map are those found by plotting the information, without adjustment from new Dongola. Upon this route, too, depends the portion of the Wady Howash, lying to the north of Kowora (q.v.).

The description given to me of the Wady Howash was extremely interesting. It was said that the sides of the wady in places were covered with coloured paintings, and that it contained numerous ruins of burnt brick, probably Meroitic in origin, and in addition many statues—colossi apparently—and pits in the ground containing ashes covered with stone slabs—possibly these were funerary pits containing human remains. The Bedayat country generally was reported as containing many stone-built ruins (*ders*), and to have numerous rock inscriptions and "Roman"—i.e. artesian—wells, like those in the western oases of Egypt, and seems likely to prove a valuable field for future archæologists.

Among the remaining places shown on the map the following may be mentioned. My informants were all Arabs, or Sudanese living in Egypt, so the names are those in use among the Arabic-speaking *bedawin* and may differ from those used by tribes speaking another language, such as the Tibbus, Bedayat and other Sudanese races.

Dendura: This is Rohlfs' alternative name Zerzura—"the oasis of the blacks." I concluded that Zerzura, if it exists at all, is a different place from Dendura. The latter was described as being as large as Dakhla Oasis, and as lying just to the west of an enormous longitudinal dune that is almost impassable, seven days due west from Bu Mungar (see also Zerzura).

Dunes: All the dune belts of the Libyan Desert are said to run from north to south. In the neighbourhood of Dakhla Oasis they were found to run 352° mag., and if, as I heard, they run parallel with the Tollab-Tikeru road, the belts appear in reality to converge slightly towards the north. Possibly the prevailing wind blows from a more easterly quarter as one proceeds westwards from Egypt, as the influence of the hot air rising from the Arabian deserts would be less felt in the western part of the Libyan Desert. Towards the Central Sudan it appears to approximate to the direction of the north-east trades normally found in these latitudes, for Commandant Tilho found the prevailing wind in Borku to blow from this direction. A dune belt that is easy to cross is said to commence about two hours to the west of Erbayana, near Kufara Oasis, and to extend for three days—I was told four—to the westward, and to die out before reaching the latitude of Bushara. A belt was also reported to exist about two hours to the west of Erwully. This belt, though about the same width as the one farther north, lying to the west of Erbayana, is perhaps only sand banked up by the Tibesti hills, though from its position it looks like the continuation of the belt near Kufara, with which it is exactly in line; Tilho's paper confirms the existence of a great dune field as far as Ertha and Borku, and also to the south of Wady Dom. The line of dunes following the Tollab-Kufara road is said to start close to the west of Kebabo, and to be about a day's journey in width from east to west. The belt is said to go to the Sudan, and to die out in the vegetation of Wanjungat. Between Wanjunga and Demi, Tilho found a "little chain of sand dunes, about fifty feet high, stretching from north-east to south-west, and extending from five to six miles in breadth," which appears to be the end of the belt described by my informant.

The dune belts form a useful check upon the accuracy of the data given me. One I saw at the end of our journey to the south-west of Dakhla, near Jebel Abdulla, is apparently the northern continuation of that which runs from El Atrun to "the Egyptian Oasis." The southern portion of the line of dunes lies farther west than the part that I saw; but a map constructed from native intelligence can hardly be expected to be very accurate, and, assuming the prevailing wind in the neighbourhood of El Atrun to blow from a direction approximating to north-east, as found by Tilho in Borku, the line of dunes would be certain to curve round somewhat towards the west at its southern extremity. The belt near Dendura is almost exactly in line with the one reported in the neighbourhood of Owana; so, too, is the wide belt to the west of Erbayana with the similar dune-field west of Erwully. Sand-free intervals in these sand belts are not uncommon, and the dying out of this belt about the latitude of Bushara that was reported to take place, may only be the commencement of one of these gaps, the line of dunes becoming continuous again farther to the south.

"Egyptian Oasis": An Ebday (i.e. one of the Bedayat tribe) who was a friend of one of my guides, told him he had once ridden from Merga (q.v.) with two *hagins* (i.e. riding camels) for five days north, following the dune belt (I was also told that the distance was ten long days from Merga with an ordinary caravan). He had then climbed a very high black hill lying in the dune belt and had seen in the distance under a cliff a huge oasis, containing a number of olive trees and much *terfa*. He was too far off to see if it were inhabited, and was afraid to go in, because he said it was an "Egyptian Oasis," and he feared that he would be killed if he did so. Another Arab told me that a cousin of his was riding along the top of a scarp about eight days somewhere to the south of Dakhla, when he saw below him a very large oasis, containing a number of olive trees, palms and wells. There was one very big ruined town that did not seem to be inhabited and a few *ezbas* (i.e. hamlets), in which a few people were to be seen. I was also told that this place was from seven to ten days from Dakhla Oasis.

Ershay: A lake of sweet water, variously described as being three miles across and five or six *feddans* (i.e. acres) in extent; also a wady of the same name that runs into it. Entering the wady near El Guttara, the lake lies three days' journey along the wady to the north. The lake is said to contain crocodiles, which seize camels when they come down to drink. There is nothing very improbable in this, for crocodiles have actually been found in the middle of the Western Sahara, in the pools of the Wad Mihero, that leads into the Wad Ighargharen, itself a tributary of the great Wad Igharghar, a valley that in prehistoric times must have contained an immense river. Presumably, as this part of the desert dried up, the crocodiles became cut off, and now exist only in the pools of the river bed—a similar state of affairs probably accounting for their presence in the Ershay Lake.

Fardy, Wady el: Another name for the Wady Tibbu, or Bahr el Ghazel, that connects with Lake Chad. Barth calls it the Barrum and the Fede. The latter name may perhaps be a corruption of the Arabic word Fardy.

There is also another Wady el Fardy that is said to run east of Jebel Kusu, through Guru, Erbayana, Buseima and Taiserbo. It crosses the Jalo-Kufara road four days south of Jalo, and then runs past Jarabub, Siwa and Bahrein to join the Nile. One account said that it also ran through the Fayum.

A large number of branch wadies are said to discharge into the Wady el Fardy from the Tibesti range. These valleys support a large population of Tibbus; but as these natives appear to be among the chief followers of the Senussi, I could not induce my informants to give me any information about this district, which appears to be one of the chief strongholds of the sect. Several wadies, however, are shown on existing maps, I do not know on what authority, as starting in Tibesti and running in this direction.

There are a number of native reports of dried-up river beds in various parts of the desert, that have never, I believe, been investigated, and may be without foundation, and information of this kind must be regarded with suspicion. But the Wady el Fardy sounds authentic, for wadies have already been reported to exist at all the points mentioned by my informants in its course. In the Tibesti range there must even now be a considerable rainfall in the rainy season, and probably in former times it was still heavier. The ultimate destination of the water that falls on the northern and eastern sides of Tibesti is still unknown. It is hardly likely that it can break back through the range and discharge towards the south, so apparently it must flow somewhere towards the north.

A plentiful supply of surface water exists in the Kufara group of oases—more than the extremely slight rainfall of the desert could possibly supply. In the Western Sahara the large oasis groups are fed by wadies of this description—the Wad Saura, for instance, brings down the rainfall from the Atlas Mountains to supply the oases of the Twat depression, while the Wad Ghirh group between Tuggurt and Biskra is supplied by the great Wad Igharghar, which takes its rise in the Central Sahara. It seems quite possible that the Kufara Oases and the Wady el Fardy are their counterparts in the Libyan Desert.

Not only are wadies known to exist at all the points along this river bed, where reported to me, but there is also known to be a large depression between Siwa Oasis and the Nile, portions of which, such as Sitra Lake, contain water and are below sea-level. The northern boundary of this great hollow has been surveyed almost throughout its entire length, the cliff running by Jebel el Ghazalat, Jebel Tarfaia, Jebel Dakar, Garet el Leben, Jebel Somara and Jebel Hashem el Gud, to the Wady Natrun. On the southern side of this great valley a well-marked boundary has been found to exist in the neighbourhood of Siwa, extending eastwards towards the Nile as far as Araj Oasis and Lake Sitra. Beyond that point it does not seem to have been surveyed. If this great depression forms part of the Wady el Fardy, it must have widened out to the east of Siwa Oasis into something like an estuary. The Wady el Fardy was described to me as being as big as the Nile Valley.

In addition to the Wady el Fardy, I heard of another great river bed known as the Wady Howar that in places was also said to be as deep and wide as the Nile Valley. The bottom of the valley was said to consist of clay and to contain much water after the rains—presumably in wells and pools—but to dry up in the hot season.

Hurry: The name of a Bedayat tribe. Also of the district that they inhabit, which contains a lake of good water, more than an Arab gunshot across from north to south, and an hour's journey from east to west. There are a few trees and palms round the lake and some cultivation. The lake lies three days east from Wanjungat, the road lying all over sand and rock, it is seven days due north from Ershay Lake, the road being all over rock with a great deal of water in the rains, but none in the dry weather. There are settlements at the east and west ends of Hurry Lake.

Iddaila: Three days to the south-west of Iddaila is a large oasis, and two days to the west of Iddaila is a large *hattia*. A road runs from Iddaila to Kufara and another runs west, hidden under the dunes.

Ko'or Wady: Lies six days west of Erbayana.

Kowora: An important Bedayat district. To the east of Kowora, after one day's journey the road is all level sand, west of which it is all rock.

Merga: The so-called "*hattia* of the Bedayat," of the *bedawin* of the Egyptian deserts. It was described as being about the size of the Tenida-Belat district in Dakhla Oasis—say ten miles each way. It contains a pool, about an acre (*feddan*) in extent, fed by a spring, or *'ain* (artesian well), which is surrounded by many palms, around which again is a belt of scrub—*argul* and *terfa*. It lies two and a half days north-west from El Atrun and three to three and a half—I have also heard four—days west from Lagia. Two and a half days to the south-west from Merga there is a high cliff with a *negeb* (i.e. pass) leading up on to the plateau on the top.

After rather more than half a day's journey over the plateau another pass is reached, leading down into the "Valley of the Bedayat" (q.v.). Merga is not regularly inhabited, but the Bedayat come there in the season to gather the dates. They also use it as a base from which to raid the caravans of Egyptian *bedawin* who go down to El Atrun to gather natron. A road runs from Merga to Kufara, Owanat (q.v.) being half-way along it. There are no Bedayat to the north of Merga. This is perhaps the place that Miani calls Ptolemy's "lake of the mud tortoises."

Colonel Tilho's native information on the question of this *hattia* agrees very closely with that I received. He, too, was told of the road from Merga to Kufara via Owanat, and also heard the place described as a pool surrounded by palms. He estimates the position as being "between the 25th and 26th degrees of longitude east and 18th and 19th degrees of latitude north." This estimate agrees well with my information so far as the latitude is concerned, but, according to my intelligence, it should be at least a degree farther east than he puts it.

No'on Lake: Belongs to the Bedayat and is about three miles across. It lies close to the hill of the same name. There is cultivation on the south-east and south-west sides. It lies one day west from Jebel Kuttum. A road runs south and another east from the lake (? destinations).

Owana: A place half-way along a road from Merga to Kufara, consisting of a well, with no vegetation in the immediate neighbourhood, but much green grass in the district after rain, on which wild asses and "bekker el wahash" (probably Barbary sheep) feed. North of the well is a cliff with a pass that takes two hours' easy travelling to traverse, and on the top is a high level oasis, the landmark for which is two rocky hills that look like one from the north; the scarp runs north-north-west and south-east from the well. Jebel Abdulla is reported to be visible from near here. The whole of this district is known as Owanat (plural of Owana). A dune belt comes down close to it from the north and dies out about two days farther to the south.[22]

Zerzura: Possibly only a generic name applied to any mythical or undiscovered oasis. I have heard it applied to Rohlfs' Zerzura (Dendura?) (q.v.)—also to the "Egyptian Oasis" (q.v.), to an oasis supposed to exist eight days somewhere to the south of Dakhla, and to a stone temple I heard of about eighteen hours' journey west of Jedida in Dakhla Oasis. The map on native information here reproduced originally appeared in the R.G.S.J., Sept., 1913. But then it was somewhat altered and a considerable amount of material was introduced into it, for which I was in no way responsible. The map is here reproduced in its original form.

The following are the principal roads that traverse the Libyan Desert: One starting from Giza, near Cairo, runs in a westerly direction through the Wady Natrun and the Wady Moghara, follows the course of the reported Wady el Fardy to El Qara, and then proceeds via Siwa, Jaabub, Jalo and Aujila to the oasis of Abu Naim and on into Tripoli. Farther to the south a caravan route, starting from the Fayum, crosses the desert to the northern end of Baharia, and just before entering the oasis is joined by roads from Wady Natrun and from Maghagha. Other routes, leaving the Nile Valley at Bahnessa and Minia, enter the oasis farther to the south, and combine to form a caravan route leaving the western side of the oasis and going, via Lake Sitra and Araj, to

Siwa Oasis. A road also runs northward from Baharia, via Wady Moghara, to Alexandria, while another leads in a south-westerly direction, by way of 'Ain el Wady, to Qasr Farafra.

Farafra is connected with the Nile Valley by a road that runs through Kairowin *hattia* to Beni Adi, near Assiut. A route that was used by the Senussi runs towards the south-west, past 'Ain Sheykh Murzuk and to the *hattia* of Bu Mungar and thence, across a field of big dunes, to Kufara. It is said to pass on its way through a large oasis. To the north-west there is a road from Farafra, crossing a small detached limestone plateau, known as El Guss Abu Said, to a well called Bir Labiyat, and then proceeding via the little oases of Iddaila and Bahrain to Siwa. Another road leads to the south from Iddaila, and passing through a little oasis, known as Nesla, leads to Bu Mungar, and on to Dakhla Oasis, running along the foot of the cliff immediately to the east of Bu Mungar. A second leads from Iddaila, over El Guss Abu Said, direct to Dakhla, along the top of the cliff above Bu Mungar.

The usual road, however, between Farafra and Dakhla runs south-east from Qasr Farafra to Bir Dikker, and then follows what is known as a *gassi*, or path swept by the wind free from sand, through a field of biggish dunes, and enters Dakhla Oasis in its north-western corner. This road emerges from the southern side of Dakhla Oasis at the town of Mut, in the form of the Derb el Terfawi, leading to Bir Terfawi and Selima Oases.

Two other roads enter Dakhla Oasis from the north—the Derb el Tawil, or "long road," that leaves the Nile Valley at Beni Adi, and, after crossing the limestone plateau, descends the cliff that bounds the oasis on the north by a pass known as El Agaba, in the eastern part of the oasis, and leads to Tenida; the other is a little-used road, called the Derb el Khashabi, that runs direct from the north-western corner of the oasis to some point in the Nile Valley to the south of Beni Adi, or perhaps goes direct to Assiut.

There are two roads in regular use between Dakhla and Kharga Oases—the northernmost leads to the well 'Ain Amur, high up on the northern side of a small detached limestone plateau, and the other, the Gubary road, runs along the foot of the cliff on the southern side of this plateau. The latter is waterless and rather longer than the 'Ain Amur road, but runs over the level, and is consequently the one most used, as the 'Ain Amur road necessitates a laborious climb up to the plateau, with a correspondingly difficult descent. It has, however, the advantage of having a well of rather bitter water about midway along it, and in consequence is occasionally used by small parties, especially in the hot weather. Several branch roads split off from the Gubary road, and lead to Beris and the places in the south of Kharga Oasis; but they are hardly ever used.

Dakhla Oasis is bounded on its western side by a field of dunes. The traces of several old roads are to be seen leading in this direction and, before the dunes came down to this part, were probably used by caravans proceeding to Kufara; but these are now, I believe, never followed. Traces of the disused road from Mut, via Owanat, to the Central Sudan has already been mentioned.

Several roads lead over the eastern cliff of Kharga depression; from the southern end of the oasis one goes, via the little oasis of Dungun, to Tumas, near Derr; a second goes, via the small oasis of Kurkur, to Aswan; a third leads in a north-easterly direction to Esna; while a fourth makes across the desert to Farshut. Esna can also be reached from the centre of the oasis by a road starting from Qasr Zaiyan. From Kharga village, in the north of the oasis, roads run to Sohag, Girga, Farshut, Qena, Luxor and Esna. But the main road running to Kharga is the Derb el Arbain, or "Forty days" route of the old slave traders, which leaves the Nile Valley near Assiut and enters the oasis at its northern end, runs through it from north to south, and then proceeds, via the wells of Shebb, Selima Oasis, Lagia and Bir Natrun, to Darfur.

The other great caravan road traversing the Libyan Desert from north to south is that starting from Benghazi, and proceeding, via Jedabya, Aujila and Jalo, to the Kufara group of oases—this was practically the route followed by Rohlfs' and the Forbes-Hassanein expeditions. From Kufara it continues, via Bushara, Asara and Tikeru, into Wanjunga and on into Central Sudan.

It will be noted that most of the roads traversing the Libyan Desert run roughly from east to west. This is unfortunate, as it necessitates their crossing the sand belts which run approximately at right angles to them, the direction of these belts being due to the strongly predominant character of the northerly winds.

The winds of the Libyan Desert are a rather interesting problem. The prevailing direction from which they blow lies slightly to the west of north, which is not quite the quarter to be expected.

All along the North African coast lies the Mediterranean. The temperature of an area of water of this size and depth changes very slowly, and would not be appreciably affected by one or two days' sunshine. In the absence of wind, the heat of the atmosphere lying over the sea is largely controlled by that of the water itself.

On the other hand, the Libyan Desert, owing to its lying nearer the equator, is subjected to a much hotter sun. Its intensely arid character prevents it from being cooled in any way by evaporation, and it is entirely unshaded by any vegetation. Under the heat of the tropical sun, the stones and sand of which it is composed very rapidly heat in the sun's rays. The air overhanging it consequently gets greatly heated in its turn, becomes lighter and so rises, and the colder, denser air from the Mediterranean has to rush in and take its place.

A very similar state of things occurs in the Atlantic and Pacific oceans, where the cold air rushes in towards the equator from both north and south to form the trade winds. These winds, however, do not blow at right angles to the equator, for the earth in its rotation slips away, as it were, from under the surrounding atmosphere, with the result that the trade winds blow from the north-east and south-east, in the northern and southern hemispheres respectively.

But instead of blowing from the north-east, as would be expected from the character of the trade winds, the wind in the Libyan Desert comes from slightly to the west of north, which at first sight appears rather puzzling.

The explanation of this peculiarity lies, I believe, in the fact that to the east of Egypt—across the Red Sea—lies a like track of country to the Libyan Desert in the shape of the Arabian Desert, where very similar conditions prevail. The Red Sea, which separates the two, being too narrow to greatly affect the situation, the air overhanging the eastern part of the Mediterranean has also to take the place of the heated atmosphere rising from Palestine and a considerable part of Arabia, and consequently tends to draw in that direction.

Various phenomena of light and electricity, seldom or never seen in other climates, are to be found in the desert. I several times saw what appeared to be a large star suddenly flash up and disappear immediately. This I believe to have been not a meteor, but some form of electrical phenomenon, as I usually saw it after a sandstorm, when the air was full of fine electrified sand.

Solar phenomena are sometimes very conspicuous in the desert, the zodiacal light that follows the sunset being often very clearly seen, in the form of a semi-elliptical portion of the sky showing brightly above the horizon, after the sun had disappeared, and shining with sufficient strength to give quite an appreciable light.

There was another phenomenon that I saw in this desert that I have never seen alluded to by other travellers. Sometimes at sunset luminous lines would appear in the eastern sky radiating from a point opposite to the setting sun. These lines were never very pronounced, but at the same time were quite clearly visible. On one occasion, instead of luminous lines, dark ones appeared instead.

Another peculiarity of this part of the desert was the way in which a sandstorm would sometimes spring up without any appreciable change in the strength or direction of the wind. I concluded this to be due to a change in the electrical condition of the atmosphere.

The connection between the winds of this desert and its geography is so close that I have included them both in this section. The chief effect of the wind on the desert sands is, of course, to be seen in the dunes. In addition to those mentioned when dealing with the native information I collected, there is a large area in the Farafra depression covered with sand hills and those in the neighbourhood of Bu Mungar which have been previously mentioned.

Several narrow belts of dunes are also to be found starting in the great depression between Siwa and Cairo. These belts, too, run roughly from north to south; but with one exception they all die out before reaching the latitude of Farafra Oasis.

The effects of the violent desert gales was everywhere to be seen. On the limestone plateau, on the way to Kharga Oasis, and on the Derb el Tawil very fine examples of sand erosion are visible.

Mr. H. Ll. Beadnell,[23] who carried out a series of weather observations over a considerable time in Kharga Oasis, estimated that the sand blew from a northerly direction for five days out of six in this district. Violent sandstorms are unpleasantly common, by far the greatest number of them coming from the predominating northerly direction. The result of this uniformity in the direction of the winds is clearly seen on the plateau. The swirling clouds of sand, driven by the furious desert gales, have in many places not only shaped the hard limestone into long ridges running up and down wind, but have even cut grooves in the ridges themselves, as though with a gigantic gouge, forming a type of desert known to the natives as *kharashef*. These ridges rise sometimes twenty feet above the level of the plateau, but more usually are only three or four feet in height, producing a surface somewhat resembling a rough sea—a very uncomfortable type of desert to have to cross with a caravan. A diminutive form of this—*kharafish*—in the shape of small ridges, often with a cutting edge, is also frequently seen, and works havoc with the soles of the soft-footed camels. Besides these forms a flat rock surface with very shallow groves, known as *rusuf*, is occasionally met with.

Some of the limestone boulders lying on the surface of the plateau are perforated in the most extraordinary way. The driving sand apparently eats its way into the softer portions of the stone, boring holes into its surface. Small pebbles are often to be seen which have been blown into these holes. These fly round and round in the excavation under the influence of a strong wind, and presumably continue the erosion of the sand blast, in the same way as a stone wears a pot-hole in a stream. In course of time the whole boulder becomes so riddled with holes as to resemble a gigantic sponge.

In several places are large patches of desert more or less closely covered with round boulders up to a foot in diameter, a type of erosion known to the natives as *battikh*, or water-melon desert.

In other places in the desert perforated rocks and small natural arches are to be seen; while near Farafra village were a number of fine "mushrooms" and table stones cut out of the chalk by wind-driven sand. Similar "mushrooms" of sandstone were, moreover, met with near the centre of the desert.

In Kharga Oasis there is an area several square miles in extent covered by curious clay ridges. These, which seemed all to be under twenty feet high, were evidently formed by the erosion of the earth by the wind-driven sand, for they all ran roughly from north to south, in the direction of the prevailing wind.

Apparently, as the sand wore away and lowered the surface of the desert, it encountered here and there harder portions of the clay which resisted its erosive action. These consequently remained protruding above the surface of the desert as the surrounding clay was eaten away by the sand blast, and consequently acted as a protection to the earth immediately to leeward of them, which remained intact above the level of the desert in the form of a ridge running in the direction of the prevailing northerly wind. I have found similar forms to the west of Dakhla and in that oasis itself.

While in the central part of the desert in my first season, I found embedded in a sand dune two short pieces of dried grass much frayed and battered;[24] so, as has already been mentioned, on leaving the camp next day, we followed the line of the sand belt, to the north as showing the direction of the prevailing wind, and so found the place from which the dried grass embedded in the dune had come.

The occurrence of this grass so far to windward of the piece I had picked up among the dunes is only another illustration of the great part the strongly predominant character of the northerly wind plays in this desert. Had we continued marching towards the north, along the same bearing as we had during the day, we should have found the oases, or *hattias*, of Bu Mungar, Iddaila and Sitra, all on the same line. The original seed, of which the grass we found were the descendants, were probably specimens carried by the wind from Sitra to Iddaila, where they took root and produced seed that was similarly carried to Bu Mungar and from thence—perhaps through another *hattia*, or oasis—to the place where we found it growing. Very probably the line of plantations of the grass may even reach to the Sudan, should there be any places along it where the seed could germinate.

ERODED ROCK, SOUTH-WEST OF DAKHLA.

It is not only in the distribution of the vegetation that the agency of this predominant wind is apparent. The sand belts follow the same direction, so, too, do the clay ridges in Kharga and elsewhere; even the hills in the desert show in many cases a distinct tendency to have their longest diameter pointing up and down this north to south line. The predominant character of the northerly winds even has an effect upon the caravan roads; that, for instance, that runs from Farafra Oasis to Dakhla lies along a hollow among the sand dunes that occupy a large area in the centre of Farafra depression, that is kept permanently free of sand by the northerly wind that continually sweeps along it, so affording an easy path through what would otherwise be a most difficult dune-field to cross.

Once at 'Ain Amur I experienced a curious storm. It was a windy morning and I had been out after gazelle. On returning towards the camp, I saw in the distance what looked like very heavy rain falling in the 'Ain Amur Wady, so hurried back to the well to gain the shelter of the ruins in its neighbourhood.

The rain, however, turned out to be only a fog—or perhaps, since the well is 1,680 feet above sea-level, it would be more correct to say cloud—only a few drops fell; but for nearly an hour the whole district was enveloped in a thick white fog, while a furious wind sprung up and blew with great violence. At the end of that time the fog cleared off, the wind suddenly dropped and a sunny and unusually hot day followed. Fog, it is needless to say, is not a common occurrence in the desert.

The word oasis is unfortunately a very vague one, to which varying meanings are applied in different parts of the world. The dictionaries usually define it as a "fertile spot in a desert." So far so good. The difficulty comes in when one attempts to apply this definition, for one is at once faced with two problems: what constitutes "fertility" and what is the size of a "spot"?

The Wad Ghirh district, for instance, in the south of Algeria, runs for some ninety-five miles from north to south, contains about forty villages, with their palm plantations, and a population of some fifteen thousand inhabitants. Each of these villages, with its palm plantations, is regarded as one oasis. The whole Wad Ghirh district being considered a group of oases.

Kharga and Dakhla Oases, which are separated from each other by about seventy-five miles of waterless desert, were considered by the ancient writers to form one oasis, known as the "great oasis."

Kharga Oasis, according to Dr. John Ball, who surveyed it for the Egyptian Government, is about a hundred and forty miles long from north to south, contains some fifteen villages and has a population of seven thousand eight hundred odd. All this is considered even now to form one oasis.

To the north-west of Kharga lies a little place known as 'Ain Um Debadib, where there is a considerable area of scrub, with a few palms and *sunt* (i.e. acacia) trees. A certain amount of ground is cultivated here by a family from Kharga village, who, however, do not always reside there. This is usually considered a separate oasis.

In the eastern part of the Farafra depression is an area, some sixteen miles by twelve, covered with scrub, among which a few date palms, which seemed to be to some extent cultivated, are also to be seen. This place is known as Kairowin. There are no permanent houses or inhabitants, though frequently *bedawin* living in tents, or brushwood huts, are to be found there with their camels. The place contains several wells, and is sometimes described as an oasis, though the natives more usually allude to it as a *hattia*.

At 'Ain Amur, half-way between Kharga and Dakhla, is a well, some ruins, a patch of scrub and a palm or two. This, however, never has any residents—the well being only used by travellers between Kharga and Dakhla. This place is usually described as a *hattia*, though I have heard even this called an oasis.

From places such as this there is a regular gradation through scrub-covered patches containing water, but no palms, scrub-covered areas containing no water, and mere patches of half a dozen bushes clustered together in the desert, called by the Arabs *roadhs*, to places that remain sufficiently damp after one of the rare desert showers to allow a few widely scattered blades of grass to grow, which the *bedawin* call *redirs*.

It is very difficult to see where to draw the line. The system adopted in Algeria of describing places like Kharga and Wad Ghirh as groups of oases—or oasis-archipelagos, as they are sometimes called—seems preferable to the Egyptian plan of alluding to them as a single oasis. It would seem advisable to confine the term oasis to a place which is actually cultivated, whether continuously inhabited or not, and to use the word *hattia* for "fertile spots" in the desert where no cultivation exists. The dividing-line, however, between a *hattia* and a deserted oasis would not be very sharply drawn.

The western oases of Egypt were known to the ancients, for some reason not very apparent, as "the Islands of the Blest"—a name that to a modern visitor has an air of being somewhat ironical.

They are usually said to lie in depressions of the plateau. So far as Baharia is concerned this is an accurate description, for it is almost entirely surrounded by cliffs; but in the case of Farafra and Kharga, the scarps of the limestone plateau only partly hem them in, and they would be more correctly said to be situated at their base. Dakhla, in the same way, lies at the southern foot of the chalk plateau that forms the floor of Farafra Oasis, and gradually rises in level as it proceeds southwards from Qasr Farafra, until it breaks down in the huge cliff that bounds Dakhla Oasis on its north and east. The little oasis of 'Ain Um Debadib, lying slightly to the west of Kharga, is also only bounded on the north by the cliff. Kharga towards the east, north and north-west is hemmed in by cliffs and hills. The cliff in places, on the eastern side, is nearly eight hundred feet in height, but is considerably lower at the northern end.

Starting from the north, on the western side of the oasis, a jumbled mass of hills, cliffs and sand dunes extend for about thirty miles towards the south to form its boundary. South of this, a long north and south belt of dunes runs parallel with the eastern scarp, and cuts off the oasis from the open desert lying to the west. At its southern end, the oasis merges into the desert without any well-defined boundary.

To anyone standing, say, on the eastern scarp and looking down on to the floor of the oasis, it would appear as flat and almost as featureless as the surface of the sea when viewed from the summit of a high cliff. Two huge flat-topped hills rise abruptly from the level oasis floor, near the eastern cliff, to the height of the plateau above it; they are known as Jebel Ghennihma and Jebel Um el Ghenneiem, and stand about thirty-five and forty miles respectively from the northern end of the oasis. Almost facing them on its western side stand Jebel Taaref and Jebel Ter. With the exception of these four hills and the smaller conical peak known as Gorn el Genna jutting up from the centre of the oasis floor, there are no conspicuous elevations to break its level monotony.

The amount of land under cultivation is extremely small compared with the total area of the oasis. Dr. Ball estimated the latter to extend to considerably over three thousand square kilometres, but states that out of this only nineteen square kilometres are under irrigation. The cultivated portions consist in some cases of patches merely an acre or two in extent. Only in the neighbourhood of Kharga village is there a really large area of continuous cultivation. Here, a long strip, some four miles from north to south, by about two-thirds of a mile from east to west, covering altogether about a thousand acres, forms a practically continuous grove of palms and cultivated land. The size of the average patch of cultivation may be taken as being some sixty-five to seventy acres. Each plot is usually known by the name of the well that irrigates it, or in cases where it contains more than one, by the name of the principal well.

The irrigation is effected entirely by means of artesian wells, some of which date back to a remote period, and are said by the native to have been the work of the Romans.

These wells and the modern native ones, which are modelled on them, are sunk by means of primitive boring appliances and lined with acacia-wood pipes. They are usually all owned by several proprietors, among whom the flow of water is distributed by methods that probably date back to a remote past. When a crop—such as rice—is being grown that requires continuous irrigation, the yield of water is divided up by means of what is known as a rice gauge. This consists of a board with a series of notches in its upper edge, through which the water flows—each proprietor being entitled to the amount that runs through a notch, whose width corresponds with the proportion of the yield from the well to which he is entitled. When intermittent irrigation is required, the owners of the well draw their water in rotation in accordance with a most complicated system. The moment at which each is to commence taking his share is ascertained by a most ingenious and intricate method of telling the time, in which one of the men converts himself into a kind of human sundial.

A Street in Kharga.

The housetops are a favourite resort of the women. To ensure privacy a row of palm leaves is stuck upright into the top of the wall. (p. 313.)

In addition to Kharga village, which is the principal centre in the oasis, a few other villages and hamlets lie scattered at intervals near the wells sunk within the oasis area.

These villages are divided into two main groups, the principal, taking them in order from north to south, are Meheriq, Kharga, Gennah and Bulaq in the northern group. South of these lies a stretch of desert for a long day's journey, containing no village and only two or three isolated wells. After this, Jaja and Dakhakhin, the two northernmost settlements of the southern group are reached. Jaja being to the east of Dakhakhin and two or three miles away. Some ten miles farther south lies Beris—the chief village of the southern group, followed by Maks Bahry (Northern Maks), and Maks Qibly (Southern Maks); five miles to the east of the latter lies the village of Dush. This constitutes the southern group.

Kharga village, though surrounded by some fine palm plantations, is a wretched, squalid place. As is often the case in desert towns, the streets in many places run through tunnels, formed by the upper stories of the houses being built out over the roadways. In Kharga, however, this peculiarity is carried to an unusual extent—many of the tunnels being so low that it is impossible to stand upright in them, and of such a length as to be completely dark. The natives say they were constructed in this manner for defensive reasons, in order that an enemy gaining access to the town should lose his way in the darkened streets.

The houses were all, so far as I saw, constructed of the usual sun-dried mud bricks, the roofs being supported on palm-trunk rafters. They were, however, peculiar in having the parapet surrounding the flat housetop surmounted by a sort of fence of palm leaves set into the top of the wall, in order apparently to heighten it and make the housetop more private, without incurring the expense of the additional brickwork. In some of the better houses the inside of this fence was plastered with clay to form a sort of wattle and daub, through which small windows were often cut so that the inhabitants could look through without being seen themselves. When a house was built beside an open street, balconies supported by an extension of the rafters were sometimes projected over the road and walled in with the usual fence, to allow the inmates of the house to get a view up and down the road.

Here and there some attempt was made to decorate the exterior of the house by rough painting round the windows—this usually taking the form of radiating lines of whitewash. One house had a sort of trefoil arch over the doorway surmounted by a projecting window, the front of which was pierced by a number of small square holes—apparently in imitation of the *meshrebia*, or lattice work, of the Nile Valley towns.

A considerable amount of rushwork is manufactured in Kharga in the form of panniers for donkeys and mats for covering the floor. The latter are made on a primitive loom stretched out upon the ground. No shuttle is used, the rushes being woven across the strings that form the basis of the mat by hand.

Kharga Oasis is richer in archæological remains than any of the others. In early times the place was evidently of greater importance than it is at present, and probably supported a larger population.

It is known to have been inhabited at a very remote period, even as far back as the reign of Thothmes III (1503-1449 B.C.). In early days it seems to have been used mainly as a place of exile. This is a use to which it seems to have been frequently put, and continues to be to this day. In A.D. 435 the Bishop Nestorius was banished to Kharga on account of his revolutionary views. Here he founded a Coptic Colony. A large Christian Necropolis, at Nadura, near Kharga village, and several mud monasteries, constructed much in the form of castles, evidently as a defence against their enemies, still remain in very fair preservation as mementos of his exile.

Ruins of ancient mud-built towns and villages are to be found in several places, notably those of Hibis to the north of Kharga village, in the neighbourhood of the temple of that name, and those of Tchonemyris, near the temple of Qasr Zaiyan. There are also the remains of the old town of Kysis lying close to the temple of the same name, which is now known to the natives as Qasr Dush.

The Romans, during their occupation of the oasis, built several forts and castles, the exteriors of which bear a striking resemblance to the old Norman Keeps to be found in England.

The most important of these forts, a building for some reason known to the natives as Ed Der—the monastery—lies in the northern part of the oasis close to the north foot of Jebel Ghennihma. It consists of an enclosure some sixty yards square, surrounded by mud-brick walls ten feet thick and about thirty in height, with a circular tower at each corner and two semicircular turrets projecting from each of its sides. From its position it was evidently intended to guard the entrance to the oasis down the wady, through which the railway now runs. The fort at present is merely an enclosure, and no trace remains of any buildings in its interior.

Here and there in the oasis are to be seen small mud-brick buildings, the interiors of which have their walls honeycombed with the little cubical niches eight inches in each direction. These are usually found at some distance from any village or existing remains. They are generally considered to have been dovecots; but it has also been suggested that they were intended to contain cinerary urns.

By far the most interesting ruin, however, to be found in the oasis is that of the sandstone Temple of Hibis, a short distance to the north of Kharga village. This, which is the only temple or public building of any importance to be found in Egypt dating from the time of the Persian dynasty, was begun by Darius I, and completed in 424 B.C. by Darius II, as Brugsch has shown from the hieroglyphics.

About a mile to the south-east of the Temple of Hibis, conspicuously placed on some high ground, are the ruins of a small sandstone building, known as the Temple of Nadura.

A mile or two to the south of the hill known as the Gorn el Gennah is a small temple known as Qasr el Guehda—a name often locally pronounced Wehda. It consists of a small sandstone building, measuring about eleven yards from north to south, by twenty from east to west.

The temple itself lies in an enclosure of mud bricks, possibly of later date, entered on the eastern side through a stone gateway.

About three miles farther to the south lies the small temple known as Qasr Zaiyan, a much smaller building than Qasr Guehda. Like it, it seems to have been surrounded by a wall of mud bricks, forming an enclosure filled with small mud-built buildings.

I did not visit the Temple of Kysis, or Qasr Dush, as the natives call it, which lies in the extreme south of the oasis. For a description of this, and for a fuller account of the antiquities of this oasis, the reader is referred to the works of Schweinfurth, Brugsch, Hoskins and Dr. John Ball.

'Ain Um Debadib, the little oasis already mentioned, is situated about twenty-two miles farther west.

Still farther to the west, the next oasis—if such it can be called—is that of 'Ain Amur, of which mention has already been made. It lies about twenty-four miles W.S.W. of 'Ain Um Debadib, close to the top of a precipitous cliff facing the northern boundary of a portion of the detached limestone plateau to which reference has already been made.

'Ain Amur stands some 1,680 feet above sea-level. The existence of a well at such a high altitude, in an excessively arid region like the Libyan Desert, is something in the nature of a phenomenon. Its presence, however, is easily explained: the top of the plateau is covered with a layer of limestone, below which is a bed of clay. Showers of rain are not quite unknown, even in this desert, and occasionally, according to the natives, there is a regular downpour. Some of the water falling on the flat limestone surface certainly finds its way through it by way of the numerous cracks to be seen on its surface. The downward progress of this water is stopped on reaching the clay, through which it can only penetrate extremely slowly. Where the strata are not absolutely horizontal, the water flows along the upper surface of the clay, protected from evaporation by the overlying limestone, until it comes to the surface at the edge of the plateau, a little distance below the summit of the cliff.

The Arab word *'Ain*, strictly speaking, means a flowing well or spring. The well at 'Ain Amur, however, did not, so far as I could see, flow at all. It consists simply of an ordinary vertical well-shaft, the water in which lies about eight feet below the ground level, and is reached by an inclined path, or stair, leading down to it from the eastern side.

The well stands near the foot of a single scraggy palm tree. A certain amount of wild palm scrub is to be seen near the well, and a short distance away is a patch of green rushes, where I was told there had formerly been another well; but this was quite filled up—probably by the wind-blown dust—at the time of my visit. The water in the well was dirty and rather bitter, but otherwise quite potable.

Water could perhaps be found at other places in the neighbourhood, as there is a long strip of green camel thorn—*argul*—running horizontally along the cliff below the plateau, at the level of the well, which lies near its western end.

Formerly 'Ain Amur must have been a place of some importance. Close to the well are the ruins of a small stone temple still showing traces of paint, and situated, like many of the temples in Kharga Oasis, in the centre of a walled enclosure of sun-dried bricks, possibly intended as a defence. The well is placed within this enclosure—little of which now remains.

About forty miles west from 'Ain Amur lies Dakhla Oasis. Like Kharga it is really a group of oases, with spaces of desert between them—or perhaps it would be more correct to say two groups, for the Belat-Tenida district on its eastern side is quite distinct from the remainder of the oasis, from which it is separated by several miles of waterless desert. The inhabitants of Belat and Tenida are consequently of a slightly different type from those of the rest of the oasis, and though only a few miles away from them, speak a rather different dialect—the hard K = Q being strongly pronounced at Belat and in the eastern group of oases, while it is slurred over in the western part and pronounced as it is in Cairo.

Dakhla Oasis differs somewhat from Kharga in that the villages are less scattered and, so to speak, more closely packed together. Owing, too, to the better water supply it is very much more fertile. Dakhla, too, is more favourably situated than Kharga, as it nestles at the foot of a great east and west cliff, three or four hundred feet in height, that protects it to a great extent from the prevailing northerly winds. Kharga, on the other hand, runs from north to south, with the result that the tearing desert gales sweep down upon it from the north with their full force. Dakhla runs east and west—with an extension towards the north at its western end, where the sheltering cliff forms a deep bay towards the north-east, measuring about six miles from north to south. The south-western portion of the oasis, in which the capital town of Mut is placed, is consequently more exposed to the prevailing winds.

Mut itself—the last place to the south-west—lies about eighteen miles from the escarpment, while most of the other villages are within five or six miles of the sheltering cliff, which form the boundary of the oasis on its northern and eastern sides. On the south the oasis merges gradually into the higher desert beyond, while to the west it is hemmed in by a huge field of dunes.

The eastern group of oases in Dakhla, in addition to the villages of Tenida and Belat, includes a number of *ezbas* (farms or hamlets), each consisting of a well or two with the surrounding palm plantations and cultivation and a few houses. Generally the whole *ezba* is owned by one individual, or at any rate by a single family.

In addition to a number of *ezbas*, the western group contains the following small towns and villages: Smint, Masara, Mut, Hindau, Qalamun, Gedida, Mushia, Rashida, Budkhulu and Qasr Dakhl—the last lying in the extreme north-west of the group, close under the shelter of the scarp. These villages vary greatly in size. Qasr Dakhl, the largest, with the *ezbas* that go with it, being estimated in 1898 to have a population of 3,758, with 3,428 *feddans* (acres) of cultivated land and 49,758 palm trees. Budkhulu, the smallest village, with its dependencies, had a population of 583, with 893 *feddans* of land under cultivation and 12,302 palms.

In addition to date palms a considerable number of other fruit trees are cultivated—oranges, tangerines, lemons, sweet lemons, limes, figs, mulberries, bananas, olives and almonds being planted under the shade of the palms. About one-fourteenth of the cultivated land is under fruit trees—principally palms—the remainder being devoted to field crops, chiefly wheat, barley, rice, clover and vegetables. Similar fruit trees and field crops are grown in Kharga.

Goats, sheep, donkeys, cattle and a few horses are kept in addition to pigeons, fowls, a few rabbits and a considerable number of turkeys. The cattle of the oases are a rather noted breed, not unlike our Channel Islanders in appearance. Buffaloes are either few, or non-existent. Camels—with the exception of about half a dozen owned by the Senussi *zawias* (monasteries) and used by the sheykhs in their visits to their headquarters in Kufara—are not kept permanently in Dakhla oases, as a fly makes its appearance in the spring whose bite is as fatal to these beasts as the tsetse fly is to horses in other parts of Africa. During the winter months, however, large herds of camels are sent by the *bedawin* of the Nile Valley to pasture in the scrub-covered areas lying on the eastern and southern sides of the oasis; but these are removed before the camel-fly appears in the spring.

Practically the whole population of the oasis is engaged in the cultivation of the land. The only manufactures of which the oasis can boast are the making of a little rough pottery and a few baskets. The women also spin small quantities of wool by means of a primitive hand distaff and spindle, and embroider their robes with the thread they produce. A small quantity of oil is also extracted from the olives, and, I believe, occasionally exported to the Nile Valley.

The buildings and villages closely resemble those in Kharga Oasis, though owing to the more wealthy character of the inhabitants the houses are frequently on a larger scale; but, as in the case of Kharga, the dwellings of the poorer natives are little better than hovels. Many of the villages are surrounded by a series of small walled-in yards into which the cattle are driven at night, and which play the part generally of farm buildings in other countries.

In some of the villages—notably Mushia, Gedida and Qalamun, which lie on the western side of the oasis, on the edge of the dune belt—the sand hills and drift sand are encroaching on the cultivation, burying the palm groves, swamping the wells and doing an immense amount of damage.

Though the depression to the north of Dakhla, in which the oasis of Farafra lies, is far larger than those in which Kharga, Dakhla and Bahariya are situated, Farafra is a miserable little place containing only about twenty wells all told, with only two oases permanently inhabited. Of these, Qasr Farafra, the larger, has a population of only about 550; while the smaller—'Ain Sheykh Murzuk—contains only one or two houses and a small Senussi *zawia*, the number of inhabitants probably not much exceeding twenty. At the time of my visit practically all the natives of this oasis were affiliated to the Senussia—and a most surly unpleasant lot they were.

Baharia, the next oasis to the north, is said to be of similar type to Kharga and Dakhla; but I did not visit it. It is peculiar owing to the large number of small isolated rocky hills to be seen scattered about the floor of the depression. Neither did I visit the oasis of Siwa, still farther north in the Wady el Fardy. It has, however, been frequently described.

NOTE

Since this Appendix was written, Hassanein Bey has visited and fixed the positions of Arkenu and Owenat (Owanet). My information upon Owanat seems to have been fairly accurate. The well at the base of the cliff, the pass leading from it, the high-level oasis above, the vegetation and the sand dunes in the district, and even the Barbary sheep, have all been verified. The position I gave it, too, from my native information was reasonably correct, being only about twenty-one miles out, as compared with an error of about twenty-five miles in the position of Kufara as fixed by Rohlfs' expedition by astronomical observations.

My estimate, however, of the nature of Jebel el Owanat—the high land above the well—seems to have been wrong. But this, I think, is due to misunderstanding on my part and not to any error on the part of my informant. "Jebel"—the term he used to describe the high land at Owanat, means literally mountain, but is a term used in the western desert of Egypt to signify the high flat tablelands of which the desert in that part is mainly composed. The oases in this district all lie near the foot of the precipitous scarps that bound these tablelands; so, as he mentioned a cliff in the proximity of the well at Owanat, I assumed the "Jebel" to be of the same character as in the neighbourhood of the Egyptian oases.

Hassanein Bey fixed the western limit of this elevated ground and also its northern and southern boundaries, but though he made a survey of some twenty-five miles to the east of the well, he was unable to fix its eastern extension. So far as it is possible to judge from his description and photographs, this elevated land seems to be of much the same flat-topped character as the "jebels" round the oases of Western Egypt, but so far as is at present known its limited area makes it correspond more to Colonel Tilho's estimate of its character of a detached massif than to a tableland strictly speaking.

It is to be hoped that future travellers before long will revisit this district and fix the eastern limit of Jebel el Owanat. Similar high ground was reported to me as lying to the north of "the Egyptian Oasis," some 130 miles to the east of Owanat, and it is possible, if this information is to be relied upon, that these two places are connected by some hill feature, of which the high land at Owanat is the western limit.

The accurate mapping of Owanat, with its permanent water supply by Hassanein Bey, should be of great assistance to future travellers, as it affords a most useful base for further exploration.

The difficulty, however, is to reach it. The old road that I surveyed to the south-west of Dakhla Oasis for some 200 miles unquestionably leads to Owanat; but it is very doubtful whether it is practicable with camels at the present time. The distance from Dakhla to Owanat in a straight line is some 375 miles, or at least fifteen days' hard travelling by caravan. A small well-mounted party travelling light, even in the most favourable part of the year, would find this an extremely formidable journey, without the use of some sort of depot or relay system.

This road has been disused probably for centuries, as in most places all traces have been completely weathered away. But from its size in the few sheltered places where it is still visible it obviously at one time was one of the main caravan routes of the desert. Moreover, there were indications upon it that it had been largely used by the old slave traders.

It can, I think, be assumed with absolute certainty that no main road of this kind can have existed that contained a waterless stretch of 375 miles—especially one over which large numbers of slaves were forced to travel, as the water supply in these caravans was always a most serious problem.

We are consequently forced to the conclusion that an intermediate well, or oasis, once existed between Dakhla and Owanat. It may have been only a well with an ordinary vertical shaft, which has long since been sanded up and obliterated; but it may be the oasis containing olive trees, on which the palm doves I found migrating from this direction into Dakhla had been feeding. The direction from which they came, viz. 217° Mag.,[25] I discovered afterwards to be almost exactly the bearing of Jebel Abdulla from Mut and so of the old road that we followed to reach it. Justus Perthes' map on a scale of 1/4.000.000, published in 1892, and also the 1/2.000.000 map, revised to 1899, published by the French Service géographique de l'Armée show an unnamed well, or oasis, by a high steep hill and another oasis to the east of it. The German map describes the oasis as being uninhabited, while the French states it to be inhabited. It has been suggested that Arkenu represents the well by the hill and Owanat the oasis farther east, and there can be little doubt that this Arkenu-Owanat district is the one to which they refer. But neither Arkenu nor Owanat can claim to be oases strictly speaking—they would both be more accurately described as wells: so it would appear that one of them—probably Owanat—represents the well and that the oasis has yet to be found. Very likely the failure of the water supply at this point led to the road becoming abandoned. A road running up from the Central Sudan, as this does, towards Cairo and the other wealthy towns of the northern part of Egypt, where slave traders could find the best possible market for their wares, must have been so convenient that it would not have been abandoned without very good cause. If this road could again be made serviceable by the restoration of this water supply, it might still prove to be one of great value.

From what I saw of that part of the desert, I feel certain that this intermediate oasis, or well, is not nearer Dakhla than Jebel Abdulla—my farthest point along the road—nor can it be much farther. It is certainly not in the immediate vicinity of that hill, but it cannot, I think, be more than 50 or, at the outside, 75 miles farther on. It probably lies rather to the east of the direct line joining the hill and Owanat, as the road seemed to be trending rather in that direction.

But the most promising side from which to reach Owanat seems to be from the east, using Bir Natrun, Legia, Selima or Terfawi as a jumping-off point.

My information as to Merga was derived from several informants whose intelligence—with one exception—all agreed in the distance and bearings from Bir Natrun and Legia, so, assuming these two places to be correctly placed on the map, the position of Merga is not likely to be very far in error. The "Egyptian Oasis"—if it exists—would make a still better starting-point. Assuming that it does, there should be no difficulty in discovering it, as it would only be necessary to follow the line of the sand dunes until it was sighted.

APPENDIX II

INSECTS COLLECTED IN THE LIBYAN DESERT

THE collections of insects made in my first two seasons in the Libyan Desert were presented to the Natural History Museum, South Kensington, who in return very kindly undertook to "name" the specimens. Unfortunately, however, they were dispersed among the different departments of the museum before they had been identified, and I am told that the specimens cannot now be traced. This is to be regretted as no other collections have been made anywhere near the parts from which they came, and it would have been of great interest to see how far the influence of the strongly predominating northerly winds of the desert had affected the distribution of the various species.

The list given below is that of the insects collected in my last season. Unfortunately the conditions under which the journey was made prevented many specimens from being obtained from the more central parts of the desert.

The majority of those here mentioned are now in the Tring Museum, where they were most kindly identified for me by Lord Rothschild. The remainder of them are in the Natural History Museum, South Kensington, to the staff of which I am indebted for their kindness in naming them.

Some of the specimens, however, sent to this museum are not included in the list, as owing "to their condition or for some other reason" they could not be identified.

I. IDENTIFIED AT TRING

Arctiidæ

Utetheisa pulchella (Linn.). Farafra, 20/4/12.

Noctuidæ

Chloridea nubigera (Herrsch.). Camp IX, Libyan Desert, 5/4/12.

Euxoa spinifera (Hubn.). Kairowin Hattia, Farafra, 12/4/12.

Agrotis ypsilon (Rott.). Bu Gerara, 4/4/12.

Cirphis loreyi (Dup.). Bu Gerara, 3/4/12.

Athetis flava (Oberth.). Meir, Dirut, Egypt, 17/3/12.

Laphigma exixua (Hubn.). Camp IX, 4/4/12; Bu Gerara, 3-4/4/12; Meir, Dirut, Egypt, 17/3/12.

Phytometra gamma (Linn.). Kairowin Hattia, Farafra, 12/4/12. Camp XI, Farafra, 6/4/12; Meir, Dirut, Egypt, 17/3/12.

Leucanitis kabylaria (Bang, Haas.). Kairowin Hattia, Farafra, 10-12/4/12.

Hypoglaucitis benenotata moses (Stdgr.). Kairowin Hattia, Farafra, 12/4/12.

Anumeta hilgerti (Rothsch.). Kairowin Hattia, Farafra, 12/4/12.

Pyralidæ

Ommatopteryx ocellea (Haw.). Camp XII, 17/4/12.

Syria Kingi (Rothsch.). (*spec. nov.*) Fifteen miles south of Bir Kairowin, 14/4/12.

Syria variabillis (Rothsch.). Meir, Dirut, Egypt, 17-23/3/12; Camp II, 23/3/12.

Syria Libyca (Rothsch.). (*spec. nov.*) Kairowin Hattia, Farafra, 12/4/12.

Heterographis adustella (Rag.). Kairowin Hattia, Farafra, 12/4/12.

Heterographis verburii (Butl.). Camp II, 23/3/12.

Heterographis samaritanella (Zell.). Kairowin Hattia, Farafra, 12/4/12.

Heterographis conversella (Led.). Camp II, 23/3/12.

Nomophila noctuella (Schiff). Camp IX, Libyan Desert, 4/4/12; Bu Gerara, 3-4/4/12; Camp XI, Farafra, 6/4/12; Camp XII, 7/4/12; Camp IV, 25/3/12; Camp V, 26/3/12; Meir, Dirut, Egypt, 17/3/12.

Pyraustidæ

Cornifrons ulceratalis (Led.). Meir, Dirut, Egypt, 17/3/12; Camp II, 23/3/12.

Noctuelia floralis (Hmpsn.). Camp II, 23/3/12.

II. IDENTIFIED AT SOUTH KENSINGTON

TINEINA

Gelechiadæ

Aproærema mitrella (Wlsm.). Meir, Dirut, Egypt, 17-18/3/12; Camp II, Libyan Desert, 23/3/12; Negeb er Rumi, Libyan Desert, 4/4/12. Seven specimens. (Tests J. H. Durrant.)

Phthorimæa eremaula (Meyr). Dakhla Road, Libyan Desert, 26/3/12; Bu Gerara, Libyan Desert, 2-4/4/12. Three specimens. (Tests J. H. Durrant.)

Plutellidæ

Plutella maculipennis (Crt.). Meir, Dirut, Egypt, 16-23/3/12; Camp II, Libyan Desert, 23/3/12; Dakhla Road, Libyan Desert, 26/3/12; Bu Gerara, Libyan Desert, 3-4/4/12; Negeb er Rumi, Libyan Desert, 4/4/12; Farafra Depression, Libyan Desert, 6/4/12; south of Bir Kairowin, 10/4/12. Fifty-three specimens. (Tests J. H. Durrant.)

Tineidæ

Trichophaga abruptella (Wlstn.). Meir, Dirut, Egypt, 17-18/3/12. Two specimens. (Tests J. H. Durrant.)

DIPTERA

Mycetophilidæ

Macrocera (?) *nana* (Macq.). Meir, Dirut, Egypt, 20-23/3/12. Three specimens. (Tests F. W. Edwards.)

Chironomidæ

Chironomus tripartitus (Kieff). Meir, Dirut, Egypt, 17-23/3/12. Two specimens. (Tests F. W. Edwards.)

Syrphidæ

Syrphus corollæ (Fabr.). Bu Gerara, Libyan Desert, 2-4/4/12. Two specimens. (Tests E. E. Austen.)

Muscidæ

Musca analis (Macq.). Meir, Dirut, Egypt, 16-20/3/12. Four specimens. (Tests E. E. Austen.)

Musca angustifrons (Thoms.). Meir, Dirut, Egypt, 16-18/3/12. Two specimens. (Tests E. E. Austen.)

TACHINIDÆ

Sarcophaginæ

Disjunctis nuba (Wied.). Bu Gerara, Libyan Desert, 4/4/12. One specimen. (Tests E. E. Austen.)

Anthomyidæ

Fannia canicularis (L.). Meir, Dirut, Egypt, 16/3/12. One specimen. (Tests E. E. Austen.)

Trypetidæ

Urellia stellata (Fuessl.). Abu Harag, Libyan Desert, 26/3/12. One specimen. (Tests E. E. Austen.)

PLANIPENNIA

Chrysopidæ

Chrysopa vulgaris (Schneider). Meir, Dirut, Egypt, 17/3/12; Camp II, Libyan Desert, 23/3/12; Dakhla Road, Libyan Desert, 26/3/12; Abu Harag, Libyan Desert, 26/3/12; Bu Gerara, Libyan Desert, 2-3/4/12; Negeb er Rumi, Libyan Desert, 4/4/12. Twenty-five specimens. (Tests H. Campion.)

HEMIPTERA

Reduviidæ

Reduvius palliles (Klug). Meir, Dirut, Egypt, 18/3/12. One specimen. (Tests C. J. Gahan.)

Jassidæ

Chlorita flavescens (Fabr.). Meir, Dirut, Egypt, 20/3/12. Three specimens. (Tests F. Laing.)

COLEOPTERA

Carabidæ

Stenolophus marginatus (Dej.). Camp II, Libyan Desert, 23/3/12. One specimen. (Tests G. J. Arrow.)

Dermestidæ

Dermestes frischi (Kug.). Bu Gerara, Libyan Desert, 2/4/12. One specimen. (Tests G. J. Arrow.)

Scarabæidæ

Aphodius hydrochæris (F.). Meir, Dirut, Egypt, 17/3/12. One specimen. (Tests G. J. Arrow.)

Aphodius granulifrons (Fairm.). Camp II, Libyan Desert, 23/3/12. One specimen. (Tests G. J. Arrow.)

Aphodius sp (?). Meir, Dirut, Egypt, 20/3/12. One specimen. (Tests G. J. Arrow.)

Tenebrionidæ

Ocnera hispida (Forsk.). Meir, Dirut, Egypt, 20/3/12. One specimen. (Tests K. G. Blair.)

ORTHOPTERA
Gryllidæ

Gryllotalpa gryllotalpa (L.). Meir, Dirut, Egypt, 17-21/3/12. Two specimens. (Tests B. Uvarov.)

APPENDIX III

ROCK INSCRIPTIONS FROM THE LIBYAN DESERT

THE graffiti shown in the accompanying plates were collected in the Libyan Desert. The majority of them occurred on the Gubary road, between the oases of Kharga and Dakhla, or in the *hattia* through which this road runs, immediately before entering the oasis of Dakhla, in its south-east corner.

In many places these rock scribings were extraordinarily numerous. It is no exaggeration to say that at some of the recognised halting-places on the Gubary road, where it is the custom for caravans to rest during the midday heat, or at the end of the day's journey, the rocks are so thickly covered with graffiti that it is almost impossible to walk without treading on them.

The collection does not pretend to be in any way a complete one, for the signs were mostly copied during a hurried journey in the hot weather of 1909; there are consequently a considerable number that have been overlooked.

Unfortunately most of them are cut on the flat horizontal stones by the roadside; so it was impossible to tell which was their right way up, as that would obviously depend upon the position with regard to them occupied at the time by the man who cut them. Some of them, however, were on more or less vertical surfaces, so that there could be no doubt as to their correct positions.

Where any of the others have been compared with signs previously reported from a different locality, from which they differed only by their position, the angle through which they have to be turned, to make their position correspond with the signs with which they are compared, is intended to be taken in a clockwise direction.

Those scribings that did not occur on the Gubary road, or in the *hattia*, were found in the following localities:—

Nos. 230-238 in the northern part of Kharga Oasis, near 'Ain el Hagar. They were mostly taken from the mouth of a shaft, cut vertically into a horizontal tunnel, excavated through the rock below to act as an infiltration gallery, to bring the water from the subsoil through which it ran to the surface at a lower level.

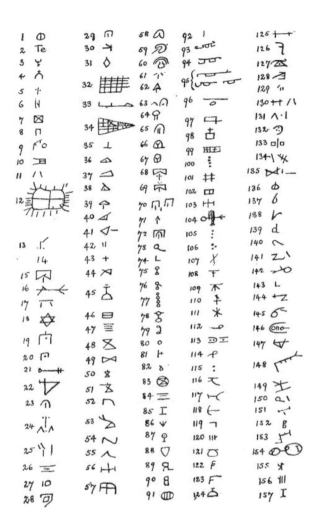

No. 219 was found on a loose block of stone at the foot of a ruined mud tower in Dakhla Oasis, near Bir 'Ain Sheykh Mufta, about three kilometres to the south-east of Smint el Kharab.

Nos. 221-228 occurred cut on a small stone ruin known as Qasr el Kadabya, about five kilometres to the south of the village of Tenida, in Dakhla Oasis.

No. 224 was seen, at the foot of the wall by a doorway, in a small stone building at the well of 'Ain Amur, on the more northerly road from Kharga to Dakhla oases.

In addition to the graffiti shown in the plates, a large number of rough drawings were seen, which want of time, unfortunately, did not allow me to copy. Many of them were of subjects that did not admit of reproduction. Among the remainder were hunting and battle scenes, drawings of a few boats, or ships—one of which was obviously intended to represent a *dahabya*—and, in addition to numerous pictures of camels, those of horses, mules or donkeys were unexpectedly numerous, considering the small use that is made of these beasts in that part of the desert.

Among the animals shown in the hunting scenes were several ostriches, which, though found in the Sudan, are quite unknown at the present time in the district where the graffiti were seen. In addition, horned game were represented in a few places; but it was impossible to determine the species which were intended to be represented.

In the battle scenes, the men were armed with bows, shields, spears and swords. I saw no guns to indicate modern drawings, or *shangamangers* that might have pointed to a Sudan origin.

The figures in every case were cut on the surface of the Nubian sandstone, a substance that is easily scratched with a knife. A portion of some of the figures given in the plates is shown by means of a dotted line, intended to show that the part thus outlined is uncertain, owing to the rock having been chipped, or to some other cause.

The Gubary road, where most of the graffiti were found, runs near the foot of a scarp that shelters it to a great extent from the strongly predominant northerly winds. But considering the amount of erosion that takes place during the frequent sandstorms from this quarter, after making all allowance for the sheltered position of the rocks upon which these inscriptions occur, their sharp-cut appearance was remarkable, seeming to indicate that they do not date from a very remote period.

Nos. 217 and 218, however, were an exception. These two inscriptions were cut one above the other, about five feet above ground level, on a vertical surface facing about north-west. The rock at this point may perhaps have been unusually soft, but both inscriptions showed most distinct signs of weathering.

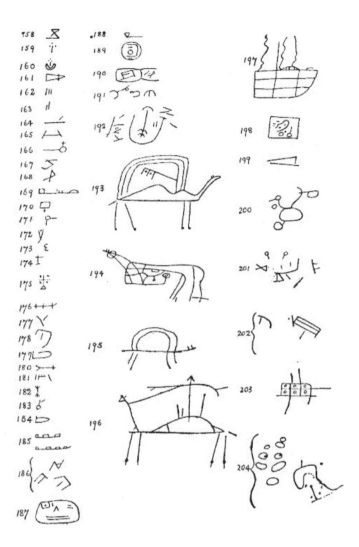

No. 217 appears to be of special interest, as it seems to be written partly in primitive Arabic characters and partly in some script, such as Tifinagh, making use of dotted letters. Inscriptions of this bilingual character have also been found in the Twat group of oases, in the Western Sahara, at Ulad Mahmud, in the Gerara District.[26]

The uncertainty as to the correct position of most of these graffiti, combined with the simple forms that so many of them show and the rough manner in which they have been drawn, renders comparisons with other drawings perhaps dangerous, and in any case requires more expert knowledge than that possessed by the present writer. But the following notes upon them may perhaps be of interest.

Many of the drawings are unquestionably tribal camel brands, as an Arab can often be seen cutting his *wasm*, or brand, on the ground during a halt, in the same manner as a white man will write his name.

These *wasms* are probably of great antiquity, and are said by the Arabs who use them to date from pre-Mohammedan times. They are used by the *bedawin* in a manner analogous to the heraldry of medieval Europe. Each tribe has its own brand, the junior branches and offshoots of the clan adopting the original *wasm* with a difference, recalling the "marks of cadency" in heraldry.

I was able, with the assistance of my men, to identify the following brands:—

The circle seen in No. 27 is a *wasm* of the Hamamla tribe shown in No. 80 and, with the added stroke, may constitute the brand of one of its subdivisions.

No. 29 is the *wasm* of the Khana tribe.

No. 37 of the Jebsia.

No. 43 that of the Zowia. It is curious that this, one of the most fanatical tribes that have been converted to the tenets of the Senussia, should make use of the emblem of Christianity as their badge.

No. 44 may be the brand of the Zoazi tribe that appears in No. 168, and also perhaps in No. 114.

No. 48, in the position shown, is the *wasm* of the Ulad ben Miriam, or, if turned as it appears in No. 158, of a Maghrabi tribe known as the Malif.

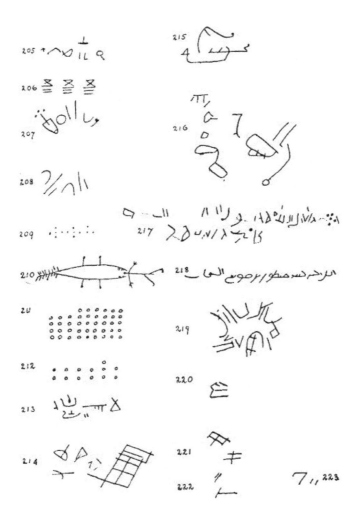

No. 75 was said to be the brand of another Maghrabi tribe, the name of which I was not able to learn.

No 85 is the mark of the Amaim, which may be also represented by Nos. 157 and 174.

No. 86, if turned through 180 degrees, would be the *wasm* of an Arab tribe from Moab, whose name I could not ascertain.

No. 87 may perhaps be inverted and intended to be the brand of the Reshaida—a dotted circle surmounted by a cross. Possibly No. 170, though the circle is represented by a square and the figure is also inverted, may also stand for this *wasm*.

The Reshaida are an offshoot of the Awazim, whose brand—a circle and cross, without the "cadency mark" of the dot—appears in No. 166, with a line added to it on the left-hand side. Reference will be made to this additional line below. Possibly Nos. 98 and 124 are also meant for this Awazim brand.

No. 109 is the *wasm* of the Orfilli tribe.

No. 156 that of the Hassun, said to be an offshoot of a tribe, whose name I could not ascertain, that have the mark Y for their brand.

Nos. 172 and 173 are both brands of the well-known Bisharin tribe.

No. 177 is the mark of the Harb tribe.

No. 179 of the Hawerti tribe.

No. 234 was said by my men to be the brand of a tribe sprung from another clan whose *wasm* may be shown in Nos. 73 and 112, but they were ignorant of the names of both of the tribes.

Many of the other marks shown in the plates are probably *derived* from these *wasms*. The *bedawin* Arabs are nearly always illiterate, but are accustomed to communicate with each other by marks scratched on the ground in the same way that gypsies make use of a "patteran." See p. 180 *ante*.

Such marks, for instance, as No. 50, derived from the Malif *wasm*, and 171 and 183, from the ♂ brand, are very possibly produced in this way.

Many of the simpler signs occurred repeatedly, and in addition the group shown in No. 2 was seen twice, and that in No. 14 several times, while the combination No. 25 in one place was repeated no less than thirty-three times in three horizontal lines. Similar marks to those No. 95 occurred in several places, generally in groups of three, placed as shown in the plate.

No. 18, the seal of Solomon, is not uncommonly seen in the rock inscriptions of the Western Sahara. It takes several forms, each of which may have a dot in the centre, thus: ✡. Its commonest form seems to be that shown in No. 18, but sometimes one of the triangles of which it is composed is drawn with a heavier line than the other, thus: ✡. It is also represented in at least one case-on the Col de Zanaga, in the Figuig district—surrounded by a waved line producing a kind of rosette ✡. In addition to these forms, the false seal of Solomon, or five-pointed star, constructed by a continuous line ✶ is also seen in this district, but I did not happen to come across it in the Libyan Desert. These signs are all much used by the native magicians.

No. 88 was apparently the tracing of a leathern sandal and was lifesize. The outline of both shod and unshod feet, sometimes the right foot being traced and at others the left, were of not infrequent occurrence. They are also found in the Western Sahara at Qasr el Jaj Ahmer, in the Geryville district, and at Guebar Rashim. The outlines of hands also occur; but I did not see any of the latter in the Libyan Desert.

Of the other signs, the mark ♦ which occurs, in combination with others, in Nos. 14 and 244, has also been found on the temple of Soleb, in the midst of an inscription. The sign L, No. 74, also appears here.[27]

Nos. 42, 43 and 49 were reported by the late Mr. Oric Bates from Marmarica.[28] So, too, were Nos. 63 and 71, if turned through 180 degrees. The small circle that appears as No. 80, and in combination with other signs in Nos. 9, 27, and in several of the groups shown in the plates, and also No. 162, if turned through a right angle, also figure in this collection. Among which, too, is the sign ∫ which may be identical with the mark ∫ in the inscription given as No. 219.

In some of the inscriptions found at the Gara esh Shorfa, in the Aulef district of Tidikelt in the Twat group of oases, the vowel dot (*tagherit*) of the Libyco-Berber script is often enclosed by a line that forms a kind of loop round it, recalling the cartouche frequently used in modern Tifinagh writing to surround the different words of a sentence; the ∤ is also sometimes enclosed in the same manner, the letters when thus treated having the following appearance: ᛒ, ᛟ. The right-hand signs of No. 63 and No. 132, No. 146 and several other of the graffiti shown in the plates may perhaps be examples of this practice, which also is very possibly illustrated by the sign ᛟ that occurs in No. 219. The cartouche treatment appears in No. 245.

Some of the more complicated signs may only be idle scratchings; drawings, for instance, such as No. 34 are often to be seen upon blotting pads, being made by some writer during the intervals of his composition. But such signs as Nos. 16, 142, 148, 149 and 153 recall the curious ligatured monograms sometimes used by the modern Tawarek in their writings, or the cryptograms, mentioned by Duveyrier and H. Barth, that the Tawarek women sometimes amuse themselves by inventing, that can only be deciphered by those to whom they have imparted the key.[29]

The circles in Nos. 203, 211 and 212 represent small cups about two inches in diameter and were used perhaps for some game such as *harubga*, or possibly for divination in the manner described by Mohammed et Tounsi.[30] Somewhat similar groups of cups have been found in the Twat Oasis group at 'Ain Guettara, and also in the Geryville district, at El Jaj Mohammed and Shellala Dahrania.

Nos. 224—the left-hand portion—242 and 243 probably represent human beings. In 224 the five fingers of two hands and the long hair in the star like a mark above them occur in several other undoubted drawings of figures that were seen, but are not shown in the plates. It is, however, doubtful whether it is the feet or the hands that are represented in Nos. 242 and 243. Among the figures that are not given in the plates, several appeared in which the hair was represented by dots instead of the lines in No. 224.

Rough drawings of camels were often seen. They are shown in Nos. 193 and 196, and possibly also Nos. 194, 195 and 131 are intended to show them. Nos. 193 and 195 may perhaps represent camels carrying a travelling tent, such as are used by wealthy women, and sometimes also by men on a journey. No. 193 may possibly represent a beast with two humps, though these, of course, are never seen in North Africa. No. 196 apparently carries a rider, mounted on a riding saddle. Among other creatures appearing in the plates, No. 210 is presumably a man being swallowed by a crocodile.

Rough drawings of camels, of a very similar type to those here reproduced, have been found by Lieut.-Col. Tilho in the oasis of Harda, in Borku; and I came across others myself in a cave, near Marsa Matru, on the North Egyptian coast. The latter were found in conjunction with drawings of a cannon being fired and of a paddle-wheel steamer, which appeared to be contemporaneous, so evidently they were of a comparatively recent date.

The drawings of ostriches and the fragments of their shells which are often to be found in the Libyan Desert, even in the neighbourhood of the Egyptian oases, has been held to show that they once existed wild in this part of the desert. But the argument is by no means conclusive; ostrich eggs used frequently to be brought from the Sudan by the old slave-trading caravans, who used them as food, and the drawings no more show that ostriches inhabited this part than the pictures of boats show that *dahaybas* once sailed over the desert in the neighbourhood, say, of Dakhla Oasis. The occurrence of these, and of drawings of antelopes and other wild animals, merely show that some of the travellers who used these roads came from districts where the creatures they represented could be seen.

LIBYAN DESERT AND ENNEDI

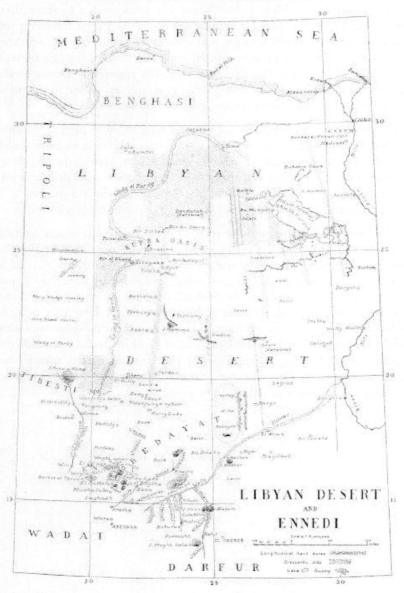

Seeley Service & Co., Ltd.

Map for "Mysteries of the Libyan Desert."

FOOTNOTES:

[1]*Trifolium Alexandrinum*, L.

[2]*Medicago Sativa* (Lucerne).

[3]An *ardeb* = 300 lbs.

[4]Peasant of the Nile Valley or oasis.

[5]"The Libyan Desert from Native Information," R.G.S.J., Sept., 1913.

[6]"Travels in the Libyan Desert," R.G.S.J., Feb., 1912.

[7]"The Farafra Depression and Bu Mungar *hattia*," R.G.S.J., Nov., 1913.

[8]"The Farafra Depression and Bu Mungar *hattia*," R.G.S.J., Nov., 1913, pp. 455-461.

[9]"Travels in the Libyan Desert," R.G.S.J., Feb., 1912.

[10]See R.G.S.J. "The Nature and Formation of Sand Ripples and Dunes," March, 1916, pp. 189-209. "Study of a Dune Belt," January, 1918, pp. 16-33. Discussion on the latter paper, April, 1918, pp. 250-258.

[11]"Customs, Superstitions and Songs of the Western Oases," Cairo, Aug., 1914.

[12]"Irrigation in Dakhla Oasis," R.G.S.J., Nov., 1917.

[13]"The Geographical Distribution of some Plants from the Libyan Desert," Cairo, Oct., 1913.

[14]*Calotropis procera*.

[15]*Malva parviflora*, L.

[16]p. 146.

[17]p. 262.

[18]"North American Deserts." Prof. D. T. MacDougal, R.G.S.J. Vol. XXXIX, No. 2.

[19]"Problems in Exploration: Africa." By F. R. Cana, R.G.S.J., Nov., 1911, p. 464.

[20]See also "The Libyan Desert from Native Information," R.G.S.J., Sept., 1913.

[21]Hassanein Bey's observations have shown that Rohlfs' position for Boema in Kufara is some twenty-five miles in error.

[22]See note on p. 319.

[23]"The Sand Dunes of the Libyan Desert." By H. L. Beadnell, R.G.S. Vol. XXXV, p. 383

[24]p. 96.

[25]See p. 90.

[26]"Note sur quelques stations nouvelles, ou peu connu, de pierres écrites du Sahara," par M. Q. B. M. Flamand.

[27]Waddington and Hanbury, "Journal of a Visit to some parts of Ethiopia," 1882. Published by John Murray, Albemarle Street, London, 268.

[28]Oric Bates, "Nomad Burials in Marmarica." "Man," Vol. XII. No. 10.

[29]"Note sur quelques stations nouvelles, ou peu connu, de pierres écrites du Sahara," par G. M. B. Flamand, p. 9.

[30]Referred to by G. B. M. Flamand, *op. cit.*

Milton Keynes UK
Ingram Content Group UK Ltd.
UKHW010630080624
443649UK00030B/534